This inaugural volume from the ⟨barcode⟩ ......ence
lives up to its name and vocation. each chapter refuses the typical
modern reflex of seeing reason and revelation as opposites and offers
fresh insight into matters at the heart of Christian theology. Readers
will find compelling biblical, historical, and theological arguments for
beating what were once opposing epistemological swords into prole-
gomenal plowshares.

> **Kevin J. Vanhoozer,** Research Professor of Systematic
> Theology, Trinity Evangelical Divinity School

This stellar collection of essays on the relationship of divine revelation
to human reason is persuasively coherent in its common focus and final
conclusions, yet penetrating in its rich details. Ranging across exegesis,
social philosophy and epistemology, ascetic theology, and dogmatics,
the authors manage a startlingly beautiful reconfiguration of reason's
shape within the particular realities of Christian faith and life. Instead
of the modernist conception of reason as an instrument of human domination, for coercive good or ill, reasoning here emerges as a creature
wonderfully nourished by God's self-giving in Christ and self-disclosure in Scripture, and thus capable of humbly yet truthfully engaging
the world of God's making. Each essay in its own way, and all of them
taken together, offer a vision that is evangelically profound and deeply
hopeful, to be received with care and thanks.

> **Ephraim Radner,** Professor of Historical Theology, Wycliffe
> College, University of Toronto

Christopher Green and David Starling have assembled a great cast
of contributors for this collection of essays on revelation and reason,
tackling topics related to how revelation and reason fit within a larger
scheme of God's self-disclosure, human knowing, and church theol-
ogizing. A stimulating series of investigations on how to understand
faith seeking a fusion of revelation and reason.

> **Michael F. Bird,** Lecturer in Theology at Ridley College,
> Melbourne, Australia.

STUDIES IN HISTORICAL
& SYSTEMATIC THEOLOGY
H
S + S
T

REVELATION *and* REASON *in* CHRISTIAN THEOLOGY

Proceedings of the 2016
Theology Connect Conference

REVELATION *and* REASON *in* CHRISTIAN THEOLOGY

*Proceedings of the 2016
Theology Connect Conference*

Edited by **CHRISTOPHER C. GREEN**
and **DAVID I. STARLING**

STUDIES IN HISTORICAL AND SYSTEMATIC THEOLOGY

LEXHAM PRESS

Revelation and Reason in Christian Theology
Studies in Historical and Systematic Theology

Copyright 2018 Christopher C. Green and David I. Starling

Lexham Press, 1313 Commercial St., Bellingham, WA 98225
LexhamPress.com

Content from "Finitude" (Daniel J. Treier, *Evangelical Dictionary of Theology*,
Baker Academic, a division of Baker Publishing Group, 2017) used by permission.

Reprinted by permission, Steven J. Duby, "Free Speech: Scripture in the Context
of Divine Simplicity and Divine Freedom," *Irish Theological Quarterly* 82, no. 3
(2017): 197–207.

Print ISBN 9781683590989
Digital ISBN 9781683590996

Lexham Editorial Team: Todd Hains, Claire Brubaker, and Danielle Thevenaz
Typesetting: Beth Shagene

This volume presents the proceedings from the inaugural Theology Connect conference, July 2016. Our mission is to spread the advanced study of Christian Theology to strategic locations around the world. We put on sustainable conferences that encourage a faithful exploration of Scripture and Christian theology.

Contents

Introduction

Is there a definite relationship between revelation and reason in Christian theology? How do these two, at times disparate, partners work together for the construction of a cohesive account of the Christian faith? Can they be paired alongside each other in the assembly of a felicitous whole? Clearly many doctrinal relationships exist within the context of a consistent presentation of Christian belief. Why decide to focus on this particular horizon with its specific set of difficulties? Why should we decide to open this hornet's nest of questions, letting them loose on the world?

The following chapters are made up of papers presented at the first Theology Connect conference, a sponsored event in Sydney, Australia, in July 2016.[1] Through this series of conferences we hope to develop a sustainable and long-lasting Christian dogmatics conference for the Oceania region. We maintain a specific set of priorities as we manage each conference.

First, Theology Connect focuses its conferences on dogmatic horizons. While the papers and plenary addresses selected for the conference include presentations on biblical, hermeneutical, and historical themes, the questions around which they orbit are those of constructive, systematic theology.

Second, Theology Connect aims to provide an opportunity for scholars from the Oceania region to participate in some of the larger, international conversations taking place in Christian systematic theology. This means that scholars from all over are invited to attend, and the themes of the conferences are not tied closely to local or regional concerns.

1. We are grateful for the reception of an initial grant from the Kern Community Foundation for the start of our series of conferences.

Third, Theology Connect prioritizes a rendering of biblical and systematic theology that is faithful to the Christian—in particular, the Reformed Protestant—tradition and also engages in constructive and at times provocative dialogue. The opinions articulated in the following chapters are not necessarily shared by all of the authors, the Australian board of advisers, or the board members of Theology Connect in the United States. Rather, this volume seeks to reflect the diverse and engaging conversation we hope for within a charitable community of Christian scholars.

REVELATION AND REASON IN CONVERSATION

With these contextual factors in mind, we invite our readers to interact with each of the papers included in this volume with an appropriate set of questions. As William Abraham's paper points out, divine revelation is a doctrine developed within a unique conceptual environment, sharing questions concerning human being, divine ontology, and the nature of epistemology (understood, for most of the history of the doctrine's development, within the Western philosophical tradition). How should divine revelation in Christian theology be understood as intelligible and tangible? Or, to put it differently, how might the doctrine of revelation be appropriately and consistently understood within the context of a Christian self-description?

One way to picture the set of questions posed by Abraham, among others, might be to envision "reason" (that is, created, human reason) and "revelation" (that is, the communicative activity of the triune God) as partners in conversation. The papers presented at the first Theology Connnect conference and selected for inclusion in this volume constitute a discussion about the way in which that conversation should proceed.

The discussion unfolds in an unapologetic way, presupposing a few important assumptions. The wording of the original conference's title, in which "revelation" precedes "reason," reflects our conviction that the gracious self-disclosure and communicative activity of God precede the work of human reason, which sees clearly only in the light that God has given. Significant, too, is that the two words are joined together with an "and," not a "versus." The kind of relationship between revelation and reason that is advocated, one way or another, in each of the essays below is not a zero-sum game in which more revelation means less reason or vice versa. Still less do we envisage the relationship as a winner-takes-all contest, in which claims of revelation subsume or displace the work of human reason altogether, or human reason asserts its sufficiency and autonomy in a manner that renders the very notion of divine revelation oppressive or redundant.

The corollary of those negations is a cheerful and confident affirmation of the harmonious relationship between divine revelation (rightly understood) and human reason (properly exercised). We maintain that the relationship between revelation and reason is in keeping with the covenant partnership into which men and women are summoned by God. The God of the Bible delights to make himself known in a manner that invites men and women into wise and responsible action as his image bearers in the world. Our faithful response to divine revelation therefore includes within it a "yes" not only to God's self-communication but also to the possibilities and limitations of the human condition. While human existence is complex and mysterious in many ways, the exercise of human reason is made free and brought to its proper end in the response that it makes to divine revelation.

This collection of essays explores different ways of positioning a harmonious and fruitful relationship between revelation and reason within the economy of grace. Each of these contributions investigates how divine revelation and human reason can be related within the context of one of the theological disciplines. We hope to challenge and encourage our readers to concentrate on the importance of this particular horizon in Christian theology. How do revelation and reason, and differing versions of their relationship, fit within a larger, responsible, and self-conscious account of the triune God and his relationship with the church and the world? When a particular construal of this relationship is offered, what are the immediate, and then the less proximate, entailments for other aspects of Christian theology? Are there some accounts that are more responsible than others with regard to the content of the Old and New Testaments? Are there some accounts that are wiser in terms of our ongoing conversation with our forerunners in the faith? What are the most important conceptual distinctions that need to be made for a faithful and relevant rendering of each of these today? To these questions we turn with each of the contributions below.

INDIVIDUAL CONTRIBUTIONS

This volume begins with a meditation on God's self-disclosure in the context of biblical narrative, written by Christopher Green, who started the first Theology Connect conference with this address, focusing on the first divine speech-act in Scripture ("let there be light," Gen 1:3). Green directs his enquiry with the following question: What does God's first command in the Bible tell us about the manner of his self-disclosure in Scripture? He argues that God's first reported discourse is self-revealing in a way that is consistent with other characters depicted in the Old Testament, indirectly offering unique insights into the nature of divine revelation.

An initial focus on epistemology follows, with keynote addresses from both Daniel Treier and William Abraham. In Abraham's essay he reminds us of the expansive terrain that lies before us when we contemplate the question of divine revelation. If revelation has public consequences, how can it operate without a generally accessible criterion of epistemic justification? Abraham suggests that revelation may bring its own rationality alongside it, as a "world constituting experience."

Daniel Treier's first essay follows this concern with public justification, but with a constructive look at divine revelation, noting the importance of human finitude and of covenantal "hearing" for framing a complementary account to more modern, ocular accounts of reason. In his second essay Treier makes particular use of Jacques Ellul's diagnosis of the modern world's deployment of technical reason and follows this with a gesture to Oliver O'Donovan's theology of culture. Treier calls us to a responsible account of human reason that is open to divine revelation and responsive to Christ's victory over all cultural powers. Treier maintains that reason is more aligned to its proper end with these factors in mind, enabling us to make public commitments to divine revelation.

The next three essays focus directly on Scripture and its interpretation. Caroline Batchelder directs our attention to the way in which humanity's vocation is described in Genesis and Isaiah, locating the

"wise knowing" that fosters human flourishing within the divine ordering and reordering activity that establish the מִשְׁפָּט ("justice") of God
in the world.

David Starling examines the way in which the relationship between
reason and revelation is depicted in 1 Corinthians 8–10, and tests the
extent to which Paul's argumentation in these chapters can be properly
characterized as an exercise in apocalyptic epistemology. Contrary to
the claims of those who view Paul's stance toward human reason as fundamentally dismissive, Starling argues that the relationship between
revelation and reason that Paul constructs within these chapters
implies an indispensable role for a chastened and charitable exercise
of human reason. In addressing the arguments of these chapters to the
Corinthians "as to sensible people," Paul seeks not merely to deflate
their pretensions but also to invite and urge them to think with true
wisdom and clear-sighted judgment.

In the final essay of this section, Chase Kuhn engages with recent
proposals that have advocated the recovery of figural readings of Scripture as a better remedy for the problems of ecclesial discord than the
Enlightenment quest for a presuppositionless hermeneutic, directed
only by the axioms and inferences of universal reason. With Stephen
Fowl as his primary interlocutor, Kuhn assesses the strengths and weak-
nesses of such figural readings and offers a preliminary evaluation of
their feasibility within an evangelical hermeneutic.

The three essays that follow shift the focus to historical theology. In
the first of them Christopher Holmes follows in the steps of Thomas
Aquinas, reflecting on the relationship between reason and meditation
in Christian theology and (therefore) in the quest for true beatitude.
Because humanity's happiness is in God, he argues, human reason is not
an end in itself. Treated as such, it becomes a hard, enslaving master,
blinded by its tendency to reject as false everything that cannot investigate and bent away from God by its delusions of autonomy. But when
the human mind submits to God, meditating on divinely revealed truth,
reason is able to fulfill its proper role as a means by which men and
women, as creatures made in God's image, exercise their intellect in
apprehension of the truth.

Bruce Pass, in the second essay of this section, traces the various senses in which Herman Bavinck uses the word "mystery" to characterize the relationship between revelation and reason. Bavinck's account of the relationship is, he argues, simultaneously modern and Reformed, bringing the dogmatics of Bavinck's Reformed Orthodox heritage into critical conversation with the epistemological concerns of modernity—nowhere more so than in his assertion that "Mystery is the lifeblood of dogmatics." By approaching the relation of revelation and reason as a paradox to be preserved rather than as a problem to be solved, Bavinck circumscribes all of our knowing, chastening human pretensions and evoking the wonder and adoration that direct our knowing toward its ultimate goal in the praise of God.

The final contribution to this section is Chris Swann's essay. He focuses on the theology of Karl Barth, taking as its starting point the stark antithesis between popular portrayals of Barth as (respectively) "hostile to reason" and "taken hostage by it." In an effort to dismantle the contradiction between these two diametrically opposed accounts of the relationship between reason and revelation in Barth's theology, Swann offers a close reading of Barth's critique of the religion of revelation in *Church Dogmatics* IV/2 §66.3. Barth's critique, Swann argues, differs radically in its motive from the revelation-denying hermeneutics of suspicion advocated by Feuerbach and his heirs, but, nonetheless, "joins hands with and even outpaces it," offering salutary lessons for those engaged in the work of contemporary systematics and theological ethics.

The fourth and final section of this volume focuses on dogmatic theology, starting with John McClean's keynote lecture, exploring the importance of Christology for delineating a fitting relationship between revelation and reason. While McClean's interest is in drawing from the heritage of the Reformed orthodox tradition, he also looks back to Chalcedon and converses broadly. McClean's essay establishes some of the more immediate and significant implications of orthodox Christology for ascertaining the relationship between revelation and reason. In his attempt to "think *in concreto*" about this relationship, he asks how the given reality of the incarnation might shape a constructive and faithful account of this theological relationship, broadly conceived.

Steve Duby approaches the question of the relation between divine action and Scripture with attention to the classical attribute of divine simplicity. Duby explores how a faithful explication of this classical doctrine allows for the transcendence and condescension of God to be held together in an account of God's self-communication in Scripture. He focuses on what bearing this noncompetitive account has on our understanding of the content of Scripture, especially increasing our comfort level with its inexhaustibility in its rich description of God and his manifold perfections.

Andrew Moody follows this by turning our attention to the nature of exemplarism—the notion that nature exemplifies Christ—as a platform for raising questions about reason's interaction with nature. Must reason first encounter Christ and special revelation in order to see creation in its proper light? Exemplarism focuses our attention as an acute case study with, as Moody says, "a complex verdict." How is the relationship between the Word of God, which is the source of all creation, and our experience of general revelation properly understood?

Mark Thompson's keynote lecture on the relationship between the doctrine of revelation—one that accounts for God's action as a communicative and redemptive agent—and the doctrine of Scripture is the final contribution offered in this volume. Thompson draws on perennial questions regarding both doctrines of revelation and inspiration and addresses them in fresh ways, with a cheerful appreciation for the rich depiction of God's communicative action within the context of Scripture (and the Reformed, evangelical tradition). In this manner the volume closes as it offers a second glance (as with Green's essay) at the importance of the Bible's depiction of God as a communicative agent for delineating the contours of the doctrine of revelation. Thompson redirects our theological enquiry to the Bible itself, finding there that in God's light "we see light" (Ps 36:9).

Abbreviations

CBQ	*Catholic Biblical Quarterly*
CD	Barth, Karl. *Church Dogmatics*. 4 vols. Edinburgh: T&T Clark, 1956–1975.
IJST	*International Journal of Systematic Theology*
JBL	*Journal of Biblical Literature*
JSNT	*Journal for the Study of the New Testament*
JSNTSup	Journal for the Study of the New Testament Supplement Series
JSOT	*Journal for the Study of the Old Testament*
JSOTSup	Journal for the Study of the Old Testament Supplement Series
JTI	*Journal of Theological Interpretation*
LW	*Luther's Works [American Edition]*. 82 vols. projected. St. Louis: Concordia; Philadelphia: Fortress, 1955–1986, 2009–.
NTS	*New Testament Studies*
RTR	*Reformed Theological Review*
SCG	*The Summa Contra Gentiles of Saint Thomas Aquinas*. Translated by English Dominican Fathers. London: Burns, Oates, and Washbourne, 1924.
SJT	*Scottish Journal of Theology*
ST I	*Basic Writings of Saint Thomas Aquinas*. Vol. I, *God and the Order of Creation*. Edited by Anton C. Pegis. Indianapolis: Hackett, 1997.
TS	*Theological Studies*
WA	*D. Martin Luthers Werke: Kritische Gesamtausgabe: [Schriften]*. 73 vols. Weimar: Hermann Böhlaus Nachfolger, 1883–2009.
WBC	Word Biblical Commentary
WTJ	*Westminster Theological Journal*

"Let There Be Light"

A Meditation on Biblical Narration and Divine Self-Disclosure

Christopher C. Green

INTRODUCTION

I would like to begin our examination of the relationship between revelation and reason in Christian theology with a very wide lens, focusing on the topic of *light* in Scripture.[1] This opens us up to a broad, cosmic context for exploring God's self-revelation and our response. In 1963 Elizabeth Achtemeier considered the role of the light established in the creation account of Genesis, its development through the Old Testament, and its function in the prologue of John's Gospel.[2] I'd like to follow her lead with a more precise focus on the creation account and God's initial reported discourse in Genesis 1:3, "let there be light." Is this initial statement in any way paradigmatic for the dramatic unfolding of God's character in the Bible?[3] Who does the God of the Bible reveal himself to be in the context of his initial command? How does light signify his action in the drama that follows?[4] With an aim to explore

1. I am grateful to John McClean, David Starling, and Michael Bräutigam, who all commented on a previous version of this chapter.

2. Elizabeth Achtemeier, "Jesus Christ, the Light of the World: The Biblical Understanding of Light and Darkness," *Interpretation* 17, no. 4 (1963): 439–49.

3. J. Todd Billings reminds us that reading Scripture involves us in a dramatic process; see his chapter "Scriptural Interpretation and Practices: Participating in the Triune Drama of Salvation," in *The Word of God for the People of God: An Entryway to the Theological Interpretation of Scripture* (Grand Rapids: Eerdmans, 2010), 195–227.

4. This reading assumes the comment of Henri Blocher, who takes his directive from James Orr's reading of the events at the onset of Genesis: "The presence of symbolic elements in the text in no way contradicts the historicity of its central

these questions, I will look briefly at some instances of initial reported speech in the Old Testament and then explore three facets of God's created light in Genesis 1. Following my description of each, I will also briefly explore how these significations are carried through in John's Gospel and may have some importance for our understanding of the contours of the doctrine of revelation in Christian theology today.

OLD TESTAMENT CHARACTERIZATION
THROUGH INITIAL REPORTED DISCOURSE

In his commentary on the book of Genesis, Robert Alter reminds us in a footnote that Rachel's first reported speech, which is directed to Jacob, significantly encapsulates her dramatized identity.[5] Rachel states to the patriarch: "Give me sons or I will die" (Gen 30:1).[6] This phrase not only typifies her impetuous nature (Alter reminds us), but it, like many initial reported statements in Scripture, gives us a clue into her inner life, her larger purpose in the story, or, to borrow a pagan term, her *destiny*. Rachel's life story ends as she dies giving birth to her second son, Benjamin (Gen 35:16-20). "Give me sons" is spoken in the plural, "or I will die."

Characters seem to come to us in one of two ways in the Bible. The process of character making either may be accelerated with an objective epithet, or it may unfold more quietly and profoundly through the narration of speech and action. Sometimes objective epithets come to the forefront with ease. David, for example, is described externally: he was "dark and handsome, with beautiful eyes" (1 Sam 16:12 NLT). Even in this case, however, we see that David's epithet is not given for the

---

meaning" (*In the Beginning: The Opening Chapters of Genesis* [Downers Grove, IL: InterVarsity, 1984], 155).

5. Robert Alter, *Genesis: Translation and Commentary* (New York: W. W. Norton, 1996), 166. Among other places, we see this phenomena in Shakespeare's works, with characters such as Edmund in *King Lear*, who in his first speech reveals that he has no commitment to family or morality, but rather he commits himself to follow his instincts. He calls Nature his goddess in his first reported discourse ("To thy law my services are bound"; act 1, scene 2). His instincts lead to his eventual death. Other candidates: Richard the Third ("I am determined to prove a villain"; act 1, scene 1) and Desdemona ("But here's my husband and so much duty"; *Othello*, act 1, scene 3). I am grateful to Mike and Kathleen Nolan for these references.

6. This is my own translation.

sake of mere historical reference.[7] It foreshadows his future struggles with a subtle hint at his (perhaps dangerously) attractive appearance. Epithets are not character-neutral, either. They often point to a composite of speech and action that we take in and associate with each persona as we read. Eglon's epithet illustrates this well, as it catalogues his oppression of the Israelites with a taint of moral judgment; he "was a very fat man" (Judg 3:17).

Without a clear epithet we are left to indirect characterization, and this is a process that places more weight on reported discourse. The advent of a character's speech situates him or her within a storied context. Shimon Bar-Efrat describes all reported discourse in the Bible as a "reflecting and exposing" of the speaker.[8] For example, Rachel's above statement models the construction of her character within the context of her own biography. Speech identifies what is going on in the heart of a biblical character, and so it opens up an extended section of subtle intentionality across a story.[9] The revealed heart of a character illuminates what he or she does, and these actions also provide a reverse testimony of the inner musings and intentions of the heart. The personal dimension also profoundly shapes the rhetorical appeal and implied audience of a biblical story, as it does with Moses' insecure self-deprecation at his calling in the book of Exodus, or Aaron's blame shifting in the story of the golden calf (Exod 4:1–17; 32:2–6, 21–24).

Initial reported discourse also opens up insights that sometimes go beyond the scope of a character's biography. Many have observed that Samson's story shares affinities with Israel at the canonical level,

---

7. Hans Frei's work on the *Wirkungsgeschichte* of the Bible in the Western world, and the development of the unfounded assumption that the Bible's meaning is only located in its extrabiblical reference, is well known: *The Eclipse of the Biblical Narrative: A Study in Eighteenth and Nineteenth Century Hermeneutics* (New Haven, CT: Yale University Press, 1974).

8. Shimon Bar-Efrat, *Narrative Art in the Bible* (Sheffield: Sheffield Academic, 1989), 64.

9. I am taking up the language of "heart" in this description without apology because it is a closer reiteration of the point of view depicted in the biblical world, even though modern terminology is much more refined with the advent of the social-scientific and psychological disciplines. Walter Eichrodt writes, "He [God] reveals himself to the individual's inmost desires and feelings as the liberating and renewing power of life ... which invites him to forget himself in a love of the whole heart and soul" (*Man in the Old Testament* [Chicago: Alec R. Allenson, 1956], 48).

both being dedicated to God with particular restrictions for the safe-
guarding of a holy vocation (Judg 13:4–5).[10] In other words, like Israel,
Samson's attention to the law of God (for Samson, the Nazirite vow)
is a matter of canonical witness. Israel, in the light of the warnings of
Deuteronomy 28, must avoid foreign women. Samson's failure in this
area stands as a warning for Israel as a whole, that if they are joined to
Canaanite women they will live in "madness, blindness, and confusion"
and will "grope about at noon as blind people grope in darkness" (Deut
28:28–29). Samson's first reported discourse makes sense along these
lines, since the trajectory that leads to his own death begins with "I saw
a ... woman" (Judg 14:2). Samson's focus on the faculty of sight in his
first statement is also no mistake; his loss of vision leads immediately
to his own death. In this sense, and inasmuch as Samson's story casts a
shadow over Israel as a whole, his initial speech functions as a warning
for Israel at the canonical level.

I would now like to transition to the question at hand, regarding
God's self-disclosure, keeping in mind these brief observations regarding the importance of reported speech for character formation in the
Old Testament. What are the implications for God's self-introduction
in the creation account of Genesis? We should start with his action.
Given the conventions for epithets in the Old Testament, it is notable
that God shows up without any external commentary. Rather, we are
introduced to him with his first act of making heaven and earth (Gen
1:1). This creative God is like a playwright who, when the curtain lifts,
walks across an empty stage and also serves as the first actor in the
drama. He not only writes the story but, while performing within it, he
sets the stage.[11] At the onset of the play, God structures the setting for
all other actors. He puts into place each of the props that will serve the

---

10. For some canonical readings of the Samson story, see Daniel Block, *Judges &
Ruth: The New American Commentary* (Nashville: Broadman & Holman, 1999), 392–93;
Brevard Childs, *Old Testament Theology in a Canonical Context* (Philadelphia: Fortress,
1985), 114–15; James L. Crenshaw, *Samson: A Secret Betrayed, a Vow Ignored* (Atlanta:
John Knox, 1978), 134; Edward L. Greenstein, "The Riddle of Samson," *Proof* 1 (1981):
247–55; Dennis T. Olson, "The Book of Judges: Introduction, Commentary and
Reflections," in *New Interpreters Bible 2*, ed. Leander E. Keck (Nashville: Abingdon,
1998), 860–62.

11. For John Calvin, creation is a *theatrum gloriae* (*Institutes* I.v.8; I.vi.2; I.xiv.20;
II.vi.1; III.ix.2).

forthcoming characters. As Genesis 1 introduces the character of this God, his agency is portrayed as one that opens up and makes possible all other agencies. So, from the very start, from without and within, God is both the playwright and protagonist of the Bible's story. God's double role cannot be encapsulated with any objective epithet, and so there is none.

God's first words in the creation account are "be light," and this is directly followed by a narrative report, "and light was" (Gen 1:3).[12] The initial command is simply made up of two words in the Hebrew text, which evinces a remarkable display of power and brevity.[13] This light of God is not described in itself. It is immediately named "day," and so it is understood as part of creation and is no emanation. This light comes before any particular manifestations of light are constructed (Gen 1:14; sun, moon, etc.).[14] Even in terms of this minimal, temporal distance between the initial light of God and the other heavenly lights, his initial command is set apart. God's first statement also dramatizes a supervenience like no other; he initiates with the smallest act, which immediately has ubiquitous effect. He also exerts little to no effort, and yet the result is universal.

God's *persona* initiates time itself through the creation of light, which comes before the distinction between day and night. In this sense God stands before time itself in the creation account. And yet, this God also moves and creates through time.[15] The narrative report of his initial command depicts him as having a particular kind of transcendence, one that stands before all temporal narratives in the Bible but that also moves freely within them.[16] In the same way he enjoys

---

12. יְהִי אוֹר וַיְהִי־אוֹר, Gen 1:3 BHS (my translation).

13. Meir Sternberg writes, "The complex of features making up God's portrayal emerges only by degrees and only through the action itself, starting with the creation of light by terse fiat" (*The Poetics of Biblical Narrative* [Bloomington: Indiana University Press, 1987], 322).

14. Achtemeier, "Jesus Christ, The Light of the World," 440–41.

15. Blocher, *In the Beginning*, 58–59.

16. Sternberg notes that God's character is constructed in the Hebrew Bible with an initial affinity for a "homogeneous portrait of God" bearing resemblance with the classical attributes, such as "omnipotent" and "omniscient"; this is subsequently brought into question by the "problematic stuff" of God's actions such as "wrath … [and] change of mind," and so on. His suggestion is that overall for God's

a presence in all settings but is not strictly identifiable with any. As playwright he creates the whole world with a simple command, but as protagonist he operates freely within that world and subjects himself to its temporal limits.

As it stands the story strips us of all resources for identifying this character's location according to the norms of the Old Testament. Rather, God acts and speaks out of himself, and as he does so, he transcends all possible epithets. All of the characters in the Bible, whether they are identified indirectly through a dramatic sequence or located with an external description, are given their backwards reference in this creative work of God. While the characterization process we undertake with this God is indirect, it is not merely indirect. It is a cumulative and dramatic process of a different kind. Meir Sternberg comments: "Though God is the Bible's hero, his portrayal may yet appear a special case. After all, most dimensions associated with character—physical appearance, social status, personal history, local habitation—do not apply to him at all. They are meant to be conspicuous by their absence, which impresses on the reader from the very beginning the message that the whole Bible will dramatize with variations: the qualitative distance that separates God from humans and pagan gods, both existing in matter and time and space and society."[17] As I see it, this creation account takes pride of place in its importance for the development of God's self-disclosing character in Scripture. With this assumption in mind, I'll offer us three implications of this observation for our consideration of revelation and reason.

GOD REVEALS HIMSELF AS DETERMINED TO DWELL WITH HUMANITY

In the initial seven days of the creation account, God's speaking forth each day reveals who he is by displaying his goal to establish fellowship with his creatures, that he might dwell with the man and woman and be "their God" (Exod 29:46; Lev 26:12; Jer 32:38; Ezek 37:23).[18] The initial

---

character "suggestion … proves more effective than statement" for the construction of God's dynamic character against the initial backdrop of his introduction, which displays his limitless power (Sternberg, *Poetics of Biblical Narrative*, 322–23).

17. Sternberg, *Poetics of Biblical Narrative*, 323.

18. Recent studies relating the temple with the creation account: Gregory K.

command, and each of the first seven days that follow, are a result of the divine word's external movement. This passage shares many similarities with the Decalogue in Exodus 20, both being key moments in the whole of the Pentateuch. Here God also speaks ten times, and as he does so he develops a larger regime, showing us what the world looks like as it stands gratefully beneath the word of God.[19]

In Genesis 1 creation is given a particular integrity beneath the authority of God's word; it has its own rhythms. There is day and night, light and darkness. "Light" in this instance is first named "day," and is "good," which betokens God's goal to establish regularity and order, and to dwell peacefully with his creation as a covenant partner (Gen 1:4). It is on account of his bringing about this light that the world is ordered according to day and night, and so it is made to be a world with rhythms, properly dignified by God's creative Word and ordered to have its own unique integrity beneath that Word.[20] The terminus of God's action here is that the man and woman should enjoy the final day of rest together with God. Depicted alongside the institution of the Sabbath, this final act of rest points to the goal that God should dwell with his people in covenant partnership.[21]

In the prologue to John's Gospel, the apostle also begins his account of the life of Christ with a special focus on Genesis 1.[22] Many of the

Beale, *The Temple and the Church's Mission: A Biblical Theology of the Dwelling Place of God* (Downers Grove, IL: IVP Academic, 2014); J. Daniel Hays, *The Temple and the Tabernacle: A Study of God's Dwelling Places from Genesis to Revelation* (Grand Rapids: Baker Books, 2016), 20–27; John H. Sailhamer, *Genesis Unbound: A Provocative New Look at the Creation Account* (Sisters, OR: Multnomah Books, 1996), 74–77; John H. Walton, *The Lost World of Genesis One: Ancient Cosmology and the Origins Debate* (Downers Grove, IL: IVP Academic, 2009), 72–92.

19. Jared Hood, "The Decalogue of Genesis 1–3," *RTR* 75, no. 1 (2016): 35–59.

20. The theme of light and darkness reverberates throughout the Old Testament and has a strong biblical heritage before it is refracted through the Johannine prologue (discussion below); see Exod 10:21–23; 13:21–22; 14:19–25; Pss 27:1; 119:105; Prov 6:23; Ezek 1:4, 13, 26–28; Isa 49:6; 60:2–3, 19–22; Hab 3:3–4; Achtemeier, "Jesus Christ, the Light of the World," 439–49.

21. Blocher writes, "He wishes to bring out certain themes and provide a theology of the Sabbath ... that was the theme closest to his heart" (*In the Beginning*, 50, 57); Sailhamer, *Genesis Unbound*, 149–50.

22. For some background on the re-creation theme in John's Gospel, see Jeannine K. Brown, "Creation's Renewal in the Gospel of John," *CBQ* 72 (2010): 275–90; John N. Suggit, "Jesus the Gardener: The Atonement in the Fourth Gospel

manifold themes and images that find their way into the Gospel of John also begin at "the beginning," and so the apostle does also, with a specific reference to Genesis 1:1 in the LXX.[23] This connects John's development of the theme of Jesus as the Light directly with Genesis 1:3. The apostle's initial identification of Christ with the Logos also reminds us of the εἶπεν ὁ θεός of Genesis 1 in the LXX (Gen 1:6, 9, 14, 20, 24, 29).[24] As in Genesis 1, the Word of God here moves to dwell with the world, but this time God's self, which is his self-expression in his creative commands, becomes incarnate in Jesus of Nazareth, the Word made flesh.

In John 1 the creative Word is personalized in Jesus of Nazareth. The apostle reiterates the common directive of God's Word and Light as established in Genesis 1: God intends to "tabernacle" with the world (John 1:14). This act of dwelling with humanity is both creative and redemptive. Both of these aspects of the Light are held together with "intentional ambiguity" so as to imply each of them, simultaneously.[25] Having invested the Light with divine and saving potency,[26] John does not want the metaphor to lose its connection with either the creation account or his forthcoming description of Jesus Christ. The prologue speaks of the "true Light" in terms of the creation account ("the world came into being through him," 1:9–10) as well as the salvation offered through the Light ("to all who received him ... he gave power to become children of God," 1:12).

Seeing this larger directive of God's light in Scripture reminds us that the doctrine of revelation cannot be dealt with in isolation from the doctrines of salvation, creation, or the church. God speaks forth his creative and self-expressive command, and he also decides to *speak himself* in the person of Christ because of an overriding intention to "tabernacle" with humanity (John 1:14). John Webster's work on Holy

---

as Re-creation," *Neotestamentica* 33 (1999): 161–68; N. T. Wright, *John for Everyone*, 2 vols. (Louisville: Westminster John Knox, 2004).

23. Ἐν ἀρχῇ, Gen 1:1 LXX.

24. Brown, "Creation's Renewal," 277.

25. Edward Klink, *John: Exegetical Commentary on the New Testament* (Grand Rapids: Zondervan, 2016), 95.

26. Klink comments that, while Genesis reflects the "lack of light's presence," which is in turn filled with the light of creation, John's account "reflects the manifestation of light's power" (Klink, *John*, 96).

Scripture brings out this aspect of revelation, which involves God's determination to dwell with his creatures as the telos of this doctrine. In Scripture, God freely decides to disclose himself *to us*. Webster emphasizes that revelation finds its end in divine and human fellowship. Revelation is "the self-presentation of the triune God, the free work of sovereign mercy in which God wills, establishes and perfects saving fellowship with himself in which humankind comes to know, love and fear him above all things."[27] Likewise, Herman Bavinck states: "For the special revelation in Christ is not meant to be restricted to himself but, proceeding from him, to be realized in the church, in humanity, in the world. The aim of revelation, after all, is to re-create humanity after the image of God, to establish the kingdom of God on earth, to redeem the world from the power of sin and, in and through all this, to glorify the name of the Lord in all his creatures."[28]

GOD'S HOLY WORKS ARE IMMEASURABLY GOOD FOR THE BENEFIT OF HIS CREATURES

A second observation concerning God's opening speech is that his commanded light illustrates the immeasurably good nature of his will. The creation of light in Genesis 1, and the subsequent distinction between light and darkness, implies that the nature of God's action is altogether holy and beneficial for the creature. Light is described as created by God, but darkness is only contrasted with that light. This distinction is established after the creation of light and then is named: "God separated the light from the darkness" (Gen 1:4).

While darkness is there at the onset of creation (Gen 1:2), no attention is drawn to it. From this point of view, the darkness itself, unlike the light, is not given any role as a signifier of God's will.[29] Darkness

27. John B. Webster, *Holy Scripture* (Cambridge: Cambridge University Press, 2003), 13.

28. Herman Bavinck, *Reformed Dogmatics*, vol. 1, *Prolegomena* (Grand Rapids: Baker Academic, 2003), 347. On this theme also see Billings, *Word of God for the People of God*, 80; Michael Horton, "Community Theater: Local Performances of the Divine Drama," in *Covenant and Eschatology* (Louisville: Westminster John Knox, 2002), 265–76; Peter Jensen, *The Revelation of God* (Downers Grove, IL: InterVarsity, 2002), 24–26.

29. Karl Barth's well-known exegesis of Gen 1 points out the importance of this word pair in his attempt to secure a position for his ontology of evil in his discussion

is named after the creation of light and so stands under the authority of God's creative Word. The Word of God simply names the darkness, demonstrating sovereignty, but as this is done he speaks forth the contrast between the two.[30] Darkness is not called "good," because it is light's foil. As Achtemeier writes, "Darkness, in the Bible, is evil and opposed to God."[31]

As in Genesis 1, the Light in John's Gospel is also contrasted with darkness. The light-darkness theme pervades the whole of the Gospel.[32] Jesus freely uses the metaphors of light and darkness in his manner of explaining the nature of the glory of God, his personal presence, and the self-assertion of those who oppose his ministry (John 3:19-21; 8:12; 9:4-5, 39-41; 12:35-36). He offers the light-darkness contrast to explain the reason why the religious leaders are incapable of "seeing"

---

of *das Nichtige* and also what he calls the "shadow side" of creation: "Just as it does not say that God created darkness, so it does not say that he saw that it was good" (*CD* III/1, 121). While I find his ontological reading of the darkness unnecessary, I find Barth's insight into the text to be shrewd.

30. See *CD* III/1, 123.

31. Achtemeier, "Jesus Christ, the Light of the World," 444. In her article Achtemeier also addresses the question raised by Isa 45:7, that Yahweh "creat[es] darkness." She mentions that this is one statement alongside others (within the Prophets) that read both darkness and light as subject to divine sovereignty (e.g., Amos 4:13; 5:8). Isaiah 45:7, however, is the Old Testament's "ultimate statement" on Yahweh's sovereignty over creation (445). This reminds of the plague of darkness in Egypt (Exod 10:21-23). Darkness is in this way subject to the will of God and stands as a predicate of God's will, but in a way that is incomprehensible and different in *kind* from light. This is artfully described in the creation account as both are named (Gen 1:5), but only the light is called "good" (Gen 1:4). Henri Blocher mentions that darkness and light, good and evil, and the story of evil's defeat in Scripture all leave us with the cross as the only definitive standpoint; see *Evil and the Cross* (Downers Grove, IL: InterVarsity, 1994), 130. If darkness/evil were, in these terms, *created* by God, it would be a *thing*, and the atonement would be unnecessary because the problem would only call for a *larger thing* to conquer it, with greater force (Blocher, *Evil and the Cross*, 131). So the nature of God's light in Gen 1 is ultimately promissory. The anticipated day of Yahweh in Amos, for instance, envisions a coming forth of eschatological darkness, which undoes the cosmos (Amos 8:9), culminating in the cross (Luke 23:44-45), and is resolved in the dazzling apparel of the angels in the resurrection (Luke 24:4). Light in the creation account means that God will conquer evil and define the difference between light and darkness definitively in the coming of the kingdom of God, or what I have called the "regime of the Word" in the creation account, which I see as prefiguring the kingdom.

32. John 3:19; 8:12; 12:35, 46; 1 John 1:5, 6; 2:8, 9, 11; Don Carson, *The Gospel According to John* (Grand Rapids: Eerdmans, 1991), 119.

the Light seen by the formerly blind man (John 9:39-41). John Painter notes that the apostle's depiction of the "light shin[ing] in the darkness" (announced in the prologue) pervades the whole Gospel with reference not only to the creation account but the incarnation and the resurrection.[33] Descriptions of night and day throughout the story also function as representations of light and darkness. Nicodemus begins in the night and subsequently moves into the light as he comes to faith (3:2). However, Judas begins his betrayal of Christ with a movement away from the light of Jesus' presence as he goes out into the night (13:30).[34] As Edward Klink says, darkness and light in John describe a "cosmic battle and a cosmic reality."[35]

With the advent of the darkness-light word pair, the light is positioned beneath the Word of God as a signifier of the will of God. This impresses us with the unadulterated holiness and goodness of God's will. Considered theologically, this is potentially a first instance of G. C. Berkouwer's "biblical *a priori*," that God is holy and not in any way the author of sin.[36] The Bible consistently depicts the will of God as holy: "God is light and in him there is no darkness at all" (1 John 1:5). In this sense the light-darkness word pair (as a predicate of God's initial, creative speech) signifies God's will for the creation of humanity as unspeakably good and objectively distinguished from darkness and rebellion. God reveals himself as he reveals that his will for the creation of humanity is not admixed with sin or evil in any compromise.

When we turn to the doctrine of revelation from the vantage point of God's holiness and unadulterated goodness, we are reminded that

---

33. John Painter, "'The Light Shines in the Darkness' ... Creation, Incarnation and Resurrection in John," in Craig R. Koester and Reimund Bieringer, eds., *The Resurrection of Jesus in the Gospel of John* (Tübingen: Mohr Siebeck, 2008), 21-46.

34. Painter, "'Light Shines in the Darkness,'" 21.

35. Edward Klink, "Light of the World: Cosmology and the Johannine Literature," in *Cosmology and New Testament Theology*, ed. Jonathan T. Pennington and Sean M. McDonough (London: T & T Clark, 2008), 79.

36. Gerrit C. Berkouwer's use of the story of the fall to illustrate the intellectual problem points out the inescapably personal nature of our response to the abstract question of sin's origin and that "causal" schemes inevitably lead to self-excusing approaches; see "The Question of Origin," in *Sin* (Grand Rapids: Eerdmans, 1971), 11-26, 523. Also see Henri Blocher, *Original Sin: Illuminating the Riddle* (Grand Rapids: Eerdmans, 1997), 105-35; Terrence Tilley, *The Evils of Theodicy* (Eugene, OR: Wipf & Stock, 2000).

revelation, when it is brought to its full fruition, subverts our sense of self-ownership.[37] God does not disclose himself to us to satisfy our convenience or intellectual curiosity. Rather, revelation must be accompanied by and received with repentance.[38] For this reason, Helmut Thielicke includes a statement on the doctrine of the Holy Spirit in his prolegomena to *The Evangelical Faith*. In his sketch of some of the intellectual questions associated with the relationship between Christian faith and modern thought, he positions his doctrine of the Spirit at the center of this discussion. Thielicke maintains, in a pivotal moment in his own prolegomena, that the Spirit provides a new self-understanding for believers conditioned by the "salvation event."[39] He draws on the parable of the prodigal son to describe how a modern person's self-understanding can be constituted by the gospel. Thielicke maintains that revelation is irruptive: "This Word cannot be integrated into something already there. It creates."[40] Thielicke's reflection here reminds us that revelation cannot be received in a merely intellectual way. It demands repentance, as the prodigal son returns to the Father. Revelation expresses God's opposition to sin and alienation, and it works in favor of what was originally intended for his creatures in the beginning.

GOD BLESSES CREATION AS A GRACIOUS AND HEAVENLY FATHER

A third aspect of God's initial creative command is that it reveals God's intention to create as Father. That is, like Rachel's opening speech, God's first command expresses a biographical intentionality. God's creative action extends across a whole week for the benefit of the crown of his creation, the first couple. The initial command that there "be light" (Gen 1:3) produces a light that is immediately converted into "day" (Gen 1:5), and then what follows is a seven-day structure, which climaxes

---

37. Billings, *Word of God for the People of God*, 75–86.

38. See Kevin Vanhoozer, *First Theology: God, Scripture & Hermeneutics* (Downers Grove, IL: InterVarsity, 2002), 227–28; Vanhoozer, *The Drama of Doctrine: A Canonical Linguistic Approach to Christian Theology* (Louisville: Westminster John Knox, 2005), 187–203. Webster writes, "Faithful reading of Holy Scripture in the economy of grace is an episode in the history of sin and its overcoming" (*Holy Scripture*, 87).

39. Helmut Thielicke, *The Evangelical Faith*, vol. 1, *Prolegomena: The Relation of Theology to Modern Thought Forms* (Grand Rapids: Eerdmans, 1974), 138–73.

40. Thielicke, *Evangelical Faith*, 1:150.

with the creation of humanity. The whole of this creative week, when understood as a natural extension of the initial creative command, expresses God's fatherly care for the first man and woman. Hence, we see the culmination of the creation account highlighted with its only use of the definite article for "the" sixth day (Gen 1:31). Also, while God is not described as Father explicitly here, another sign of paternal love can be found in Genesis 5:1, where the making of an image of oneself is an act of begetting, as Seth is begotten in the "image of" Adam. If Adam and Eve are made in God's image, is this not also an indication of God's paternal love for the first man and woman at the climax of the creative week?[41]

Throughout the creation account God intends to bless and benefit the first couple. This exemplifies his gracious provision for humanity. In this context טוב can be understood covenantally: "beneficial."[42] God provides a partner for the first man because it is not "good" for him to be alone (Gen 2:18). "Good" in these introductory chapters signifies God's intention to bless.[43] A counterexample also helps us with this: there is a day that is not called good, and about which the text only says "and it was so" (Gen 1:7). This is the second day, the day for separating the waters above from those below. This day also foreshadows the collapse of both sets of waters in the flood narrative (Gen 7:11).[44] Since the water canopy does not benefit the first couple in any immediate way, and perhaps because it may foreshadow the coming of the flood, the second day is not said to be "good."

When the word "good" is understood in this way, the whole of the creation week builds into a portrait of worship, mutual fellowship, and rest, culminating in the Sabbath. All of the initial creation days surround the first couple with blessing. In this light the defiance of Adam and Eve also makes transparent sense. The man and the woman insist on taking a fruit and asserting their own self-sufficiency; they seek to know what is *best* as they both aim to benefit themselves in opposition

---

41. For instance, in Luke's Gospel, Adam is the "son of God" (Luke 3:38).

42. "טוב," in Francis Brown, S. R. Driver, and Charles A. Briggs, *The Brown-Driver-Briggs Hebrew and English Lexicon* (Peabody, MA: Hendrickson, 1997), 373–75.

43. Sailhamer writes, "In this chapter something is 'good' only if it directly benefits mankind" (*Genesis Unbound*, 119; see Gen 2:9, 17; 3:5, 22; 26:29).

44. Alter, *Genesis*, 32; Gordon J. Wenham, *Genesis 1–15* (Waco, TX: Word, 1987), 181.

to God and each other.[45] This ingratitude provides us with an indirect testimony to God's fatherly care in the creation account. The first couple, in their attempt to supplant the word of God, denies what the creation account tells us directly: that all that took place as a result of the divine speech was accomplished for the "very good" benefit of the man and woman (Gen 1:31).

The light in John's Gospel furthers God's aim to benefit creation as Father. God sends the eternal Word for the salvation of the world. This Logos has divine status and dwells eternally with the Father (John 1:1). Herman Ridderbos finds the shared divinity between the Father and the Logos to be explanation enough for the apostle's interest in the creation account. As John compares the incarnation with other examples of God's self-mediation in Scripture, he finds no other suitable comparison available except for the speaking and shining forth of God's Logos and Light in the creation account.[46] He sees John's adaptation of Genesis 1 to be a reworking of its content due to the historical manifestation of the eternal Word "with the Father" (e.g., 1 John 1:1–3).

This Logos is also identified with the μονογενής of the Father (John 1:14), and so Jesus' healing is understood as an expression of the Father's "work" (5:17). When Jesus heals on the Sabbath, he tells the religious leaders that this is lawful because he, as God's unique Son, is doing the personal work of the Father in the maintaining and restoring of creation.[47] This identification attributes the creation week specifically to the Father. Jesus' contemporary work on the Sabbath, in his hearkening back to creation, serves to manifest the glory of the Father in

---

45. Blocher writes, "By posing each as absolute, they absolutize their difference" (*In the Beginning*, 173–74).

46. Herman Ridderbos writes, "When the evangelist wants to express the glory of him whose witness he is, he cannot speak of this glory in any other way but in divine categories. ... That is why the evangelist falls back on the dynamic creating word in the beginning of all God's ways, the word that called forth light out of darkness and created life: the Logos of life that was from the beginning. ... What is said of the Logos can be said of the Light, too: that it has been with the Father from the beginning" ("The Christology of the Fourth Gospel: History and Interpretation," in *Studies in Scripture and Its Authority* [Grand Rapids: Eerdmans, 1978], 68).

47. In John 5, Jesus identifies his work in healing on the Sabbath with the Sabbath of the creation account, which is ongoing, perhaps because it does not end with an "evening and morning" statement, as do the other days of Gen 1; Blocher, *In the Beginning*, 57; Klink, *John*, 275–76.

his unique Son, which is a reiteration of the glory not fully shown to Moses in the exodus.[48] The unique glory invested in the Son indicates a qualitative difference between the Son and the "children of God" (1:12), who only partake in fellowship with the Father through the Son (14:6), and in doing so become "children of light" (12:36).

Considered theologically, God's revelation finds its culmination in our joyful reception of his self-disclosure as the triune God: Father, Son, and Holy Spirit. If we continue our brief look at John's Gospel, Philip asks Jesus in the upper room that he reveal the Father (14:8), which shows a practical blindness in response to the Light of the world, who is always shining (9:5). Jesus responds to this request by teaching the disciples about the coming of the Holy Spirit, and these words of exhortation are a reiteration of the Father's intention; they "belong to the Father who sent me" (14:24).[49] This teaching cannot be received without the comforting work of the Spirit himself, which will only be realized when Jesus breathes on the disciples after the resurrection (20:22).[50] This coming of the Paraclete will complete the revelation of the triune God for the disciples, as the Spirit will teach them "everything" (14:26).

The disciples, Jesus says, will be left with the peace and joy of Christ's presence among them in the Spirit, which will mark them with "a courageous serenity."[51] This joy and peace springs abundantly from the heart of the triune God, who shares his Light with the world. God's glory reflects his own, internal joy. Karl Barth, among others, identifies the glory of God with the disclosure of all of his perfections. God's vitality puts his inward serenity and joy on display: "All together and without exception [the divine perfections] take part in the movement of God's self-glorification and the communication of His joy. They are

---

48. Klink, *John*, 111.

49. See Don Carson, *Jesus and His Friends: An Exposition of John 14–17* (London: Paternoster, 1995), 69.

50. Klink sees in this act fulfillment of Jesus' prayer in John 17:23, "I in them and you in me," completing the revelation of the triune God in the Spirit's inauguration of the mission of the church (*John*, 861–66).

51. Carson, *Jesus and His Friends*, 87. Carson points out that Jesus imparts his *own* peace to the disciples with a first-person possessive: "my peace." This is a peace that is open to suffering, as is Christ's, and is not "as the world gives" (John 14:27); see Carson, *Jesus and His Friends*, 83–88.

the coming into being of light outside Him on the basis of the light inside him, which is Himself."[52]

CONCLUSION

In the first chapter of Genesis, God's first speech in the creation of light is explicative of his self-revealing work in creation and salvation. The initial creation week is started with the creation of light and is manifest in a series of subsequent days. In response to God's opening statement, creation is made to be a regime of shalom beneath God's Word. God's intention to bring about this result is discernible across the narrative, which is, when taken on the whole, a reflecting and exposing of God's character as Father, who acts for the sake of his creatures without compromise.

In John, the Light that creates and re-creates is Jesus, and so the backwards reference to Genesis 1 is unmistakable. As in the creation account, the Light in John's Gospel is the external movement of the divine Word toward a dwelling with humanity, a manifestation of God's holy will and an expression of his fatherly action. However, in John's Gospel the accent is placed on how these divine operations are accomplished in person, in Jesus of Nazareth.

This refraction of God's creative light through the prologue to John's Gospel also reminds us that the doctrine of revelation cannot be detached from the dynamic unfolding of God's glory and light in the Bible's witness to the economy of grace. God's self-revelation cannot be detached from his goal to save, redeem, and establish fellowship. Also, revelation cannot be apprehended or properly understood without repentance. Finally, God's revelation finds its end in our joyful acknowledgment of him in his life as Father, Son, and Holy Spirit.

---

52. *CD* II/1, 647. More recently, Kevin Vanhoozer's explication of the divine perfections also observes divine light as an objective category; see *Remythologizing Theology: Divine Passion, Action and Authorship* (Cambridge: Cambridge University Press, 2010), 247–51.

WORKS CITED

Achtemeier, Elizabeth. "Jesus Christ, the Light of the World: The Biblical Understanding of Light and Darkness." *Interpretation* 17, no. 4 (1963): 439–49.

Alter, Robert. *Genesis: Translation and Commentary*. New York: W. W. Norton, 1996.

Bar-Efrat, Shimon. *Narrative Art in the Bible*. Sheffield: Sheffield Academic, 1989.

Barth, Karl. *Church Dogmatics*. 4 vols. Edinburgh: T&T Clark, 1956–1975.

Bavinck, Herman. *Reformed Dogmatics*. Vol. 1, *Prolegomena*. Translated by John Vriend. Grand Rapids: Baker Academic, 2003.

Beale, Gregory K. *The Temple and the Church's Mission: A Biblical Theology of the Dwelling Place of God*. Downers Grove, IL: IVP Academic, 2014.

Berkouwer, Gerrit C. *Sin*. Grand Rapids: Eerdmans, 1971.

Billings, J. Todd. *The Word of God for the People of God: An Entryway to the Theological Interpretation of Scripture*. Grand Rapids: Eerdmans, 2010.

Blocher, Henri. *Evil and the Cross*. Downers Grove, IL: InterVarsity, 1994.

———. *In the Beginning: The Opening Chapters of Genesis*. Downers Grove, IL: InterVarsity, 1984.

———. *Original Sin: Illuminating the Riddle*. Grand Rapids: Eerdmans, 1997.

Block, Daniel. *Judges & Ruth: The New American Commentary*. Nashville: Broadman & Holman, 1999.

Brown, Francis, S. R. Driver, and Charles A. Briggs. *The Brown-Driver-Briggs Hebrew and English Lexicon*. Peabody, MA: Hendrickson, 1997.

Brown, Jeannine K. "Creation's Renewal in the Gospel of John." *CBQ* 72 (2010): 275–90.

Calvin, John. *Institutes of the Christian Religion*. Edited by John T. McNeill. Translated by Ford Lewis Battles. 1536 ed. Philadelphia: Westminster, 1970.

Carson, Don. *The Gospel According to John*. Grand Rapids: Eerdmans, 1991.

———. *Jesus and His Friends: An Exposition of John 14–17*. London: Paternoster, 1995.

Childs, Brevard. *Old Testament Theology in a Canonical Context*. Philadelphia: Fortress, 1985.

Crenshaw, James L. *Samson: A Secret Betrayed, a Vow Ignored*. Atlanta: John Knox, 1978.

Eichrodt, Walter. *Man in the Old Testament*. Chicago: Allenson, 1956.

Frei, Hans. *The Eclipse of the Biblical Narrative: A Study in Eighteenth and Nineteenth Century Hermeneutics*. New Haven, CT: Yale University Press, 1974.

Greenstein, Edward L. "The Riddle of Samson." *Proof* 1 (1981): 247–55.

Hays, J. Daniel. *The Temple and the Tabernacle: A Study of God's Dwelling Places from Genesis to Revelation*. Grand Rapids: Baker, 2016.

Hood, Jared. "The Decalogue of Genesis 1–3." *RTR* 75, no. 1 (2016): 35–59.

Horton, Michael. *Covenant and Eschatology*. Louisville: Westminster John Knox, 2002.

Jensen, Peter. *The Revelation of God*. Downers Grove, IL: InterVarsity, 2002.

Klink, Edward. *John: Exegetical Commentary on the New Testament*. Grand Rapids: Zondervan, 2016.

————. "Light of the World: Cosmology and the Johannine Literature." In *Cosmology and New Testament Theology*, edited by Jonathan T. Pennington and Sean M. McDonough, 74–89. London: T&T Clark, 2008.

Olson, Dennis T. "The Book of Judges: Introduction, Commentary and Reflections." In *New Interpreters Bible 2*, ed. Leander E. Keck, 722–888. Nashville: Abingdon, 1998.

Painter, John. "'The Light Shines in the Darkness' … Creation, Incarnation and Resurrection in John." In *The Resurrection of Jesus in the Gospel of John*, edited by Craig R. Koester and Reimund Bieringer, 21–46. Tübingen: Mohr Siebeck, 2008.

Ridderbos, Herman. *Studies in Scripture and Its Authority*. Grand Rapids: Eerdmans, 1978.

Sailhamer, John H. *Genesis Unbound: A Provocative New Look at the Creation Account*. Sisters, OR: Multnomah, 1996.

Sternberg, Meir. *The Poetics of Biblical Narrative*. Bloomington: Indiana University Press, 1987.

Suggit, John N. "Jesus the Gardener: The Atonement in the Fourth Gospel as Recreation." *Neotestamentica* 33 (1999): 161–68.

Thielicke, Helmut. *The Evangelical Faith*. Vol. 1, *Prologomena: The Relation of Theology to Modern Thought Forms*. Translated by Geoffrey W. Bromiley. Grand Rapids: Eerdmans, 1974.

Tilley, Terrence. *The Evils of Theodicy*. Eugene, OR: Wipf and Stock, 2000.

Vanhoozer, Kevin. *The Drama of Doctrine: A Canonical Linguistic Approach to Christian Theology*. Louisville: Westminster John Knox, 2005.

————. *First Theology: God, Scripture & Hermeneutics*. Downers Grove, IL: InterVarsity, 2002.

————. *Remythologizing Theology: Divine Passion, Action and Authorship*. Cambridge: Cambridge University Press, 2010.

Walton, John H. *The Lost World of Genesis One: Ancient Cosmology and the Origins Debate*. Downers Grove, IL: IVP Academic, 2009.

Webster, John B. *The Domain of the Word*. London: T&T Clark, 2012.

————. *Holy Scripture*. Cambridge: Cambridge University Press, 2003.

Wenham, Gordon J. *Genesis 1–15*. Waco, TX: Word, 1987.

Wright, N. T. *John for Everyone*. 2 vols. Louisville: Westminster John Knox, 2004.

2

The Public Character of Revelation

Divine Speech and Finite Reason

Daniel J. Treier

The doctrine of divine revelation is a complex nexus of challenges. Any particular account of revelation needs to clarify its scope and focus: for instance, the plausibility of Christian truth in relation to alternatives (apologetics)? The particular character of Christian theological reasoning (theological prolegomena)? An account of Christian theology's authoritative sources and their relationships (theological encyclopedia)? A Christian account of reasoning in general (a theological epistemology)? In some distinction from all of these alternatives, the present essay focuses on how *concepts* of revelation intersect with late modern challenges to the *plausibility* of authoritative divine communication.

"Modern" people have come to see faith and revelation on one hand, and knowledge and reason on the other, as fundamental opposites. Eric Springsted tells of surveying his students and discovering that "the vast majority thought faith was 'believing something without proof.'"[1] They remained unable to grasp the concept of trust: instead, "faith was a 'personal' choice (albeit in a shallow sense of 'personal'). ... The idea of faith as knowledge gained by interpersonal dealings, or as a matter of being linked to a tradition, a history, or a community, didn't make sense because traditions, history, and communities didn't make sense at any deep level."[2] Springsted points out that "in the modern world Mark Twain could get a laugh by claiming in the mouth of a schoolboy that

---

1. Eric O. Springsted, *The Act of Faith: Christian Faith and the Moral Self* (Grand Rapids: Eerdmans, 2002), ix.
2. Springsted, *Act of Faith*, x.

'faith is believing what you know ain't true.'" While a medieval person "would not have gotten the joke,"[3] modern philosophy of religion implies that faith could only be rational at all if we provide grounds for God's existence and offer evidence for divine revelation.

But this intuitive modern contrast between faith and reason is profoundly problematic. Modernity perceives revelation to involve primarily personal or even private realities; in epistemological terms these realities count merely as claims regarding experience—hardly a basis for public argument. Faith leaps into an intellectual abyss. By contrast, in theological terms "revelation" involves divinely ordered reality being communicated accessibly to all, at least in principle. Meanwhile, modernity perceives reason to involve primarily public or even universal realities; in epistemological terms these count as claims regarding undebatable truths, by virtue of procedural standards combined with personal neutrality. Again, by contrast, in theological terms "reason" involves human practices of recognizing and responding to an ordered world. While in principle its realities are accessible to all who encounter them, in practice they are encountered in particular circumstances that providentially limit the contingent possibilities of human understanding.

In unfolding a theological response to this set of contrasts, first I will provide a conceptual narrative of a gradual but tragic shift concerning revelation: away from the biblical emphasis on communication and hearing, toward a visual emphasis on illumination and seeing. Once classical plausibility structures collapsed and no longer undergirded the widespread acknowledgment of divine revelation, for modern thinkers revelation appeared to involve a subjective claim of inner experience or genius rather than an objective disclosure of reality. Second, I will provide an alternative biblical account of revelation that incorporates visual metaphors secondarily, subsequent to the oral concepts that are fundamental to divine self-communication. Third, I will provide a corrective account of revelatory divine communication that addresses human finitude and not just human fallenness. Finitude has been relatively neglected among traditional doctrines of revelation

---

3. Springsted, *Act of Faith*, 6.

since fallenness has been the preoccupation of conservative reactions against modernity. Fourth and finally, I will suggest a couple of corollary implications for a theological account of human reason.

A CONCEPTUAL NARRATIVE:
FROM HEARING TO (NOT) SEEING

So, first of all, a brief narrative of a long conceptual shift regarding revelation. The Bible itself takes a word-centered and speech- or hearing-oriented approach. Fully defending that broad claim is of course impossible here. For the moment, suffice it to say that revelation itself is not the Bible's preeminent concept for either theological or general knowledge. The root metaphor underlying the concept "revelation" is visually oriented, suggesting a movement from hidden to disclosed, from unseen to seen. In a related sense revelation as a biblical concept is apocalyptically oriented, suggesting a history and a hope of dramatic unveilings. As Peter Jensen highlights, however, the biblical concept of most interest for theological authority is the knowledge of God, with this knowledge of God belonging in the larger narrative context of the gospel.[4] Moreover, the Bible frequently construes this knowledge of God in terms of wisdom.[5] As a motif, revelation occurs when God dramatically moves along the narrative of the gospel, within which he communicates the divine light and life.

Facing the unfolding challenges of the Greco-Roman context, early Christian apologists pursued philosophical and cultural engagement grounded in appeals to the Logos. The surrounding (neo-)Platonic environment encouraged Christians increasingly to construe the knowledge of God in visually oriented terms. Thus they often depended on the metaphor cluster of light and illumination.[6] God, who is himself light,

---

4. Peter Jensen, *The Doctrine of Revelation*, Contours of Christian Theology (Downers Grove, IL: IVP Academic, 2002).

5. See this case made in Daniel J. Treier, *Virtue and the Voice of God: Toward Theology as Wisdom* (Grand Rapids: Eerdmans, 2006), chap. 2.

6. The surrounding account seems to be consistent with the tracing of key sources in works such as René Latourelle, *Theology of Revelation: Including a Commentary on the Constitution "Dei Verbum" of Vatican II* (repr., Eugene, OR: Wipf & Stock, 2009). Regarding complexities over illumination in particular, see also briefly Carl R. Trueman, "Illumination," in *Dictionary for Theological Interpretation of the Bible*, ed. Kevin J. Vanhoozer (Grand Rapids: Baker Academic, 2005), 316–18;

is self-expressive: the Father begetting the Son, who is the Word, in the Spirit. This light of the divine self-communication provides illumination for humans to see reality as it is. Ambiguity arises over the object of illumination: the subject matter, or our unseeing eyes? Still, the emphasis on illumination accords with the dominant medieval construal of salvation's end: God's illumination leads humans toward the beatific vision.

Such an illumination-oriented account is objectivist, but not in the early modern sense of pursuing distance or neutrality in relation to the object. Rather, the objectivity of knowledge stems from the object giving itself to the mind of the knowing subject(s).[7] This objective giving invites various forms of relationship. With respect to a personal God, in whose mind the relevant conceptual forms reside, this objective giving invites relationships of participation. God gives the human knower(s) a creaturely part in God's self-knowledge insofar as the very forms of true ideas reside in the divine mind. The Logos in whom all of reality holds together is not merely some divine attribute or operation or externalization but a Person, by whose Spirit people come to know the triune God. So the human knower participates not just in God's self-knowledge but in God's self-communication and accordingly—at a suitable level—in God's own blessed fellowship.

The attractions of such an account are not solely apologetic or philosophical but also properly theological, as the Johannine echoes suggest. Nevertheless, cultural attractions ebb and flow. The affinity between revelation and reason began disintegrating at least by the later Middle Ages. If the church's epistemic authority had not already begun to disintegrate with the Great Schism, then it certainly disintegrated in the Reformation era.[8] Traditional metaphysics further disintegrated during

---

furthermore, Lydia Schumacher, *Divine Illumination: The History and Future of Augustine's Theory of Knowledge* (Oxford: Wiley-Blackwell, 2011), places the metaphor in a wider epistemological context than just Christian theology's construal of divine revelation.

7. Mark A. Bowald, "Objectivity," in *Dictionary for Theological Interpretation of the Bible*, ed. Vanhoozer, 544–46.

8. For a provocative account with theological insights highlighting both of these time periods, see William J. Abraham, *Canon and Criterion in Christian Theology* (Oxford: Clarendon, 1998). Yet in response see Daniel J. Treier, "A Looser 'Canon'?

early modernity's Copernican revolution. In the end the objective givenness of revelation's illumination gave way to its subjective—and therefore episodic, merely private, apparently arbitrary—possibility. Beauty—along with the goodness, truth, and unity of being—would now reside in the eye of the beholder.

At least some theological attractions of such an account remain. Some of its cultural attractions remain as well, at least in the eyes of those who call for "reenchanting" the world with a sacramental ontology, according to which a world of signs invites participation in divine things.[9] The point here is not that such an illumination-oriented account is simply unbiblical or entirely caused its own demise. More modestly, though, when an exceedingly complex set of cultural factors pulled revelation and reason apart, this illumination-oriented account left Christians vulnerable to the appearance of irrationality—not just in the core mysteries of faith but also in our very stance toward the world. Once seeing with the mind's eye gave way to "seeing is believing"—for yourself—with Christendom's unified authority and plausibility structures disintegrating, believing went from being publicly necessary to optional and then to increasingly implausible.

A BIBLICAL ALTERNATIVE: FROM HEARING THE WORD TO BEHOLDING WISDOM

So far, the implied moral of this story is that we should recover the Bible's orientation toward speech and hearing when it comes to knowledge of God. To summarize the virtues of this more biblical orientation: First, a word-oriented account addresses the apocalyptic dimensions of revelation. God's communication makes knowledge of God possible in a salvation history that incorporates divine interruptions into particular contexts. Second, a word-oriented account addresses the need for interpretation alongside these interruptions themselves: God's mighty acts are communicative, and God's communication is active.

Relating William Abraham's *Canon and Criterion in Christian Theology* to Biblical Interpretation," *JTI* 2, no. 1 (2008): 101–16.

9. See Hans Boersma, *Heavenly Participation: The Weaving of a Sacramental Tapestry* (Grand Rapids: Eerdmans, 2011), and in response Daniel J. Treier, "*Heavenly Participation: The Weaving of a Sacramental Tapestry*—A Review Essay" (with a response from Hans Boersma), *Christian Scholar's Review* 41, no. 1 (Fall 2011): 67–71.

God does not leave humans to their own interpretative devices, and this communicative orientation honors the objective givenness for which illumination-oriented accounts were groping. Third, from a related angle, communication is more (inter)personal: a word-oriented account helps to avoid a dichotomy between "personal" and "propositional" notions of revelation, along with a related dichotomy of whether divine self-communication is purely objective or instead requires a successful response to count as revelation.

Fourth, a further way to champion a communication-oriented account is Trinitarian, in terms of Word and Spirit.[10] The Spirit helps to make the Word public precisely by making the hearing more deeply personal—as divine transcendence is reflected in the possibility of the most radical indwelling. The Logos is not preeminently an impersonal rational structure that humans hope to see with the mind's eye, but God's communication in person—the substance that (who) holds all creation together. The claim is not that such a Word-oriented account will make Christianity appear to be more rational or convincing to modern unbelievers. Instead, a Word-oriented account could make Christianity appear less irrational to Christians, giving them more confidence in the gospel as they face late modernity.

Yet proposing this moral for the story requires addressing a series of potential objections, particularly from Scripture.

1. Does not the Old Testament, especially the Psalter, contain visually oriented texts—the heavens declaring God's glory, the firmament showing God's handiwork (Ps 19)?

2. Does not the Old Testament, especially the wisdom literature, contain creation-oriented texts that emphasize human recognition rather than divine communication?

3. Does not Romans 1:18–20 establish a *locus classicus* for bringing these Old Testament antecedents into a New Testament theology of creation's general revelation and human recognition?

---

10. For a resolute champion of a Trinitarian perspective see Colin E. Gunton, e.g., *A Brief Theology of Revelation* (Edinburgh: T&T Clark, 1995).

4. Does not the New Testament, notably John's Gospel, use illumination metaphors related to knowing God?

5. Does not 2 Corinthians 3–4 treat textual communication as problematic while celebrating visual metaphors, metaphors related not just to creation but to knowledge of God in Jesus Christ?

6. More generally, does not biblical material regarding creation order or even natural law support at least the rudiments of natural theology?

To address these questions briefly:

1. Indeed, some Old Testament texts establish the objective givenness of visually oriented divine self-revelation. But those texts generally run in tandem with communication metaphors; accordingly, they do not establish the priority of the visual over the oral. They certainly do not assert the reality of independently adequate or saving pagan knowledge of God on a visual basis.

2. Indeed, likewise, some Old Testament texts establish the objective givenness of the Creator's communicated wisdom. But again they do not assert the reality of independently adequate or saving pagan knowledge of God on a visual basis. Instead, Job 28 and Ecclesiastes emphasize the elusiveness of humans grasping what Lady Wisdom in Proverbs 1, 3, and 8 apparently offers. Wisdom's offer of divine self-communication and self-expression in the created order is quite limited, and it has a particular context, the covenant community.

3. Indeed, Romans 1:18–20 establishes a kind of general revelation. But two strong qualifications immediately follow: its minimal content (God's eternal power and divine nature) and its negative result (human distortion and subsequent liability for judgment).

4. Indeed, John 1:9 makes the intriguing statement about Christ's light enlightening everyone. But John 3:19–21 generalizes that humans love darkness rather than light. John 5:31–47 and 8:31–59 critique mistaken searching of the Scriptures, even or especially within the covenant community. The overarching theme of testimony, along with John's theology of the Logos, makes the Gospel word-oriented. The beholding of God's glory in Christ via the Spirit's witness is particular to the apostles before it becomes any more general for later generations.

Therefore, the meaning of enlightenment in John 1 must be seen in this larger context. Divine speaking illuminates, rather than the other way around.

5. Indeed, 2 Corinthians 3–4 indicates the propriety of visual metaphors. But the visual metaphors properly apply to those who have heard God's Word in the Spirit, those who are then free to seek further transformation as they gaze on Christ's image. The emphasis of the larger context rests on the greater glory of the Spirit's life-giving ministry; that greater glory reflects the more dazzling and enduring glory of Jesus Christ, in comparison with the previous and merely human mediation comprising Moses' ministry. Veiled hearts prevent understanding unless the divine communication becomes fully personal in this way.

6. Indeed, the Old Testament does appeal to creation order, even as having some kind of relation to the Torah (Isa 24:5), by which all the earth's peoples could be called to account. But Oliver O'Donovan suggests two crucial distinctions that mitigate against a more full-blown account of "natural law": a distinction between ontology and epistemology, and a distinction between whole and part.[11] The ontological reality of the created order does not ensure its postlapsarian epistemological recognition. Partial recognition of the created order does occur, among unbelievers and not just believers, yet the recognition remains episodic and the resulting obedience only partial because of competing first principles. Instead of the fear of the Lord leading to full-orbed wisdom, too often unbelief fragments human participation in God's shalom.

In sum, the claim is not that the Bible has no place for visual metaphors or even a concept of illumination in its theological epistemology. To the contrary: in principle creation highlights divine power and wisdom. Failures to recognize such divine revelation, however, entail that humans need redemption in order to know the true God or even to see creation truly. Because reconciliation with the triune God happens through hearing the word of forgiveness in Jesus Christ by the Holy

---

11. Oliver O'Donovan, *Resurrection and Moral Order: An Outline for Evangelical Ethics*, 2nd ed. (Grand Rapids: Eerdmans, 1994), especially 85–91.

Spirit, oral metaphors are conceptually prior to visual ones. The Spirit enables people to read the letter of Scripture in the freedom of the gospel, and only in that light to read the book of nature properly from cover to cover. Otherwise, humans read the created order more like an encyclopedia: experts learn a lot about bits and pieces, and others access a little of that knowledge, yet no overarching unity appears to be more than alphabetical. Accordingly, oral metaphors must take precedence. Having heard the word, by the Spirit we can then see everything in the light of its truth.

A NEGLECTED ASPECT: FROM ACKNOWLEDGING THE FALL TO CELEBRATING FINITUDE

Beyond the epistemic plausibility of divine illumination, modern theologies of revelation faced an additional fork in the road. Modernist or liberal theologies, reacting to tensions between universal or public reason and historical events or personal experiences, addressed human finitude as much or more than fallenness. Conservative theologies reacted by relating special revelation primarily to that fallenness.

While these conservative theologies rightly treated the biblical history of God's self-communication as integral to the history of redemption—and vice versa—prelapsarian humanity already needed and experienced divine self-communication, as God's walking and talking with Adam and Eve testifies. Hence an evangelical account of revelation must not only address human fallenness but also appreciate our finitude.

The thought of Martin Heidegger provides a convenient basis for generalizing about the quasi-"existentialist" accounts of finitude that became influential among modern theologians.[12] Heidegger recognized some challenges that human life contexts place on the development of authentic personal identity. We experience the world in terms of anxieties we have in the face of death, in terms of social expectations to which we conform, and in terms of uses we have for things, which

---

12. For a lengthier sketch of Heidegger's thought in relation to the Bible, see Daniel J. Treier, "Ecclesiastes in Dialogue with Modernity: A Matter of Life and Death," in *Reading Ecclesiastes Intertextually*, ed. Katharine Dell and Will Kynes, Library of Biblical Studies (London: Bloomsbury T&T Clark, 2014), 295–308.

disclose what they are. Yet Heidegger's thought displays the crucial difference that belief (or not) in bodily resurrection makes for how to construe the relational character of human existence.

The Bible places human limits in a set of relational contexts, to which (for instance) the use of various prepositions can attest.[13] We live "in" a series of spheres of reality. The limits established by these spheres need not be threatening impositions. They can instead comprise liberating gifts—liberating humans from the desire to become gods, to direct our own lives. Yet these limits can only be received as gifts by embracing the hope of resurrection: resurrection hope directs people to their true end, eternal life, promising that no earthly limit threatens a definitive end to their existence. Relationship with God and the new humanity in Christ will ultimately help them to find, rather than feeling the need to create, their true selves. Proper theological treatment of human finitude will recognize our need for the revelatory promise of redemption.

But emphasizing finitude is not just another way of indicating that divine revelation addresses fallen people who need good news. Both the Bible and the book of nature depict finite human existence in terms of several relational spheres of reality. These relational spheres indicate that most human knowing depends on testimony, and this emphasis on testimony underscores the epistemic viability of appeals to divine revelation. To depend on God telling us so, particularly through the Bible mediating the witness of fellow humans, is in character with the rest of human existence. Thus, consider briefly how the following relational spheres of life together both limit us humans and undergird our meaningful agency.

- Human lives unfold "in" (1) the context of *the created cosmos*—whose order points to their life-giving Creator and to limits shared with fellow creatures;

---

13. This theological sketch of finitude borrows major portions of Daniel J. Treier, "Finitude," in *Evangelical Dictionary of Theology*, 3rd ed., ed. Daniel J. Treier and Walter A. Elwell (Grand Rapids: Baker Academic, 2017), 317-19—used with permission here.

- "in" (2) the context of *a body*—which provides both a medium for action and particular limits on human agency;
- "in" (3) the context of *family*—whose members are God's agents for giving and sustaining earthly life and personal identity;
- "in" (4) the context of *time*—whose passage gives each person a particular history, shaping opportunities for developing personal identity into enduring character;
- "in" (5) the context of *place*, or meaningful spaces—whose particular location gives shape to personal identities and opportunities through the love of particular neighbors and friends, both human and nonhuman. Given these contexts of body, family, time, and place, humans are nameable. Being named, they have bodies that can be located, relationships that can be enacted, and thus lives that can be narrated.
- Hence human lives are already oriented in many respects, yet their intentionality may and must be directed "at" (6) *work*,
- "at" (7) *play*,
- and/or "at" (8) *rest*, at any particular time-place within a broader history and neighborhood. Humans are unique among earth's embodied creatures in having responsible agency—in being able to contemplate their ultimately religious self-transcendence, embodiment, families, times, and places.[14]
- Accordingly, if humans are to realize their true end, then these activities ought to comprise ever-deepening participation "in" (9) *Jesus Christ and his body*, the church,
- "by" (10) *the Holy Spirit*. This participation in Christ and his body raises the question of how fully humans should ever be "at home" in the contexts of this present earthly age.

We can generalize about this set of relational realities that limit human lives and direct them toward their true end. But generalization quickly encounters irreducible particularity. Because the Creator has given us bodies through which to engage a world, humans are oriented by the love of particular family members, neighbors, and friends, and

14. See here the account of personhood in Robert Spaemann, *Persons: The Difference between "Someone" and "Something,"* trans. Oliver O'Donovan, Oxford Studies in Theological Ethics (Oxford: Oxford University Press, 2007).

by particular activities in particular time-places. Human agency is a gift, bringing particular yet limited opportunities for giving gifts—even the self—to God and others. Such possibilities may be narrower or wider, but they are not endless. Receiving this gift of agency from the Creator establishes its lawful context: Humans need divine instruction regarding how to give good gifts to others, and how to receive gifts, in a manner that genuinely counts as worship.

So in two respects genuine human freedom is not limitless. First, we appropriate prior forms of possible action within each newly particular context. These relational realms we find ourselves "in" simultaneously limit our possibilities and mark out spaces that contain concrete opportunities for action. Second, then, we become accountable for responses to suffering we undergo and for stewardship of gifts we are given—accountable ultimately to God, proximately to the various others who mediate the suffering and the gifts. A definitive biblical contrast ensues concerning the fundamental human response within these relational contexts. In the Old Testament this contrast involves whom or what we fear: God, or someone or something else? In the New Testament the contrast undergoes a conceptual shift to focus on faith: Will humans fundamentally fear someone or something else, or be defined by God's promise of resurrected life? Such faith is the form that the fear of God takes once Israel's Creator has redeemed humanity in Jesus Christ.

Such an account of human finitude again signals how divine self-communication is a more suitable focus than divine "revelation" as such. It prioritizes oral, rather than visual, metaphors as being most suitable for the located, limited, yet self-transcending creatures that God has made humans to be. Humans are those with whom God walked and talked in the garden—a proto-Word. Humans are those to whom God gave the tree of life—a proto-sacrament. The interpersonal communication and personal presence that comprise fellowship—these we needed, and God gave right from the beginning. In that context of fellowship humans could discover and delight in, even denominate, the wonders of the world God made. When we soon fell, God pursued us and spoke to us, involving various forms of creaturely mediation in our redemption and return to rightful worship. God's word and Spirit restore the vision necessary to see salvation's glory and creation's wisdom; vision does not restore our ability to hear (and to obey: note the conceptual overlap between those responses).

The primacy of word over vision in a Christian account of revelation is fitting in light of the gospel's primacy for the knowledge of God.[15] The good news not only involves what God has already done but also continues to have a promissory character, so that its proclamation elicits faith in what people cannot yet see. In part, then, the oral priority in divine revelation stems from the fall, from a cosmic curse and the personal need of redemption. The point of the present account is to complement that truth, though, by showing that the oral priority in divine revelation also aligns with human finitude. God has related to us as speaking and hearing creatures right from the beginning. Finite creatures could not have a comprehensive worldview unless God, who alone has a God's-eye perspective, spoke first. The world in its givenness presented opportunities for human naming and cultivation. For all its visual tableau, however, the world with its relational realms comprised a historical order in which the God who is essentially Spirit talked with us. Once humans fell from this grace, from the garden all the way to the incarnation, God often accommodated himself to them by taking visual form. Yet, thus getting attention with visual forms, God simultaneously veiled himself in unveiling himself. We most fully know God when the Spirit makes divine presence real in word and sacrament, transcending the otherwise human limits that make us self-transcending creatures—when, in other words, God communicates to establish communion with us.

CONCEPTUAL IMPLICATIONS: FROM "REVELATION" AS DIVINE SPEECH TO PRACTICES OF FINITE REASON

Therefore, an account of divine revelation that reflects the Bible's emphasis on verbal communication should begin with what is often called special revelation, namely God's word as it variously takes human form(s). Such a verbally oriented account can quickly acknowledge the reality of what is often called general revelation, namely creation's varied forms of testimony regarding God its Creator. All humans ought

---

15. As emphasized in Jensen, *Doctrine of Revelation.*

to respond to such testimony by fearing God in faith. But how can they believe if they have not heard? The primacy of Scripture as divine self-testimony follows from the primacy of the gospel and the triune God's self-communication in Jesus Christ.

Those who have heard this good news do not stop with initial faith; they press on toward developed obedience, seeking deeper understanding of the good news and its implications for all of life. All Christians are amateur theologians, learning to practice this craft of faith seeking understanding in the twin contexts of created reality and cultural reasoning. Theology as a disciplined, communal craft comprises a crucial aspect of the church's faithful witness in response to hearing God's word. Still, because we hear this word by the Spirit, in the contexts of God's loving work in the world, theological wisdom rightly seeks to integrate its witness with the full panoply of truth that creation and cultural history seem to communicate.

On acknowledging in this way that "all truth is God's truth," we need to consider the application of "general revelation" terminology to nontheological realms of study. Evangelical support for liberal arts education frequently appeals to this conceptual framework. Yet there is good reason to worry that general revelation is not the best category for authorizing such engagement with wider learning. One concern is that the definition of "revelation" gets overstretched: Not all truths are heard from God in the same way or speak about God as directly. If studying biology or sociology depends primarily on general revelation, then such spheres of human knowledge reduce to theological claims in some trivial way. Or revelation simply establishes that God as Creator is the ultimate source of knowledge, again in a trivial way: God is not primarily a rival source of knowledge among academic disciplines, or else "God" becomes a gap filler in human knowledge—pushed aside easily and often. Another concern with basing wider learning on general revelation is that the motivation behind such learning gets pinched. If studying biology or sociology depends primarily on general revelation, then such spheres of human knowledge reduce to instrumental means serving "spiritual" ends. Truths about physical life or human society become unimportant in themselves, interesting only for what they might indirectly reveal about divine character. Here God is not just a rival source of knowledge but rival subject matter.[16]

Theology then makes a false peace with the intuition that God does not care very much about the world he created or the cultural histories he providentially sustains. All truth is God's truth, however, because God's self-disclosure communicates that God loves the world. How can we communicate that commitment without worshiping the creature instead of the Creator? Partly by celebrating human finitude properly, as a divine gift. This gift indicates both that creaturely goods are to be occasions of delight, in all their particularity, and that they are to be occasions of worship, in all their limitations. Created goods direct us to listen and respond to the speech of the One who confers the freedom to enjoy them rightly.

————————

Of course, further concerns might arise concerning the communication-oriented account of revelation proposed here. One possible concern focuses on Christians: such an account could reinforce the worst sort of logocentric, propositionalist, dead yet divisive orthodoxy. Or, more minimally, such an account could reinforce the naive hope that hearing or knowing more about God will produce more loving obedience. In response, excessive biblical literacy may not be a very plausible contemporary worry.[17] But the form of the word's primacy advocated here is not cognitively oriented in any case. To the contrary: in principle a

————————

16. This concern about general revelation is expressed in chap. 1, "Faith Seeking Understanding," of Daniel J. Treier, *Good News: An Evangelical Introduction to Christian Theology* (Grand Rapids: Baker Academic, forthcoming)—used with permission here.

17. John Sullivan, "Reading Habits, Scripture and the University," in *Bible and the University*, ed. David Lyle Jeffrey and C. Stephen Evans, Scripture and Hermeneutics 8 (Grand Rapids: Zondervan, 2007), 216–39, reflects anecdotal worries over increasing biblical illiteracy, whereas Byron R. Johnson, "The Case for Empirical Assessment of Biblical Literacy in America," 240–52, denies that social-scientific evidence demonstrates the increase—further discussed briefly in Daniel J. Treier and Craig Hefner, "Twentieth- and Twenty-First Century American Biblical Interpretation," in *Oxford Handbook of the Bible in America*, ed. Paul Gutjahr (Oxford: Oxford University Press, 2017), 129–48.

more communication-oriented, less revelation-oriented, conceptual framework is less likely to exacerbate problematic rationalism.[18]

Another possible concern focuses on non-Christians: What difference would it likely make in the public square to get revelation's conceptual house in order? Even if the proposed conceptual narrative and biblical alternative were right, is it not impossible to recover some purported golden age or receive an opportunity to rewrite past mistakes? And how could focusing on divine speech make revelation seem to be more public rather than less?

In response, the biblical and historical truth of the matter should transcend pragmatic immediacy. Practically speaking, though, a communication-oriented account could foster a properly missional approach that is less apologetic (whether defensively on the right or culturally on the left) while more enduringly soteriological and ecclesial. Revelation is very public indeed if the Creator God's speech announces truth to everyone, and God's Spirit can address Christ's saving word personally to anyone. We should hardly ignore apologetics or avoid philosophical epistemology altogether. But late modernity's typical assumptions about knowledge are periodically relevant, not intellectually decisive, for a Christian theological approach to revelation. Strands of philosophical epistemology increasingly recognize how dependent human beings are on testimony.[19] This dependence on testimony for nearly all knowledge is fitting in light of human finitude, with its embodied relationships that are substantially enacted by speaking and hearing. In light of their fallenness, humans further depend on particular testimony about God's redeeming grace, given the need for forgiveness in Christ and the Spirit's regeneration. Dependence on testimony, in light of the fall, is an extension of what humans face in light

---

18. The recent work of James K. A. Smith, most notably *Desiring the Kingdom: Worship, Worldview, and Cultural Formation*, Cultural Liturgies 1 (Grand Rapids: Baker Academic, 2009), has rightly challenged the excessively cognitive focus of much Christian worldview thinking, especially in educational spheres. Some caveats about the biblical "foolishness of preaching" are needed, however, lest Smith's work be misused to offer a distortedly noncognitive picture of Christian transformation at the other extreme.

19. As noted in Kevin Vanhoozer and Daniel J. Treier, *Theology and the Mirror of Scripture: A Mere Evangelical Account*, Studies in Christian Doctrine and Scripture (Downers Grove, IL: IVP Academic, 2015), 85–100.

of finitude—not some kind of philosophical abnormality concocted by desperate apologetics.

Hence, believing again that testimony is integral to most if not all human knowing, with testimony to their faith making a viable claim of personal knowledge in an inevitably pluralistic public square, Christians might worry less about the church's conformity to cultural plausibility structures. Instead we should focus more on our fidelity to biblical truth and conformity to Christ's love. We let our light shine before others so that they may see good works, yes—but in the hope that this sight will draw them toward the city of God, where they may *hear* people heralding the good news.

WORKS CITED

Abraham, William J. *Canon and Criterion in Christian Theology*. Oxford: Clarendon, 1998.

Boersma, Hans. *Heavenly Participation: The Weaving of a Sacramental Tapestry*. Grand Rapids: Eerdmans, 2011.

Bowald, Mark A. "Objectivity." In *Dictionary for Theological Interpretation of the Bible*, edited by Kevin J. Vanhoozer, 544–46. Grand Rapids: Baker Academic, 2005.

Gunton, Colin E. *A Brief Theology of Revelation*. Edinburgh: T&T Clark, 1995.

Jensen, Peter. *The Doctrine of Revelation*. Contours of Christian Theology. Downers Grove, IL: IVP Academic, 2002.

Johnson, Byron R. "The Case for Empirical Assessment of Biblical Literacy in America." In *The Bible and the University*, edited by David Lyle Jeffrey and C. Stephen Evans, 240–52. Scripture and Hermeneutics 8. Grand Rapids: Zondervan, 2007.

Latourelle, René. *Theology of Revelation: Including a Commentary on the Constitution "Dei Verbum" of Vatican II*. Reprint, Eugene, OR: Wipf & Stock, 2009.

O'Donovan, Oliver. *Resurrection and Moral Order: An Outline for Evangelical Ethics*. 2nd ed. Grand Rapids: Eerdmans, 1994.

Schumacher, Lydia. *Divine Illumination: The History and Future of Augustine's Theory of Knowledge*. Oxford: Wiley-Blackwell, 2011.

Smith, James K. A. *Desiring the Kingdom: Worship, Worldview, and Cultural Formation*. Cultural Liturgies 1. Grand Rapids: Baker Academic, 2009.

Spaemann, Robert. *Persons: The Difference between "Someone" and "Something."* Translated by Oliver O'Donovan. Oxford Studies in Theological Ethics. Oxford: Oxford University Press, 2007.

Springsted, Eric O. *The Act of Faith: Christian Faith and the Moral Self*. Grand Rapids: Eerdmans, 2002.

Sullivan, John. "Reading Habits, Scripture and the University." In *The Bible and the University*, edited by David Lyle Jeffrey and C. Stephen Evans, 216–39. Scripture and Hermeneutics 8. Grand Rapids: Zondervan, 2007.

Treier, Daniel J. "Ecclesiastes in Dialogue with Modernity: A Matter of Life and Death." In *Reading Ecclesiastes Intertextually*, edited by Katharine Dell and Will Kynes, 295–308. Library of Biblical Studies. London: Bloomsbury T&T Clark, 2014.

———. "Finitude." In *Evangelical Dictionary of Theology*, 3rd ed., edited by Daniel J. Treier and Walter A. Elwell, 317–19. Grand Rapids: Baker Academic, 2017.

———. *Good News: An Evangelical Introduction to Christian Theology*. Grand Rapids: Baker Academic, forthcoming.

———. "*Heavenly Participation: The Weaving of a Sacramental Tapestry*—A Review Essay." *Christian Scholar's Review* 41, no. 1 (Fall 2011): 67–71.

———. "A Looser 'Canon'? Relating William Abraham's *Canon and Criterion in Christian Theology* to Biblical Interpretation." *JTI* 2, no. 1 (2008): 101–16.

———. *Virtue and the Voice of God: Toward Theology as Wisdom*. Grand Rapids: Eerdmans, 2006.

Treier, Daniel J., and Craig Hefner. "Twentieth- and Twenty-First Century American Biblical Interpretationn." In *Oxford Handbook of the Bible in America*, edited by Paul Gutjahr, 129–48. Oxford: Oxford University Press, 2017.

Trueman, Carl R. "Illumination." In *Dictionary for Theological Interpretation of the Bible*, edited by Kevin J. Vanhoozer, 316–18. Grand Rapids: Baker Academic, 2005.

Vanhoozer, Kevin J., and Daniel J. Treier. *Theology and the Mirror of Scripture: A Mere Evangelical Account*. Studies in Christian Doctrine and Scripture. Downers Grove, IL: IVP Academic, 2015.

3

The Personal and Cultural Character of Reason

Christ's Triumph over Modern Technique

Daniel J. Treier

A contemporary Christian account of divine revelation ought to resist or even reverse late modernity's intuitive associations. So I argued in a prior essay, "The Public Character of Revelation: Divine Speech and Finite Reason." Divine revelation should not be treated as primarily personal or even private. Human reason should not be treated as a pre-eminently public or even universal "source" of authoritative, "scientific" knowledge. Instead, divine revelation involves divinely ordered reality being communicated publicly—in principle, to all. Reason involves creatively faithful practices of recognizing and responding to the realities of God's cosmos. These practices depend on personal faculties being deployed in various communal contexts.

Accordingly, an account of revelation should recover the biblical focus on communication and hearing, within which visual metaphors of illumination and seeing have a properly secondary place. Accounting for humans' need of divine revelation in terms of finitude, not just fallenness, actually supports such a communicative focus because our limitations involve the gift of relationships, and these relationships make our knowing heavily dependent on testimony. Here, then, we need to develop a theological account of human reason consistent with that revelatory focus on the word. Such an account of reason should orient human knowing ultimately to the wisdom rooted in fearing the Lord and hearing with faith. Such wisdom can make appropriate space for exploring the world in the light of its Creator's glorious presence and for engaging creation's checkered cultural history in the wake of the fall.

This account of human reason will unfold in a series of steps. First, I will briefly sketch an account of late modern rationality's increasingly technical orientation, since "technique" has become a regime that dominates how humans think. Next, a preliminary account of human reason's three aspects—its personal character, its communal practice, and its cultural products—will deflate "reason" from a purportedly universal "source" set in opposition to revelation and faith. Then I will address the contemporary public context of Christian reasoning, at least in certain "Western" social strata, by sketching a theology of culture with which to address modernity's technological regime. The primary framework for this theology of culture will emerge from the work of Oliver O'Donovan. His political theology and ethics help us to understand Christian practical reason in light of the resurrected Christ's reign over all other earthly powers.

FROM TECHNIQUE TO TECHNOCRACY

First, a contemporary theological account of reason must grapple with the modern dominance of its instrumental and procedural aspects: the regime of "technique." Well known in the philosophical realm is Martin Heidegger's phenomenology of how people come to know things in terms of their use(s). Of course, generalizations about "modern" individualism and objectivity in the wake of René Descartes, along with subjectivity in the wake of Immanuel Kant, are similarly well known. But, for present purposes, Jacques Ellul highlights a particularly important aspect within the modern transformation of rationality: the way in which modernity's knowledge regime intersects with its societies' technological apparatus.

Ellul defines "technique" in a way that has epistemological, not just technological, import: "the totality of methods rationally arrived at and having absolute efficiency (for a given stage of development) in every field of human activity."[1] Ellul emphasizes the priority that modernity

---

1. The following account is consistent with my own reading of primary texts, but I cannot do better than this summary from my colleagues (with whom I have taught Ellul): Jeffrey P. Greenman, Read Mercer Schuchardt, and Noah J. Toly,

places on efficiency, on the one best way of achieving desired results as quickly and completely as possible. Technique involves methods and not just machines, becoming more than the sum of any individual means while encompassing economic, organizational, and human realms. Technique thus defined has seven major characteristics.[2] (1) *The automatism of technical choice*: technique fosters finding the one best way apart from meaningful human judgment. (2) *Self-augmentation*: technique fosters commitment to its continual development. (3) *Monism*: technique functions as a whole and is not divisible into various characteristics here and there. (4) *Technical universalism*: technique in modernity has newly universal ambitions and thus promotes sameness everywhere. (5) *The autonomy of technique*: technique always ends up working independently of other considerations, making efficiency trump any moral or even spiritual norm. Above all, though, (6) *rationality*: technique systematizes everything through discourse and logic. And (7) *artificiality*: technique struggles with nature and supposedly creates anew—although, ironically, in seeking to overcome necessity with human freedom, it creates new forms of necessity.

In the realm of knowledge, modernity's self-understanding as the era of newfound "science" ironically generates yet simultaneously masks tension between the instrumental and procedural aspects of "reason" thus defined. Is knowledge to be pursued for its own sake, with *procedures* as objectively and purely neutral as possible? Or is knowledge to be pursued for its practical usefulness, with *instrumental* value for technological development and hence social benefit?

Rather than generalizing about this ironic regime at even greater length, it is worth considering its effects on Christian thinking under three headings.

First, its effect *on Christian scholars and public intellectuals*: As C. Stephen Evans has suggested, Christian scholars have become increasingly afraid to make Bible- or tradition-based claims in the public square.[3]

Understanding Jacques Ellul (Eugene, OR: Cascade, 2012). The quote is from Ellul's *Technological Society*, trans. John Wilkinson (New York: Vintage, 1964), xxv, cited in Greenman, Schuchardt, and Toly, *Understanding Jacques Ellul*, 22.

2. Quoted and summarized from Greenman, Schuchardt, and Toly, *Understanding Jacques Ellul*, 30–34.

3. See C. Stephen Evans, "Afterword: The Bible and the Academy: Some

Science has created the illusion that truly rational claims can claim procedural neutrality and thus, in principle, universal assent. By contrast, historically normal realms of human disagreement, including so-called ultimate questions of meaning, now seem to be almost automatically causes for skepticism: if not everyone will agree, or at the very least acknowledge the validity of one's arguments, then one cannot claim that one knows—or maybe even that there is truth to know. Accordingly, Christian intellectuals tend to make even specifically Christian claims in terms that are as neutral as possible; witness for instance the debates over natural law or the political theory of John Rawls.

Second, the effects of the regime of "technique" *on biblical and theological scholars*: Long-standing debates over so-called historical criticism and "reading the Bible like any other book" reflect the frequent assumption that genuine scholarship must appeal to procedural reason as neutrally as possible. Evangelicals themselves have become leaders in defending this ideal, not just embracing the validity-oriented hermeneutics of E. D. Hirsch Jr. but even insisting that the integrity of biblical authority depends on doing so. For those recently interested in "theological interpretation of Scripture," to question aspects of procedural reason has led to charges of embracing "postmodernism" and/or "pragmatism," associated with crass versions of instrumental reason.[4]

Third, then, the effects of the regime of "technique" *on pastors and laypersons*: Instrumental reason can become precisely the problem, intensifying alienation between the people of God and the public square in general, not to mention the academy in particular. Modernity has generated the paradigm of "application," defined over against "observation" and "interpretation," for how we (instrumentally) engage the Scriptures. Laypersons' frequent expectation is that pastors' sermons,

---

Concluding Thoughts and Possible Future Directions," in *The Bible and the University*, ed. David Lyle Jeffrey and C. Stephen Evans, Scripture and Hermeneutics 8 (Grand Rapids: Zondervan, 2007), 304–10, as discussed briefly in Daniel J. Treier and Craig Hefner, "Twentieth- and Twenty-First Century American Biblical Interpretation," in *Oxford Handbook of the Bible in America*, ed. Paul Gutjahr (Oxford: Oxford University Press, 2017), 129–48.

4. For a strong champion of Hirsch's approach, see the hermeneutics of Walter C. Kaiser Jr. For an overview of theological interpretation of Scripture vis-à-vis alternatives, see Daniel J. Treier, *Introducing Theological Interpretation of Scripture: Recovering a Christian Practice* (Grand Rapids: Baker Academic, 2008).

to be spiritually fruitful, must provide concrete steps of application.[5] Both laypersons and pastors as well as scholars tend to desire a formulaic method or procedure for moving sequentially from observation to such application via one right interpretation. The very act of interpretation, though, is viewed as unfruitful unless it eventuates in a certain kind of application. Theological schools and biblical scholars are faulted for their arrogance and abstraction when they do not meet this ideal. Moreover, laypersons and pastors often reflect either overconfidence about Scripture's plain meaning and concrete application on one hand or else timid and helpless confusion on the other. This dialectic between overconfidence and confusion may simply be the nonacademic corollary to the increasing skepticism among Christian intellectuals about bringing robust biblical thinking into the public square.

Elsewhere I have suggested that a rigidly sequential, two-step picture of biblical interpretation may be holding people captive.[6] Framing the exegesis of Scripture more theologically, and the nature of theology more holistically in terms of "wisdom," helps to resist the regime of technique. Without extensively repeating that material here, next I will briefly sketch a theology of human reason that further develops the possibilities of such premises.

A BRIEF THEOLOGY OF HUMAN REASON

First, *rationality's personal character*: Reason is an activity that engages certain faculties of particular human persons. There is a revealing ambiguity connected with several relevant English words, including "theology" and "tradition"; they can designate both discursive products and the intellectual and communicative activities that generate them. So it is with "reason"; meanwhile its overarching biblical motifs, "knowledge of God" and "wisdom," similarly encompass not only discursive products or content but also cognitive activity in the former

---

5. For concern over the homiletical problems with two-stage hermeneutics, see Richard A. Muller, "The Study of Theology," in *Foundations of Contemporary Interpretation*, ed. Moisés Silva (Grand Rapids: Zondervan, 1996), 630–31.

6. E.g., Daniel J. Treier, "Christology and Commentaries: Examining and Enhancing Theological Exegesis," in *On the Writing of New Testament Commentaries: Festschrift for Grant R. Osborne on the Occasion of His 70th Birthday*, ed. Stanley E. Porter and Eckhard J. Schnabel (Leiden: E. J. Brill, 2013), 299–316.

case ("knowing God") and even a state of being in the latter ("being wise"). "Philosophy" itself, classically, designates such an overlapping state of being and activity ("love of wisdom")—as well as the discourse and content that result.

Particular persons think. Speaking of a social unit thinking is minimally at one metaphorical remove from this personal reality. An individual person thinks as an inner activity, in connection with all that he or she is—not least "spiritually," before God. This activity not only expresses the person's existing character but also affects future character. Martha Nussbaum is among many who are helping to broaden our contemporary conceptions of reason and the identities of its practitioners. She helpfully suggests that emotions can be pointers to deeply held reasons.[7] Thus, Christian thought was not simply hidebound in the biases of a given era when it appropriated the classical picture of reason's self-involvement. Christians have properly theological reasons for engaging the profoundly personal and contextual character of human knowing.

Biblical wisdom material does acknowledge the realities of instrumental and procedural reason. Much of what passes for "wisdom" is a matter of skill—of learned and/or calculated behavior. But neither totally nor even primarily, for wisdom begins with fearing the Lord. And that is the foundation for what the Bible means by "knowing" God and "understanding" God's will.[8] Viewed from the other side, the rich realities of relating to God are very frequently depicted in cognitive terms, with vocabulary that involves reason. So it will not do to isolate modern, scientific, or skill-oriented, knowing altogether from the deeply personal knowing with which the Bible deals—treating the former as intellectual and the latter as something merely experiential or relational. Of course, distinctions can be made; but from a biblical, Christian perspective both ordinary and scientific knowing have their place within the holism of true wisdom. Reason is an activity of persons,

---

7. Martha C. Nussbaum, *Upheavals of Thought: The Intelligence of Emotions* (Cambridge: Cambridge University Press, 2001).

8. See especially Daniel J. Treier, *Virtue and the Voice of God: Toward Theology as Wisdom* (Grand Rapids: Eerdmans, 2006), chap. 2.

not of machines geared for either the most efficient results or the most complex understanding.[9]

Second, *rationality's communal practice*: If reason is an activity of particular persons, nevertheless it is undertaken via language, in social contexts, within a developing history, and therefore with contingent standards of excellence—roughly the import of what Alasdair MacIntyre means when he speaks of a "practice."[10] The insights of virtue epistemology signal that lifelong learning is itself learned, while reliable knowing involves people of truth-conducive character participating in communities of study and deliberation.[11] If philosophy of science after Thomas Kuhn and Michael Polanyi teaches anything, then both the personal factors behind creative hypotheses and the communal factors behind intellectual paradigm shifts need due acknowledgment.[12] When we simply aggregate "reason" as a depersonalized philosophical source that supposedly competes with the authority of revelation, we run roughshod over these aspects of personal character and communal practice. Character and practice affect both theological reception of revelation and societal employment of reason.

Third, *rationality's cultural products*: If we should not primarily speak of "reason" in a reified sense as a philosophical source, then how should we understand the products of reasoning as an activity? Reasoning does generate concepts to think with, ideas to think about, and beliefs to hold. But it also generates institutions to think within and texts to communicate with.[13] These institutions and texts, as well as the linguistic

---

9. A striking account of the dangers of trying to make human thinking machinelike appears early in Brian Brock, *Christian Ethics in a Technological Age* (Grand Rapids: Eerdmans, 2010).

10. Alasdair MacIntyre, *After Virtue: A Study in Moral Theory*, 2nd ed. (Notre Dame: University of Notre Dame Press, 1984), 186–87.

11. See, e.g., W. Jay Wood, *Epistemology: Becoming Intellectually Virtuous*, Contours of Christian Philosophy (Downers Grove, IL: InterVarsity, 1998); Linda Trinkaus Zagzebski, *Virtues of the Mind: An Inquiry into the Nature of Virtue and the Ethical Foundations of Knowledge* (Cambridge: Cambridge University Press, 1996).

12. See Thomas S. Kuhn, *The Structure of Scientific Revolutions*, 2nd ed. (Chicago: University of Chicago Press, 1970), and especially Michael Polanyi, *Personal Knowledge: Towards a Post-Critical Philosophy* (Chicago: University of Chicago Press, 1958), which comes from a Christian and a practicing scientist.

13. For an account of concepts, see Kevin J. Vanhoozer and Daniel J. Treier, *Theology and the Mirror of Scripture: A Mere Evangelical Account*, Studies in Christian

habits they appropriate and replicate, exert personally and socially forming power. In short, the activity of reasoning depends on testimony, so it produces "culture" or "cultures" (depending on theoretical preferences for emphasizing the singular or the plural). Such cultural activity involves not just static products but dynamic feedback loops, as texts and institutions shape the concepts, ideas, and beliefs of persons through their communal practices.

To integrate human reason's elements of personal character, communal practices, and cultural production, it is helpful to borrow from culture's metaphorical roots in agriculture.[14] Reason's cultural products comprise not only the fruit harvested from previous cultivation but also the seeds of subsequent personal character and communal practices. Such an account of human reason makes sense of the Bible's emphasis on *walking* and *growing* in wisdom. But, of course, metaphors always break down, and picturing the dynamics of reason in terms of a social field does not mean that persons simply plant themselves. Christians should think about reason not just culturally but salvation-historically, in terms of *God's communicative activity* that superintends social forces and gives personal freedom. Furthermore, now that Christian thinking often seems to be on the defensive in the public square, and certainly should feel itself to be deeply at odds with the regime of technique, an account of reason should not only address social forces and personal freedom generally. It should also specifically orient the church's public intellectual witness regarding revelation. In other words, a contemporary Christian account of reason—and especially how the church's witness should engage the wider culture with faith seeking understanding—is best developed not via philosophical epistemology but instead as an aspect of a theology of culture. For developing such a theology of culture, particularly to address the forms of human action called "technology," the work of Oliver O'Donovan is uniquely helpful.

Doctrine and Scripture (Downers Grove, IL: IVP Academic, 2015), especially 181–90; for an introduction to accounts of institutions that are broader than organizations, see Jonathan Leeman, *Political Church: The Local Assembly as Embassy of Christ's Rule*, Studies in Christian Doctrine and Scripture (Downers Grove, IL: IVP Academic, 2016), especially chap. 2.

14. See the deflationary account in D. Stephen Long, *Theology and Culture: A Guide to the Discussion*, Cascade Companions (Eugene, OR: Cascade, 2008).

THE PUBLIC CONTEXT OF CHRISTIAN REASONING

O'Donovan's contributions to an evangelical understanding of Christian public life can be traced under four headings, loosely related to major monographs preceding his current trilogy: (1) God's kingship and the history of salvation, (2) Christ's resurrection and creation's moral order, (3) the Spirit's freedom and society's authoritative judgment, and (4) the monk's cell and common objects of love.

God's Kingship and the History of Salvation

Though it might count as his second major monograph, *The Desire of the Nations* takes logical priority for the present concern. There O'Donovan develops political theology as a Christian tradition that means more than just "what theology says about politics."[15] Political theology emerges from acknowledging the lordship of God in Christ. Political theology therefore develops an analogy between the divine and human rule that modernity is determined to keep separate: political theology talks about God as King.[16]

The twofold suspicion behind modernity's separation of divine and human rule is that politics corrupts morality, and theologians corrupt politics. By contrast, political theology avers that reflection on the history of God's saving reign in Christ can provide the needed concept of authority that modernity lacks. The biblical history of salvation, with its very political concepts, deserves attention that is genuinely historical, neither fundamentally suspicious nor simply Whig.[17]

The Bible's crucial affirmation regarding this history of salvation is that providence works to fulfill the promise of Yahweh's redemptive reign. Political theology therefore understands legitimate authority to involve (1) God's saving victory as its efficient cause; (2) the act of judgment as its formal cause; (3) the possession of land and God's law as its material cause; and (4) God's praise as its final cause. Accordingly, legitimate earthly political authority involves (1) the exercise of power

---

15. Oliver O'Donovan, *The Desire of the Nations: Rediscovering the Roots of Political Theology* (Cambridge: Cambridge University Press, 1996). What follows is a summary that sometimes hews very closely to the book's own language.

16. O'Donovan, *Desire of the Nations*, 1–5.

17. O'Donovan, *Desire of the Nations*, 6–11, 12–21, 21–29.

(in light of God's saving victory), (2) the execution of right (in the act of judgment), (3) the maintenance of tradition (in land and law), and (4) acknowledgment (in the service of acknowledging the ultimate Ruler with praise). Thus, God provided military, judicial, kingly, and prophetic mediators of such authority.[18]

Christian believers, in this time between the divine reign "already" inaugurated in Christ and its consummation "not yet" fully realized, both separate from and influence "secular" governing authorities (chap. 3). Jesus' act of representation inaugurates God's triumphant reign as he both stands alone and really presents us in himself before God. His (1) advent makes God's reign present anew; his (2) passion undertakes the climactic act of judgment that sets the world right; his (3) resurrection inaugurates a new humanity in appropriate continuity with Israel's public tradition; and his (4) exaltation orients the church, that inaugurated new humanity, to living by faith in the consummation of God's reign (chap. 4).

Leaving aside O'Donovan's innovative but less compelling fourfold account of the sacraments that matches this paradigm,[19] his larger ecclesiological point concerns the obedience of rulers (chap. 6) and the redemption of society (chap. 7) associated with Christendom. Christendom is neither an end in itself for which the church ought to strategize nor an automatic evil the church ought always to resist. In undertaking her mission, the church must not act coercively, but she may hope for societal transformation of various kinds resulting from divine blessing upon her witness.

In many respects modern liberal society resulted from the church's missionary success enabling Western civilization to bite the political hand that fed it—feeding it (1) freedom, with the advent of Christ's divine authority triumphing over other powers in earthly history; feeding it (2) mercy, with the passion of Christ's divine forgiveness providing the definitive act of judgment that reorients all others; feeding it (3) natural right, in light of the communal life that emerges from maintaining but relativizing Israel's tradition; and feeding it (4) openness to speech, in light of the exalted Christ's pouring out of the Holy Spirit

18. O'Donovan, *Desire of the Nations*, 30–49, 49–66.
19. O'Donovan, *Desire of the Nations*, 174–92.

THE PERSONAL AND CULTURAL CHARACTER OF REASON

of prophecy. Instead of true freedom, though, modernity champions indeterminate autonomy; instead of mercy, modernity simply opposes all suffering; instead of natural right, modernity champions absolute procedural equality; and instead of openness to speech, modernity offers totalized (both egalitarian and competitive) speech.[20]

But it was not so from the beginning. Political authority as we know it emerged from God's temporary provision for managing a fallen world. In a sense such political powers rival properly divine rule, but they were defeated when Christ announced and accomplished God's definitive act of judgment. They have been temporarily reauthorized for certain limited tasks until the enactment of that judgment is fully consummated. Christ indeed claims every square inch of the cosmos as his own (to echo Abraham Kuyper's famous phrase), but not simply through an abstract claim as Creator. Christ ultimately stakes this claim through a concrete history of salvation that reestablishes comprehensive divine sovereignty. Such sovereignty involves taking even every thought captive (2 Cor 10:1–6).

At this point it is worth making explicit the crucial premise that political theology is the proper biblical starting point for a Christian theology of culture. That is true historically, if (for instance) the discussions epitomized by H. Richard Niebuhr's *Christ and Culture* are any indication.[21] But it is also true dogmatically, if O'Donovan is correct that the Bible's dominant theme in its history and praise—even to the point of how God chooses to identify himself—is Yahweh's kingship. And the crucial moment of God's royal victory is Christ's resurrection.

CHRIST'S RESURRECTION AND CREATION'S MORAL ORDER

Thus, the resurrection of Christ is integral to political life, and O'Donovan's earlier monograph *Resurrection and Moral Order* offers the ethical

---

20. O'Donovan, *Desire of the Nations*, 252–71, 271–84.

21. The criticisms of Niebuhr's typology (*Christ and Culture* [New York: Harper, 1951]) offered, e.g., in Craig A. Carter, *Rethinking Christ and Culture: A Post-Christendom Perspective* (Grand Rapids: Brazos, 2003), and D. A. Carson, *Christ and Culture Revisited* (Grand Rapids: Eerdmans, 2008), are noteworthy, many of them surely legitimate. Yet Niebuhr himself qualified the claims for his typology more than critics sometimes acknowledge, and he plausibly claimed to have identified key biblical motifs that recur in the church's perennial disputes over cultural engagement.

framework with which to understand that claim.[22] That framework involves four principles.[23] First, the *realist* principle relates practical reason to created order: there is truth outside ourselves to know, including moral truth to which human actions must correspond. Yet, second, the *evangelical* principle relates that created order to the gospel: the good news liberates people for constructive moral action in social space. For, third, the *Easter* principle underscores Christ's resurrection as the distinctive moment when liberated human action becomes possible. This moment mediates between the rival alternatives of creation and kingdom ethics: in the resurrection God reaffirms the created order in Christ, yet God also indicates its historical need for redemptive transformation. Fourth, then, a complex *church* principle ensues, which acknowledges a subjective element of moral authority following and participating in the prior objective authority of Christ.

The resurrection indicates that redemption is "of" creation, not "from" it. The objective order of creation remains, ontologically speaking; yet the need for redemption suggests that, epistemologically speaking, there are subjective barriers to human recognition of that creation order—subjective barriers that work decisively against many appeals to natural law (chap. 1). As for the order of creation, it involves the "kinds" of things that God has made; while God is free, God has exercised the freedom to make an ordered world. That ordered world also involves "ends" for things; while creaturely freedom involves the exercise of will, that exercise is only meaningful within an ordered field of meaning, not in a modern struggle of will as the polar opposite of nature. Beyond redeeming natural kinds and ends, though, Christ's resurrection transforms cultural agency and contexts: we live by grace alone through faith alone, needing divine forgiveness and judgment to address what would otherwise be the totalitarianism of immanent history (chap. 2).

Epistemologically speaking, then, humans learn of particular things in relation to the totality of things in the world; they learn of other things while being within that very world themselves; and they learn of

---

22. Oliver O'Donovan, *Resurrection and Moral Order: An Outline for Evangelical Ethics*, 2nd ed. (Grand Rapids: Eerdmans, 1994). Again, a summary follows using some of the book's own language.

23. O'Donovan, *Resurrection and Moral Order*, ix–xxi.

these things without comprehensive knowledge of world history's end (chap. 3). Human learning must unfold in relation to Christ the Logos, distinguishing between true and false forms of the one reality in him (chap. 4). The Spirit evokes humans' free response to this reality that Christ has redeemed, converting them not only out of alienation from God and God's world but even out of alienation between reason and the will (chap. 5)—both knowing and doing the good.

Authority is the objective correlate of this freedom that is received in Christ by the Spirit. There are natural forms of authority such as beauty, age, community, and strength, not to mention truth. Then there are political forms of authority—naturally, in terms of might and tradition; morally, in terms of addressing injured right. Justice involves public right action, which has only a proximate status for the present; Christ has reauthorized secular political authority, but only temporarily until he institutes fully his own triumphant rule (chaps. 6-7). Further implications of this account for personal ethics must be left aside here, especially since O'Donovan has returned to ethics in his current trilogy.

The Spirit's Freedom and Society's Authoritative Judgment

O'Donovan's third major monograph in this sequence, his political ethics entitled *The Ways of Judgment*, unfolds the implications of his earlier claim that "the authority of secular government resides in the practice of judgment."[24] Such judgment "*is an act of moral discrimination that pronounces upon a preceding act or existing state of affairs to establish a new public context.*"[25] Much of this stunning material addresses political institutions and not the current focus of Christian engagement with culture, especially public reasoning. Suffice it to say that O'Donovan's is a unique blend of what we might call two-kingdoms duality and neo-Reformed one-reality perspectives. So, for instance, he accepts the two-kingdoms element of the Reformers' distinction between gospel and law, acknowledging that political judgment does not enact God's transforming redemption but only temporarily promotes earthly justice. Yet he commends the earlier tradition of political theology in which the church's bishops may urge rulers to exercise clemency in

---

24. Oliver O'Donovan, *The Ways of Judgment* (Grand Rapids: Eerdmans, 2005).
25. O'Donovan, *Ways of Judgment*, 7, emphasis original.

certain cases—in which it may be forward-looking for earthly societies to limp after God's gracious forgiveness in the way they provisionally enact judgment (e.g., chap. 6).[26]

For present purposes the book's crucial section is part 3, "Life Beyond Judgment: Communication." This treatment of communication, or sharing in common, addresses how particular Christians as rational persons should relate both to each other in the church and to fellow humans in the world at large. In other words, how does the Spirit lead people into freedom in Christ?

O'Donovan suggests that being appropriately counterpolitical means being neither apolitical nor totalizing about politics. For Christians, not everything is "political" in the sense of earthly judgment. We anticipate a postpolitical reality that realizes creation's ideally prepolitical state in light of the triune God's saving history: judgment associated especially with the Father, representation with the Son, and communication with the Spirit. The church is a postpolitical reality, in principle God's paradigm society—and thus at present both political and counterpolitical (chap. 13).

"Communication," defined in terms of biblical *koinonia*, involves holding something as common, as "ours." Communication as *koinonia* does not simply give and/or take, as in "this mine is yours and yours is mine"; such "exchange" is preliminary, but communication means mutually possessing and sharing. The word is the paradigm object of communication because of meaning; meaning epitomizes that which humans can both perceive and possess—what we can share. O'Donovan addresses work, private interest, place, and power in the light of communication thus defined, while he finds law and church to transcend any particular society as defined by its cultural institutions (chap. 14).

On this account, work is primary and consumption secondary; work involves "every human activity that enhances the material of communication."[27] Private interest is only a moment of rest between acts of

---

26. On this emphasis see further Oliver O'Donovan and Joan Lockwood O'Donovan, eds., *From Irenaeus to Grotius: A Sourcebook in Christian Political Thought* (Grand Rapids: Eerdmans, 1999), which represents the classic Christian political tradition as a viable source of contemporary insight, via not only primary source selections but also the O'Donovans' editorial framing and introductions.

27. O'Donovan, *Ways of Judgment*, 250.

communication. Places "are the precondition for social communication in material and intellectual goods," with the neighborhood (sharing common space) and not the market (for exchange) being fundamental.[28] Places make society a concrete universal, preventing any one society from being an all-encompassing whole—instead celebrating local representation. After all, distant communication has always been associated dangerously with power. While any society involves the organization and relations of institutions, the church is not just one social institution among others. Along with God's law, the church is an institution that transcends particular societies.

The church must be understood in terms of both household and city, mediating between private and public in addressing both material sharing and verbal communication (chap. 15). Ecclesiological and anthropological details go beyond the scope of the argument here, but in that material (chap. 16) O'Donovan certainly introduces additional questions to ponder about persons vis-à-vis communities. For the moment it is enough to draw out this implication: political theology must help Christians to celebrate the God-given pre- and postpolitical realities of human culture. The church's cultural engagement ideally fosters the communication of meaning rooted in Jesus Christ as the creation's true King.

THE MONK'S CELL AND COMMON OBJECTS OF LOVE

O'Donovan uses the monk's cell as a way to address how persons and communities relate. How does the command to "judge for yourselves" (Luke 12:57–59) relate to the command to "judge not"? According to O'Donovan, we must judge "of" ourselves: both "from" ourselves, involving reflection, and "on" ourselves, involving our own case. If individualism becomes a worry in light of this spiritual preoccupation regarding personal judgment, then a distinction must be made. One, problematic, kind of individualism involves independently prepolitical atoms that contract together out of self-interest. But another, appropriate, kind of personal interest involves postpolitical subjects who achieve genuine individuality. The newly modern problem was the reflective subject

---

28. O'Donovan, *Ways of Judgment*, 255.

emerging as a center of public interest, in a way that presumably reduced prepolitical, atomistic motivation down to self-preservation. The affective independence of this individual modern subject's conscience paralleled the earlier theopolitical king: everyone became his or her own ruling subject. Whereas initially Protestantism democratized monastic spirituality for particular persons, soon (according to O'Donovan) the early modern aftermath of the Reformation undermined necessary communal institutions. Thus, emerging skepticism over social forms produced problematic individualism rather than healthy individuality.

By contrast, O'Donovan claims that properly speaking "*the subject is realized in the church, the church completed in the subject.*"[29] The church is the end of the personal subject and not vice versa; properly sober self-conception opens into communication (see Rom 12). While the church is vital to human flourishing, communication remains a personal activity, and individual freedom a meaningful good. Accordingly, the church both is and is not political. It *is* political in this sense: it is a society-transcending human community with institutions of authority; while the church judges not, it is judged by the Holy Spirit and, in some ways, it proleptically mediates divine authority. Yet in another sense the church is *not* political: it is a communal anticipation of the eschaton, when there will be no institutions of judgment—neither state nor church.[30]

At this point two possible critiques arise concerning O'Donovan's project. One critique concerns his emphasis on the eschatological immediacy of Christ's rule and, hence, the postlapsarian rather than prelapsarian character of earthly government. Does O'Donovan accurately recover a core claim of the earlier Christian tradition of "political theology"—that earthly government is God's response to the fall—as he claims? If so, is this earlier tradition correct? Does it leave him championing an individual beatific vision that lacks adequate emphasis on redemption's bodily and social dimensions? For a postlapsarian account

---

29. O'Donovan, *Ways of Judgment*, 314, emphasis original.
30. Jonathan Leeman develops the helpful image of the church as an embassy, thereby paying needed theoretical attention to its institutional character (which is not altogether the same as its political character; see *Political Church*).

of government apparently suggests that the eschaton does not involve humans in communal coordination.[31] Moreover, does O'Donovan's perspective require overextended claims about "judgment" being an activity-oriented concept in Scripture?[32] For then he might be delimiting the divinely reauthorized vocation of earthly government too narrowly. Might government have other appropriate functions—beyond moral discrimination that establishes a new public context—that would more clearly include prelapsarian and/or eschatological elements of social coordination?

Another, possibly related, critique concerns O'Donovan's lack of emphasis on covenant. In all likelihood he avoids the concept out of concern over modern contractualism.[33] Yet is not kingship also a readily abused biblical concept? If "covenant" is integral to Scripture's history of salvation, then must we not attempt to clarify its distinction from "contract" rather than leaving it aside? If so, would more "horizontal" emphasis on social institutions of the "people of God" be appropriate?

Perhaps the lectures that preceded *The Ways of Judgment*, published as the little book *Common Objects of Love*, partially reflect O'Donovan's response to these worries.[34] The first chapter, "Objects of Love," seeks an Augustinian answer to the questions of how humans can reason

---

31. The trend reflected in the writings of N. T. Wright, and in J. Richard Middleton, *A New Heaven and a New Earth: Reclaiming Biblical Eschatology* (Grand Rapids: Baker Academic, 2014), celebrates the cosmos-affirming significance of Christ's resurrection, as O'Donovan does. But this trend creates prima facie tension with O'Donovan's emphasis on personal immediacy with God. David Lyle Jeffrey cautions against taking the trend too far and losing the classical Christian critique of worldliness in "(Pre) Figuration: Masterplot and Meaning in Biblical History," in *"Behind" the Text: History and Biblical Interpretation*, ed. Craig Bartholomew et al., Scripture and Hermeneutics 4 (Grand Rapids: Zondervan, 2003), 363–92, especially 377–82, 387–90.

32. To clarify this issue and what is at stake, see Craig Bartholomew, R. W. L. Moberly, and J. Gordon McConville, eds., *A Royal Priesthood? The Use of the Bible Ethically and Politically: A Dialogue with Oliver O'Donovan*, Scripture and Hermeneutics 3 (Grand Rapids: Zondervan, 2002), especially the chapters by Jonathan D. Chaplin and James W. Skillen (along with O'Donovan's responses).

33. This lack of emphasis is discussed variously in Bartholomew, Moberly, and McConville, *Royal Priesthood?*, as well as O'Donovan in response to them. In his response to McConville, O'Donovan expresses his worry about a "fatally easy" slide from "covenant" to "contract" in the modern mind.

34. Oliver O'Donovan, *Common Objects of Love: Moral Reflection and the Shaping of Community* (Grand Rapids: Eerdmans, 2009).

collectively and historically. This answer lies in the coinherence of knowledge with love, corresponding to the coinherence of God's Word and Spirit. Moral reflection and moral deliberation likewise coinhere; furthermore, all of these rational enterprises presume a social context and activity. The original form of the question at stake is "What shall *we* do?" not "What shall *I* do?" or "What shall *they* do?"

The second chapter, "Agreement to Share," indicates that the love involved in founding a community is not reciprocal but object oriented; together "we" love some other object. Our love then becomes reflexive via words. We become a society when we develop transcendental representations that perpetuate an identity in a tradition of love. But we do not develop such societies all on our own; we find ourselves placed, by divine providence, with each other and with the objects to love. Modernity sought to hide the realities of providence and tradition within its tradition of supposedly having no tradition. But in fact, O'Donovan argues, a properly "secular" society needs an eschatological faith to sustain its identity. The main claim here is that an Augustinian account of the secular deals with the not-yet of God's kingdom, not a supposedly neutral public square. Thus, rather than appealing to the language of covenant regarding these horizontal relationships, which could fall easily into a contractual mindset, O'Donovan focuses instead on personal desire and the external object(s) by which desire can bind communities together—for both good and ill.

This little book's third chapter, "A Multitude of Rational Beings United," treats "publicity" as modernity's most distinctive form of representation—reflecting O'Donovan's observations from fifteen years ago, prior to the advent of social media! Mass communication slops together news, advertising, and entertainment in a Babel that, lacking the gospel and the Holy Spirit, rebelliously apes Pentecost. Modernity signals that a crisis of representation is the dominant issue of contemporary politics—as reflected in its desperate attempt to create common interests, its fevered pace of communication, and its obsession with the visual-erotic. By contrast, O'Donovan writes, "There is a visible sign of the Kingdom of God in the community that waits upon it [that is, the church's existence is a witness to the true meaning of secularity]. Its apparent passivity is an active power in the designs of saving providence. Not by creating images, but by being itself a true reflecting image, it [the church] serves the victory of the representative."[35]

COMMUNAL PRACTICES, PERSONAL FAITH, AND PUBLIC CONSEQUENCES

Thus O'Donovan teaches biblical Christians to view both theology and culture in significantly political terms, but his notion of politics is strikingly epistemological: a matter of judgment. His epistemology is then strikingly ethical: a matter of preeminently practical reason. His ethics in return is strikingly epistemological: a matter of reflection and deliberation relating to reality, not just externalized duty or intuitive discernment. Such a theology of culture resists accounting for reason in primarily instrumental or procedural terms.[36]

Once technology appears in this more evangelical and sapiential light, then machines can be acknowledged as possible developments of creation's good order; methods, as possible developments of humanity's good freedom; and means, more generally, as necessary elements within agents' good pursuit of ends. Accordingly, in a culture permeated by technique, Christian practical reasoning should reflect both restraint and hope. Already my prior essay has accounted for *faith* as the form that fear of God takes when we hear the good news of Jesus Christ. Earlier this essay has accounted for *love* as the inescapable counterpart of knowledge, which we seek together and represent to each other in response to God's world. Now we account for *hope*: because God is King; because Christ is the risen Lord who has reaffirmed the order of the creation he is redeeming; because the Spirit enables those who are in Christ to begin realizing once again the true freedom for which humans are made; and because the church's very existence—however fallible—testifies to a postpolitical future when God's judgment will be complete. Such hope, however, elicits *restrained expectations* for the present: restraint regarding how transparently we can apply scriptural

---

35. O'Donovan, *Common Objects of Love*, 72.

36. O'Donovan's current ethical trilogy (*Ethics as Theology* [Grand Rapids: Eerdmans, 2013–2017]) is too intricate and expansive to incorporate within this short account of his implied theology of culture. While I have read and marked these later works, I have not yet fully learned or inwardly digested them. For present purposes, though, they extend rather than alter the main lines sketched here.

prooftexts in concrete cases of discernment; regarding how effectively
we can discern tactics of cultural engagement; and regarding how accurately we can predict the future—even the relatively near-term consequences of possible actions.

If there were space to expound such hopeful restraint further, then
O'Donovan's theology of culture might suggest additional implications
for human reason such as the following. (1) *God's kingship and Christ's
resurrection provide a helpful supplement to the rationale behind the more
classically Reformed account of archetypal and ectypal knowledge.* All true
human knowing corresponds to—that is, it has a certain form of creaturely participation in—the Son's knowledge of the Father, in God's
inner Word. That Word, by the Spirit, is expressed in a suitable creaturely form once the Son assumes humanity in Jesus. While the focus of
this divine self-communication is how to live in the light of God's love,
ultimately anything we come to know of God's world—when we come
to know it truly—must relate to properly fearing our King. The Christ
in whom all things hold together both shares in God's knowledge of all
things as they truly are and mediates to human brothers and sisters a
creaturely share in such knowledge.

(2) *The Spirit's gift of creaturely freedom, however, must limit rhetorical
appeals to human "participation" in divine knowledge.* Of course, the life-
giving Spirit sustains all human beings in their cultural and intellectual
practices, both personally and communally. More specifically, the Spirit
gives new life to those who are in Christ by making God's Word present—
enabling them to participate in divine self-knowledge more integrally,
with less fragmentation: as creatures with whom God makes a home,
to whom God gives a share that makes the knowledge common. So the
vocabulary of participation has its place. But "in Christ" the Christian is
now putting on a new self, inaugurally enjoying the restored reality of
genuine freedom. Hence participation in God cannot have such strongly
ontological overtones as to negate the human subjects' distinction from
the divine Creator whom they serve. Perhaps the etymological overlap
between "culture" and "cultus" is suggestive: human knowing is an
aspect of worshiping our King, in whose knowledge we come to participate—yet of whom we remain but humble servants.

(3) Human subjects not only remain distinct from the God in whose knowledge they gain a creaturely share; *they also remain sufficiently distinct from one another to be personal agents, and thus it can be misleading to say that everything is political.* While maintaining an emphasis on freedom, O'Donovan still makes Augustinian allowances for common objects of love—true and/or false—to influence human knowing. His more distinctive and challenging contribution regarding the intellectual dynamics of self, others, and society lies in his account of public judgment and practical reason. Christ has reauthorized earthly governments simply to enact judgment. Politics does not exist to effect the new creation, and it does not completely encompass the communal activity of the original creation. Even efforts at temporary betterment only occur properly when governments attempt to create a new public context in addressing injured right. More recently, O'Donovan's account of practical reason is consistently restrained when addressing how much if anything humans can know about the future in deliberating about the purposes they form as agents. Therefore, Christian practical reason about engaging culture ought to reflect twofold restraint: regarding the function of government and regarding Christian political attempts to advance God's kingdom. Our agency as redeemed persons in community bears witness to a future society that is, at least in important respects, postpolitical.

(4) Furthermore, *such restraint regarding public judgment and practical reason should extend to theoretical reason as well.* Christ's resurrection may reaffirm the created order and its cultural history, but it surely did not authorize modern science to function as simply another triumphant power, threatening to supplant the earthly government that Jesus' kingship subordinated. Christ's reign confronts scientific ideals of both disinterested procedure and technological effectiveness. The ideal of knowledge for knowledge's sake tempts even some Christians, for fear of "postmodernism," and it may appear to be a fitting modern analogue to "contemplation" as classically defined. Yet the grain of truth involved here, that the Creator loves his world and by studying it we may herald his glory, does not overcome the weeds of idolatry. Knowledge purely for knowledge's sake would choke out the love of God and neighbor that should be ingredient in all cultural endeavors.

After all, it is questionable whether an ideal of disinterested knowledge has ever been met; the monetary arrangements of contemporary universities and scientific research, not to mention philosophy of science, indicate otherwise. Even early Baconian celebrations of modern science lauded its technological amelioration of human woes. Even champions of the pure ideal of intellectual disinterest operate parasitically on larger cultural capital. So Christians have better ways of promoting the careful study of God's world. Not coincidentally, relating theoretical reason to larger questions of practical reason will address the prophetic connection between idolatry and injustice. Every human being has a practical stake in the conduct even of culture's theoretical activities. Toppling certain theoretical idols will make more transparent the idolatries and injustices of the regime of technique—which increasingly affect the lives of every person on planet Earth.[37]

Human understanding is a matter of cultural products and not just personal character or communal practices. Admittedly, Christians must take the sum total of current knowledge, or at least opinion that passes for "reason," with due seriousness. But most fundamentally we must acknowledge the authority and herald the reality of Christ our King. It can be awkward to encounter the Bible's warfare metaphors (e.g., 2 Cor 10:1-6). Certainly it would be unwise to appropriate them in contemporary contexts without apologetic savvy and pastoral sensitivity. Yet taking every thought captive to Christ involves a struggle far beyond

---

37. Brent Waters reflects on the tensions arising for O'Donovan's locally oriented account of communication in light of the global market with its technologically enhanced speed ("Communication," in *The Authority of the Gospel: Explorations in Moral and Political Theology in Honor of Oliver O'Donovan*, ed. Robert Song and Brent Waters [Grand Rapids: Eerdmans, 2015], 143–59). Hans Ulrich rightly seeks to extend O'Donovan's concern for how political theology reveals the true "ways of judgment" to the contemporary cultural need for understanding the true "ways of life"—and therefore to extend the ways of judgment to address the act of discernment ("The Ways of Discernment," in *Authority of the Gospel*, 179–95). My goal in this essay is to pursue that task a bit further in the belief that O'Donovan's theology of culture is largely correct, while also acknowledging its incompleteness in some respects. In particular it may be underdeveloped regarding some aspects of communal coordination, a concern that Brian Brock develops in terms of emphasizing the (separating) judgment of Babel at the expense of the (reconciling) gift of Pentecost ("What Is 'the Public'? Theological Variations on Babel and Pentecost," in *Authority of the Gospel*, 160–78).

flesh and blood, engaging an adversary whose basic tactic is deception. The history of modern thought involves not only incredible leaps in scientific understanding and technological development but also seemingly constant theoretical paradigm shifts.[38] Today's "assured results" may contribute to that development but often give way to tomorrow's new understanding. As with other cultural powers, then, Christians should simultaneously be grateful for these fruits of creation's goodness and aware of the fall's curse. We should be neither fearful nor foolish when the world deems us to be out of intellectual fashion. Sometimes, on the supposedly "wrong side of history," there we can see the risen Lord seated at God's right hand, having been vindicated in the climax of salvation history.

Thus, in my view, O'Donovan's evangelical realism supports a deflationary account of much that people call human "reason" within a broader theological celebration of God's cultural gifts. I offer this reading cautiously, on two grounds: on one hand, it is often just a reading of his texts, laboring to understand the broader biblical patterns of thought that together they unfold; on the other hand, this reading is undoubtedly selective, laboring to discern the import of these thought patterns for a set of questions that O'Donovan has not always addressed explicitly.

---

38. William A. Wilson, "Scientific Regress," *First Things* 263 (May 2016): 37–42, highlights the Open Science Collaboration's testing of one hundred published psychology experiments from three of the field's most prestigious journals: "Of the studies that had originally reported positive results, an astonishing 65 percent failed to show statistical significance on replication, and many of the remainder showed greatly reduced effect sizes." Such problems pertain beyond the social sciences, with similar results for instance appearing in pharmaceutical studies from top journals. As Wilson notes, the academic establishment often responds to such problems by appealing to "the self-correcting nature of the scientific method" over time, via peer review, research competition, and objective reality—eventually overcoming "sloppiness, bad luck, and even fraud." Wilson suggests, however, that this response could itself be treated like a hypothesis to test—and it would fail. Scientific bureaucracy accumulates more and more unreliable results accompanied by more and more power—and thus more and more attraction for opportunistic people and practices that exacerbate the problems. It seems to me that in the wrong hands an argument like Wilson's could be taken too far—not least by Christians who might use it simply to deny the credibility of any scientific claim they dislike. That danger notwithstanding, Wilson rightly calls for resisting when "cultural trends attempt to render science a sort of religion-less clericalism."

Nevertheless, in light of this political theology of culture, as well as Ellul's critique of technique and a biblical theology of wisdom, an account of human reason should most basically involve a faculty affecting, and affected by, personal character and communal practice. Thus, it produces a pluriform harvest that is continually planting new seeds. Such cultural activity is a gift of God. Reason involves the distinctive faculties and practices by which people study the world, use words to make thoughts their own, and make common the word—both capital letter and lowercase. Yet in a fallen world such reasoning may reflect the order of creation in only fragmentary ways, or it may even actively resist God's renewal of creation. With reason Christians ought to serve the Creator in the world Christ is reclaiming, both exploring that world and proclaiming his triumph. But, in the current waiting period until this King's final return, no human activity or authority—intellectual or otherwise, the world's or even the church's—may rival the Spirit's living Word!

WORKS CITED

Bartholomew, Craig, et al., eds. *A Royal Priesthood? The Use of the Bible Ethically and Politically: A Dialogue with Oliver O'Donovan*. Scripture and Hermeneutics 3. Grand Rapids: Zondervan, 2002.

Brock, Brian. *Christian Ethics in a Technological Age*. Grand Rapids: Eerdmans, 2010.

———. "What Is 'the Public'? Theological Variations on Babel and Pentecost." In *The Authority of the Gospel: Explorations in Moral and Political Theology in Honor of Oliver O'Donovan*, edited by Robert Song and Brent Waters, 160–78. Grand Rapids: Eerdmans, 2015.

Carson, D. A. *Christ and Culture Revisited*. Grand Rapids: Eerdmans, 2008.

Carter, Craig A. *Rethinking Christ and Culture: A Post-Christendom Perspective*. Grand Rapids: Brazos, 2003.

Ellul, Jacques. *The Technological Society*. Translated by John Wilkinson. New York: Vintage, 1964.

Evans, C. Stephen. "Afterword: The Bible and the Academy: Some Concluding Thoughts and Possible Future Directions." In *The Bible and the University*, edited by David Lyle Jeffrey and C. Stephen Evans, 304–10. Scripture and Hermeneutics 8. Grand Rapids: Zondervan, 2007.

Greenman, Jeffrey P., Read Mercer Schuchardt, and Noah J. Toly. *Understanding Jacques Ellul*. Eugene, OR: Cascade, 2012.

Jeffrey, David Lyle. "(Pre) Figuration: Masterplot and Meaning in Biblical History." In *"Behind" the Text: History and Biblical Interpretation*, edited by Craig Bartholomew et al., 363–92. Scripture and Hermeneutics 4. Grand Rapids: Zondervan, 2003.

Kuhn, Thomas S. *The Structure of Scientific Revolutions*. 2nd ed. Chicago: University of Chicago Press, 1970.

Leeman, Jonathan. *Political Church: The Local Assembly as Embassy of Christ's Rule*. Studies in Christian Doctrine and Scripture. Downers Grove, IL: IVP Academic, 2016.

Long, D. Stephen. *Theology and Culture: A Guide to the Discussion*. Cascade Companions. Eugene, OR: Cascade, 2008.

MacIntyre, Alasdair. *After Virtue: A Study in Moral Theory*. 2nd ed. Notre Dame: University of Notre Dame Press, 1984.

Middleton, J. Richard. *A New Heaven and a New Earth: Reclaiming Biblical Eschatology*. Grand Rapids: Baker Academic, 2014.

Muller, Richard A. "The Study of Theology." In *Foundations of Contemporary Interpretation*, edited by Moisés Silva, 533–688. Grand Rapids: Zondervan, 1996.

Niebuhr, H. Richard. *Christ and Culture*. New York: Harper, 1951.

Nussbaum, Martha C. *Upheavals of Thought: The Intelligence of Emotions*. Cambridge: Cambridge University Press, 2001.

O'Donovan, Oliver. *Common Objects of Love: Moral Reflection and the Shaping of Community*. Grand Rapids: Eerdmans, 2009.

———. *The Desire of the Nations: Rediscovering the Roots of Political Theology*. Cambridge: Cambridge University Press, 1996.

———. *Ethics as Theology*. 3 vols. Grand Rapids: Eerdmans, 2013–2017.

———. *Resurrection and Moral Order: An Outline for Evangelical Ethics*. 2nd ed. Grand Rapids: Eerdmans, 1994.

———. *The Ways of Judgment*. Grand Rapids: Eerdmans, 2005.

O'Donovan, Oliver, and Joan Lockwood O'Donovan, eds. *From Irenaeus to Grotius: A Sourcebook in Christian Political Thought*. Grand Rapids: Eerdmans, 1999.

Polanyi, Michael. *Personal Knowledge: Towards a Post-Critical Philosophy*. Chicago: University of Chicago Press, 1958.

Treier, Daniel J. "Christology and Commentaries: Examining and Enhancing Theological Exegesis." In *On the Writing of New Testament Commentaries: Festschrift for Grant R. Osborne on the Occasion of His 70th Birthday*, edited by Stanley E. Porter and Eckhard J. Schnabel, 299–316. Leiden: E. J. Brill, 2013.

———. *Introducing Theological Interpretation of Scripture: Recovering a Christian Practice*. Grand Rapids: Baker Academic, 2008.

———. *Virtue and the Voice of God: Toward Theology as Wisdom*. Grand Rapids: Eerdmans, 2006.

Treier, Daniel J., and Craig Hefner. "Twentieth- and Twenty-First Century American Biblical Interpretation." In *Oxford Handbook of the Bible in America*, edited by Paul Gutjahr, 129–48. Oxford: Oxford University Press, 2017.

Ulrich, Hans. "The Ways of Discernment." In The *Authority of the Gospel: Explorations in Moral and Political Theology in Honor of Oliver O'Donovan*, edited by Robert Song and Brent Waters, 179–95. Grand Rapids: Eerdmans, 2015.

Vanhoozer, Kevin J., and Daniel J. Treier. *Theology and the Mirror of Scripture: A Mere Evangelical Account*. Studies in Christian Doctrine and Scripture. Downers Grove, IL: IVP Academic, 2015.

Waters, Brent. "Communication." In *The Authority of the Gospel: Explorations in Moral and Political Theology in Honor of Oliver O'Donovan*, edited by Robert Song and Brent Waters, 143–59. Grand Rapids: Eerdmans, 2015.

Wilson, William A. "Scientific Regress." *First Things* 263 (May 2016): 37–42.

Wood, W. Jay. *Epistemology: Becoming Intellectually Virtuous*. Contours of Christian Philosophy. Downers Grove, IL: InterVarsity, 1998.

Zagzebski, Linda Trinkaus. *Virtues of the Mind: An Inquiry into the Nature of Virtue and the Ethical Foundations of Knowledge*. Cambridge: Cambridge University Press, 1996.

4

Divine Revelation

William J. Abraham

INTRODUCTION

The concept of revelation is a basic concept. It cannot be reduced to some other concept or a conjunction of other concepts; definitions invariably turn out to be synonyms or semantically related to the very idea of revelation for their elucidation. We learn the concept in our linguistic communities just as we learn other concepts. Thus we first learn it as applied to creatures; we then learn how to apply it by analogy to God. Just as we first learn how to understand and use concepts such as "creation" and "father" as we grow up in linguistic communities and then fix their meaning appropriately when applied to God, so too we learn to use the concept of revelation and its neighbors, say, the concept of manifestation, by developing its analogical extension to the divine. This does not mean that the concept is rigid and static. On the contrary, we do not need to have a precise and formal account of the necessary and sufficient conditions of revelation at the outset; we work informally, making judgments and adjustments as we go along, using our formal descriptions as useful boundary markers and incentives for further conceptual refinement. Equally, the analogical extension of a concept such as revelation can have a retroactive effect leading to the enrichment of our initial conception of revelation as applied, say, to human agents. This last observation underlies the misleading claim that the true meaning, say, of "father," "creation," or "revelation," lies in their predication as applied to the divine.

Philosophical reflection on divine revelation has a long and con-voluted history. Theologians have been tempted to short-circuit the

examination of divine revelation by looking for "the" biblical conception of revelation and then resisting or marginalizing the work of
philosophy. The motivation for this way of operating stems from the
assumption that Scripture is the normative instantiation of divine revelation and thus should act as both source and norm for our understanding of divine revelation. Several objections stand in the way of
this procedure. First, the claim that Scripture should be seen first and
foremost in terms of divine revelation is itself a developed theory of
divine revelation; it begs a host of questions that can at best be the last
word rather than the first word. Second, as a theory it is a relatively
early development in the wake of the canonization of various texts in
the Jewish tradition, but it is a development that rested on a confusion
of divine revelation with divine speaking or divine inspiration or both.
Third, in order to pick out "the" biblical conception of divine revelation,
one already needs to have some notion, however vague, of what revelation is; without this, it is impossible to identify and chart the concept of
divine revelation in Scripture.[1] Finally, to think of Scripture in terms
of divine revelation is to think of Scripture first and foremost in epistemic categories; there are other fundamental ways of conceiving of
Scripture, say, in soteriological categories, that deserve attention and
are equally if not more compelling.

In this essay the relevant historical considerations that have cropped
up in the Christian tradition will be woven into the philosophical issues
that arise in and around the topic of divine revelation.

THE CONCEPT OF REVELATION

The concept of revelation belongs in a family of concepts such as manifest, show, disclose, divulge, and make known, where the basic meaning
is that something formerly hidden is now available to be acknowledged,
received, pondered, and shared. George Mavrodes' schema is especially
illuminating: m reveals a to n by means of k.[2] Thus Mulligan reveals
his name to Murphy by telling Murphy who he is. In the case of God,

---

1. See Rudolf Bultmann, "The Concept of Revelation in the New Testament," in
Existence and Faith (New York: Meridian, 1966).

2. George Mavrodes, *Revelation in Religious Belief* (Philadelphia: Temple
University Press, 1988), 88.

God reveals his name to Moses by telling Moses, "I am that I am." *M* represents the agent of revelation; *a* represents the content of revelation; *n* represents the recipient of divine revelation; *k* represents the mode or means of revelation. This schema is purely formal. It can be filled out in a great variety of ways depending on the material claims about divine revelation on offer, say, in Judaism, Christianity, or Islam. There is no comprehensive agreement on exactly what and how God has been revealed; on the contrary, there is massive disagreement that has at times spilled over into violence. Even within the Christian tradition, there is significant disagreement; contested doctrines of divine revelation have flourished especially in the modern period, when epistemological issues became prominent within theology and philosophy.

There are helpful taxonomies of divine revelation. One can envisage a form of divine revelation given through communication, say, by divine speech-acts, and a form of divine revelation given by manifestation, as found in examples of personal and mystical experience. In the former case God reveals Godself by speaking to someone, telling them this or that; in the latter case God reveals Godself by giving someone a glimpse of his glory or by providing conscious awareness of the divine presence. One can also think of a distinction between general, special, and even extra-special revelation. General revelation is divine revelation given through the natural order and conscience; special revelation is felicitously represented by the divine revelation given to the great eighth-century prophets of Israel; extra-special revelation is, say, the full, final, and definitive revelation given in Jesus Christ. In addition, one can ruminate on a distinction between universal and personal revelation. The former is available or meant to be made available to everyone; it is publicly salient; the latter is intended for this or that individual in his or her particular circumstances; it is personally or privately salient. General revelation in conscience, making us aware of various moral truths, is available to everyone; the special revelation of the prophets or the extra-special revelation in Christ, once given, is to be shared initially by the people of Israel but then with the whole world. The latter then engenders proposals as to how this is to be carried out, whether in oral or written form, and whether through the essential institutions of a religious community or not.

It is also common to distinguish between propositional and non-propositional revelation. Given that anything said about God can readily be couched in terms of propositions, this distinction is better captured by speaking of divine revelation through speech-acts and divine revelation through non-speech-acts. Thus God spoke to Moses by way of his call and promises at the burning bush. When no one, not even Moses, believed the promise of divine deliverance, God then revealed his covenant commitment to Israel through his acts in liberating Israel from oppression under Pharaoh. God continued to provide divine revelation in Israel through divine commandments of various kinds, whether moral, ceremonial, or civil; equally, God continued to provide divine revelation through appointing various leaders, assisting Israel in times of adversity, and disciplining her by sending her into exile. Thus we might say that revelation supervenes on other acts God performs.

We can capture this last observation by noting that revelation is a polymorphous concept. Like human activities such as farming or teaching, an agent reveals certain things by performing this or that action in, with, and through which the revelation is achieved. Thus one farms by plowing fields, checking the weather, milking cows, going to market, poring over breeding records, and the like. One teaches by providing syllabi, giving lectures, asking questions, evaluating exams, and the like. So in revelation, one reveals this or that by speaking, helping out a neighbor in need, making promises and keeping them, and the like. God reveals by acting in nature, in conscience, in making a covenant with Israel, coming in the incarnation, raising Jesus from the dead, and the like. Given this, not all revelation may be intentional, even in the divine case, for God may permit certain things to be revealed even as the primary intention may be that of salvation. Also, given the polymorphous character of divine revelation, the content of divine revelation can be manifold. It can focus on the character and nature of God or involve the hidden depths of the human condition. Thus divine action in redemption can reveal the depths of human alienation and sin.

Not every action performed by an agent is necessarily revelatory. Most of the actions we perform are not picked out and identified as revelatory; revelation is predicated only of those acts that unveil what was previously hidden. If every act is revelatory then there are no contrasting actions that would enable us to learn the concept. Thus the action of my third finger on my left hand in typing this entry is not revelatory. We know mostly from the relevant context what to pick out as revelatory. So failing to bow at an important ceremony could reveal my ignorance, my clumsiness, or my desire to insult the chief marshal of the day. Or it may simply be an accidental omission on my part that reveals next to nothing about me. The same applies to God. The details of God's actions in providence, for example, are invariably hidden from us. God is active in everything that happens to bring good out of evil; but we may not be able to specify what God is doing beyond this very general ascription of action. Without specification we do not even know the underlying divine action on which divine revelation might supervene.

Revelation is not necessarily a success concept, say, like winning a race, where coming first is a necessary condition of winning the race. The crucial issue here is the place of human reception in accepting whether divine revelation has occurred. Given certain conceptions of divine action, God necessarily achieves what he intends to do. On this view revelation is a guarantee of successful reception by the intended recipient. Over against this, it is easy to envisage a situation where God fully intends to reveal his faithfulness to Israel through repeated avowals of love and care through a prophet, but lots of intended recipients reject the authenticity of the prophet, make ridicule of his message, and kill him. Certainly it would be odd to say that no one will pick up on divine revelation, but this is a contingent claim about the likelihood of success given other assumptions; it is not an essential feature of divine revelation. It is surely also the case that one can recognize divine revelation and then go on to reject it. Even more controversially theologically, it is possible to appropriate divine revelation and then walk away from it for good. At this point the discussion of divine revelation takes us directly into debates about human freedom, grace, and predestination. We have moved from purely formal conceptual considerations into theology proper. There is no uncontested way of demarcating the boundaries that can be drawn at this point; philosophy and theology necessarily overlap.

Divine revelation can be seen as a gift of divine grace in two senses. First, it is a matter of grace because divine revelation is given as a matter of divine freedom rather than divine necessity. Even divine revelation in nature presupposes that God has designed creation in such a manner so as to reveal his power and wisdom through the created order. Divine freedom is even more visible in special and extra-special revelation. God acts in generosity and grace to make Godself known. Second, given any serious doctrine of sin, God also supplies assistance in the recognition, reception, and understanding of divine revelation. Technically, this assistance is identified as prevenient grace, that is, the grace that comes before the gift of justifying and sanctifying grace. Given these theological considerations, it is common to distinguish between divine revelation and divine illumination. Divine illumination is the divine action involved in enabling the recipient of divine revelation to pick up, entertain, and appropriate the gift of divine revelation in salvation. This action is characteristically associated with the work of the Holy Spirit, although not exclusively so because of the unity of divine action in the agency of the Trinity. In medieval epistemologies divine illumination was extended to embrace any knowledge whatsoever. Thus divine illumination accompanied knowledge of any proposition in that knowing is predicated of human agents who require divine assistance at every level of their agency. For an agent to know that two plus two equals four or that Ireland is an island requires a concurrent act of the Holy Spirit in the illumination of the mind. What was originally a doctrine about knowledge of God in divine illumination in salvation was pressed into service to explain epistemic success across the board. Such a development does not preclude but complements the appropriation of analogies between physical light, following the science of the day, and spiritual light.

In theories of global illumination within epistemology, what is happening is that everything is being assimilated to the faith of the church as furnished by divine revelation; inside the world of faith, knowledge is being conceived within a horizon in which nothing takes place without appropriate divine action making it possible. We might say that reason operates within the bounds of faith, where faith is understood to be the comprehensive creed of the church worked out with such care in the medieval period. Hence faith is intimately related to divine revelation indirectly in that sense of faith captured by the term *fides*. *Fides* means in this instance the creedal or intellectual content of the Christian tradition, and it can be used in a neutral sense as when we speak of the Jewish faith or the Mormon faith.

However, there is another sense of faith that is even more directly related to divine revelation. That sense is captured technically by the term *fiducia*, where *fiducia* essentially means trust. *Fiducia* represents the apt way in which the believer should normatively respond to divine revelation as that revelation supervenes, say, on the recital of the mighty acts of God or on the proclamation of the promises of God. Trust assumes the presence of mental assent but goes beyond that to include a living appropriation in thought, will, disposition, and action, of what is given in divine revelation.

As already noted, the presence of faith in the believer is brought about through the assistance of divine grace. Humanly speaking, faith is not a matter of passive reception or credulous make-believe, for faith comes by hearing the good news of the gospel and by acting on the promises of God. Moreover, faith in this sense of living and abiding trust can in part be ignited and sustained by the testimony of other believers who have taken up, say, the promises of God and found that they are generously fulfilled. Such faith is not a work in the sense of a mere performance of works of piety or works of charity, for the believer is put in the right before God not by works but by faith. However, faith without works is dead. The mark of faith in God, like the mark of faith in a doctor, is that one acts on what God has communicated or promised, just as in having faith in a doctor one acts on what he or she asserts or recommends.

Positing a logical and material relationship between divine revelation and divine action entails a significant implication for any doctrine of God. It means that the fundamental category for thinking about God is that of action and agency. God is rightly conceived as the one who acts. More specifically, God is best thought of as an agent, not in the sense of one more agent among or alongside other agents, but in the sense of the utterly singular and unique agent on which everything depends. This leads to the ancillary question as to what to do with other categories that are often canvassed as logically more primitive alternatives to that of agency, such as Being, Being beyond Being, Process, Serendipitous Creativity, Event, and the like. The relevant rule to follow at this point is that of consistency. If the category in question is compossible with the fundamental predication of agency and action to God, then it is permitted. Whether it should be positively adopted will depend on other crucial factors such as, say, its accuracy and its potential enrichment of the doctrine of God. Thus if we take Being or Being beyond Being to mean that God should be conceived along purely abstract or impersonal lines, then they should be rejected. On the other hand, if these concepts help us to express in an apt way the indivisibility of God into parts as represented by early doctrines of divine simplicity, or if they help us to articulate the unchanging character of God in his faithfulness to creation and redemption as represented by some doctrines of immutability, then they are acceptable and deployable.

REVELATION, SCRIPTURE, AND TRADITION

Specific, material claims about past divine revelation have been central in Judaism, Christianity, and Islam. Hence debates about the recording, preservation, and transmission of divine revelation have been canvassed in all three traditions. Each has been understood as a religion that depends crucially on canonical texts and their interpretation.

On one historical reading, understandings of the varied sacred texts in Judaism and Christianity were from the beginning couched in terms of divine speaking. The standard way to proceed was to begin with a vision of divine revelation assimilated to divine speaking to prophets. This notion was a common one in the Greco-Roman world and was readily assimilated within Judaism.[3] It is false to claim that there are no claims about divine speaking outside Israel; on the contrary, the claim was a common one in the ancient Near Eastern world. The differences lay in the content of claims about divine speaking, not in the deployment of the idea of divine speaking. The natural corollary of this emphasis on divine speaking was to think of divine revelation in terms of a divine word. Extending the origins of the part to the whole,

---

3. John R. Levison, *Of Two Minds: Ecstasy and Inspired Interpretation of the New Testament* (North Richland Hills, TX: Bibal, 1999).

it became virtually canonical to speak of the texts through which divine speaking was transmitted also in terms of a divine word.

This development dovetails nicely with the crucial place of speaking in cases of human revelation. In many instances what we say reveals what we are thinking or doing in our non-speech-acts. Thus lifting my finger in an auction can be taken as a bid, a signal to a companion to fetch a drink, an effort to ward off a bee, or a failed attempt to scratch my ear. One obvious way to resolve what action is performed is to ask the agent and hear what he or she says. In this instance, speaking accompanies a single bodily movement and resolves the ambiguity that may not be determined by the context. In the case of God, divine speaking becomes even more important because, aside from claims about incarnation, God does not have a body. The long-standing practice of conceiving Scripture in terms of the word of God fits with the historical origins of its creation, the place of prophecy in divine revelation, and the privileged place of speaking in determining the intentions and purposes of agents in their actions.

This emphasis on Scripture as the word of God spills over into theories of the divine inspiration of Scripture. In the history of the discussion it was common for centuries to construe divine inspiration in terms of divine dictation, a position that was abandoned under pressure from the results of historical investigation in the nineteenth century. Even a cursory study of the texts shows that it is mistaken to think of Scripture being dictated by God, for the authors make it clear that they are engaged in the kind of ordinary acts that are central to the production of texts. They are not simply taking down what God says, in a manner analogous to the way a secretary takes down what is dictated by the manager of the company. Moreover, while instances of divine speaking may be recorded and enshrined in Scripture, it is an obvious error to extend divine speaking to the whole of the text, in terms of its content or in terms of its writing, transmission, collection, and canonization. Expressed in more conceptual terms, it is as much a mistake to confuse divine inspiration and divine speaking as predicated of human agents as it is to confuse divine inspiration and divine speaking as predicated of God. Yet this confusion persists when contemporary doctrines of Scripture transpose older theories of divine dictation and divine inspiration into the theories of divine authorship and then go on to think of the production of Scripture in terms of double authorship.[4] Scripture, it is thought, is at one and the same time fully the action of its human authors and fully the action of God. Conceptual genealogical excavation is crucial for either exposing or defending this move and the hermeneutical consequences that are implied.

One reason for the persistence of the identification of divine revelation with Scripture lies in the normative place assigned to Scripture in theology. The very idea of canon as a norm or rule of faith rather than more modestly as a list of books betrays this persistence. Equally, the effort to safeguard a doctrine of inerrancy and infallibility as predicated of Scripture occupies the same conceptual space. If Scripture is spoken by God, and if God does not speak in a trivial manner, then it is prima facie natural to infer that what Scripture says, God says, and that what God says is true. Doctrines of propositional revelation as applied to Scripture also fit naturally with this inference.

Such a vision immediately runs into trouble on two fronts. First, even if we grant the premises, it may well be the case that God communicates his will through a host of literary genres where the conclusion to a global vision of inerrancy does not follow. Thus God could supply information by means of myth or parable; in this instance it would be a mistake to read the materially straightforwardly as true. Second, the actual texts of Scripture make all sorts of assertions that on the face of it are morally otiose, theologically questionable, or otherwise false. One way to preserve a doctrine of inerrancy once this was recognized was to interpret the relevant text in terms of allegory. Both Origen (184/5-253/4) and Thomas Aquinas (1225-1274) essentially preserved the inerrancy of the text by seeking out figurative meanings of texts that proved to be problematic given what they were convinced was the case on extrabiblical grounds. Thus the defense of inerrancy, contrary to widespread popular and academic misunderstanding, requires the rejection of a literalist hermeneutics of Scripture.

Recent defenders of inerrancy are implicitly committed to such a stance. In order to save the truth of the text, they resort to an appeal

---

4. See the criticisms of this approach in Karl Rahner, *Inspiration in the Bible* (New York: Herder & Herder, 1961), 16.

to original autographs, or to appraisals of authorial intention that rework the meaning of the text, or to efforts to shift to a figurative interpretation. The deeper origins of such moves lie in an initial confusion of Scripture with divine revelation that at one point rested on the confusion of divine inspiration with divine speaking. The repair of this damage requires a radical recognition of this conceptual mistake, a rethinking of the meaning of canon as a list, and a more felicitous soteriological doctrine of Scripture that sees its primary function as a critical means of grace. This in no way requires the jettison of special or extra-special divine revelation; it simply requires a more nuanced account of the way Scripture mediates such revelation.

The construal of Scripture *tout court* as divine revelation also required careful attention to the exact delineation and limits of the scriptural canon. For a millennium it was common to see the writings of various fathers and ecumenical councils as divinely inspired and thus informally to include them in the Scriptures of the church. Aquinas effectively ended the confusion on this in the West.[5] However, at the Council of Trent (1545–1563), what was designated as tradition over against Scripture was also taken to be dictated by the Holy Spirit, requiring the same kind of assent as was required of Scripture. Equally interesting, the move to identify in a formal way the exact books belonging in the canon was postponed until after the Reformation, when success in persuading opponents depended on knowing which texts were truly canonical.

While all the protagonists may have agreed that the church had a hand in determining the outcome of this debate both in terms of production and official endorsement as canonical, this agreement did not resolve whether the church or Scripture was the final court of appeal in settling theological disputes. Catholics argued initially for the former. Protestants insisted that in actually canonizing this or that text, the church was establishing the primary norm for its own teaching; the church was binding itself to Scripture as norm. John Calvin (1509–1564) provided a different way of avoiding any appeal to the role of the church in determining the books of Scripture by an appeal to

5. Yves M.-J. Congar, OP, *Tradition and Traditions: An Historical and a Theological Essay* (New York: Macmillan, 1967), 92–93.

the inner witness of the Holy Spirit as the grounding source of the identity of Scripture. The general consensus that has emerged over centuries of detailed debate in the West is that Scripture is the fundamental norm of church doctrine; insofar as the church plays a role, she does so by acting as the divinely appointed and infallible interpreter of Scripture. The climax of the latter development rests in the doctrine of papal infallibility adopted at Vatican I (1869-1870) and reaffirmed with appropriate updating at Vatican II (1962-1965).

The historical study of Scripture has played a decisive role in the way debates about divine revelation have proceeded in the modern period. Study of Scripture in part was a pivotal spur to the cultivation of historical investigation. Aggressive disputes about the origins and meaning of Scripture, about the content and place of church tradition at the boundaries and interpretation of Scripture, and about the place of the church and her Scriptures in the political arena meant that historical research was inescapable for the various contestants. Without shoring up their historical assertions, they could not make progress against opponents. Initially the issue was simply that of the material results of historical investigation. Were the relevant historical claims embedded in theology on offer actually warranted by the results of historical study? Only careful historical work could answer this kind of question. Benedict De Spinoza (1632-1667) on the Jewish side and David Hume (1711-1776) on the Protestant side pushed the debate to a whole new level when they proposed that the very nature of historical investigation casts doubt on traditional theories of divine revelation that identified divine revelation with Scripture. Both of them ended up outside their respective religious traditions; but their work signaled a much more radical attack on divine revelation that remains in place today.

As Ernst Troeltsch (1865-1923) later argued, the crucial insight is that one cannot make decisions about what has happened in the past without relying on the principles of criticism, analogy, and correlation.[6] Thus the historian necessarily queries the sources consulted, makes critical decisions about what really happened by going beyond a naive

6. See Ernst Troeltsch, *Writings on Theology and Religion* (London: Duckworth, 1977), 10.

acceptance of what one found in one's source, informally comparing putative events and actions with analogous situations today, and by locating both of these operations in terms of causal theories about how the world operates. Where earlier appeals to historical investigation could falsify this or that historical claim required by theological assertions about divine revelation in the past, the outcome of the later arguments cut to the very core of any claim about direct divine action in history. One might think of this as a radical naturalizing of historical investigation; the only causal agents permitted in any critical understanding of the past were those natural and human agents that every historian used as the default position in making decisions about what happened. What this in turn meant was that the standard claims about the place of divine action in the origins and content of Scripture were ruled out of court as a condition of the historical study of Scripture. If specific divine actions are disallowed, then the claims of divine revelation that supervene on these divine actions are equally disallowed. At one stroke the whole edifice of appeal to past divine revelation was undermined, and new ways to secure the truth of theological claims had to be found.

In effect the study of Scripture now had to be carried out in terms of a functional atheism. What lies at the source of this development is the more general philosophical claim that one cannot engage in the study of any text, including the texts of Scripture, without commitment to prior ontological and related epistemological claims. The crucial mistake in the neighborhood is the claim that only nontheistic ontological and related epistemological assumptions can satisfy the principles of criticism, analogy, and correlation. Ernst Troeltsch clearly recognized this when he noted that he himself worked as a historian already committed to a very specific vision of the God-world relation; otherwise crucial ontological and epistemological questions were being begged at the outset. Troeltsch was an idealist who saw God exclusively at work in, with, and through natural and human agents; his theological claims were secured not by appeal to special revelation but by appeal to religious experience. Correlation is a purely formal desideratum. It simply requires that understanding of the past rests on assumptions about causal powers; it does not by itself specify what those causal

powers must be. Theists are committed to causal powers, including the
causal agency of God. If this option is ruled out, then we are appealing
not to a formal conception of correlation but to a material one. The
debate then naturally moves to one of the boundary between history
and theology; more importantly, it moves the debate into the arena of
ontology and epistemology.

DIVINE REVELATION AND EPISTEMOLOGY

Revelation is in fact a very important epistemic concept. Appeal to
divine revelation figures naturally in debates about the warrants and
justification of theological proposals. It is often seen as a foundation, or
ground, or reason for claims about God. Hence it belongs in the family
of terms generally listed as reason, experience, intuition, conscience,
testimony, and perception. Those who have attempted to develop a
quadrilateral of Scripture, tradition, reason, and experience implicitly
recognize this placement of divine revelation within the field of epistemology. However, it is a category mistake to lump together Scripture
and tradition on the one hand with reason and experience on the other.
The former are constituted by materials, persons, and ecclesial practices; unless they are radically reconceived in epistemic categories, they
fail to fit into the field of epistemology. The latter terms are genuinely
epistemic concepts, even though these in turn are really placehold-
ers for a network of concepts that are summarized under reason and
experience for heuristic purposes. Moreover, epistemological problems
cannot even begin to be resolved merely by adding up this list of items;
to persevere in this practice is to fall into intellectual self-deception.

It has been exceptionally common to look on claims about general
revelation as a form of natural theology or as a theological warrant for
natural theology. This observation is mistaken. Claims about general
revelation constitute claims about how God is manifest or made known
through his action of creating and sustaining the universe. Claims about
natural theology are claims about how to derive sound and valid inferences from propositions about various features of the universe such
as the basic existence of the world or the beauty and order to be found
within the world. The former is a matter of direct perception; the latter
is a matter of deductive or inductive inference or arguments to the best

explanation. It is striking that the cosmological, teleological, and moral arguments generally focus on those features of the universe that also show up in claims about general revelation, that is, the contingency of the universe, its beauty and order, and human recognition of moral goodness in conscience. However, perceiving God in the universe and making good arguments for the existence of God are two radically distinct enterprises. Given that some actions of an agent (in this instance a creative agent) may more characteristically and more aptly reveal the presence and character of the agent, it is natural to pick out certain features of the universe as better focusing general revelation in creation. It is logically contingent that these same elements show up in classical forms of natural theology; they are quite distinct in their provenance and require different modes of reflection for their evaluation.

In the modern period theology tended to deploy a standard account of the relation between natural theology and divine revelation. One first established the existence of God by means of proofs of the existence of God; one then filled out the bigger picture by appeal to divine revelation, especially to special and extra-special revelation. Claims to special revelation differ, of course, in their venues and content; so one also had to develop an argument for the authenticity of the special revelation that formed the second leg of the journey. One first came to believe in the existence of God by means of proof; one then got to special revelation by appeal to miracle. So the presence of miracles was taken as the ground for special revelation. In the language of John's Gospel, one argued to the authenticity to Jesus as a bearer of divine revelation because no one could perform the miracles he performed unless God was with him (John 3:2).

This widely repeated schema generally presupposed what we now identify as evidentialism and internalism. It satisfied the assumption that one was not entitled to a belief unless one had good propositional evidence for that belief; equally it could satisfy the assumption that a rational agent had to have access to the grounds on which they based their beliefs. It also fitted nicely with classical foundationalism in that it was compatible with the claim that only certain kinds of belief could be treated as basic beliefs, that is, those that were self-evident, incorrigible, or evident to the senses. Theism and Christian theism were clearly not basic beliefs.

Immanuel Kant (1724-1804) and Hume demolished this whole way of thinking. The standard story is that Kant undermined the conventional proofs for the existence of God, and Hume, in addition to challenging the standard proofs, undermined the appeal to divine miracle as a warrant for special revelation. The epistemological crisis arising from this epochal development remains to haunt theology even today. Initially the crisis was addressed on the side of unbelief by the invention of various forms of atheism. On the side of belief, the immediate effect was to turn to religious experience as the fundamental ground for a revisionist account of the Christian tradition, or to turn afresh to special revelation as the exclusive ground of Christian faith and practice, arguing that revelation and reason were effectively in tension with each other. The first option was taken up by Friedrich Schleiermacher (1768-1834) and his heirs; the second by Søren Kierkegaard (1813-1855) and his followers. The enduring result is skepticism about the prospects of appeal to divine revelation. Even those committed to divine revelation tend to argue that no good independent reason can be given for commitment to special divine revelation; divine revelation is to be received as a matter of faith, not argument.

Schleiermacher's appeal to religious experience as a warrant for theological proposals was revolutionary in its day.[7] There were precursors of it in the tradition of spiritual senses that shows up in a pronounced way in mysticism and ietism. The latter were often treated with great suspicion on two grounds. First, they were associated with the perennial dangers of heresy and attack on ecclesiastical authority. Mystics and pietists too readily challenged the epistemic and executive authority of the institutions of the church as represented by various ecclesiastical hierarchies. From the days of Montanism in the second century, they were under an intellectual cloud as unreliable and likely to lead to sectarian division and schism. Second, appeal to religious experience, while it may have garnered some support by analogy with sense experience, was seen as much too subjective compared to the

7. See especially Friedrich Schleiermacher, *On Religion: Speeches to Its Cultural Despisers* (Cambridge: Cambridge University Press, 1988).

objectivity of natural theology and special revelation. The standard response was to dismiss it by speaking of religious experience as belonging to the world of superstition, "enthusiasm," and emotionalism. Thus religious experience was not likely to be truth conducive; if anything, it was likely to be misleading and invariably subject to presumption and self-deception.

However, it is possible to refigure the epistemic insight genuinely but obscurely articulated by Schleiermacher and later developed by Rudolf Otto (1869-1937) as a form of appeal to divine revelation understood in terms of manifestation of the divine. To take a mundane example, suppose Mulligan enters a room dressed from head to toe and he finds Murphy sitting in the corner armchair. When Mulligan removes his hat, he reveals that he is bald. As noted earlier, this is a case where revelation takes the form of the manifestation of a present state of affairs. It is relevantly different from the case where Mulligan tells Murphy over the phone that he is completely bald and has saved a small fortune over the years because he has not needed any attention from the local barber. The latter is a case of revelation through communication. Yet in both cases we can say that revelation supervenes on other acts performed by Mulligan; thus the polymorphous character of the concept of revelation is kept in place. Mulligan reveals that he is bald by removing his hat; there is no speech act of communication. The analogue in the case of divine manifestation is obvious. It involves those instances of religious experience where the subject finds herself aware of, say, the presence and love of God. It is now common to treat these cases of divine manifestation as instances of perception of the divine. The philosophical questions are sufficiently complex to be marked off for epistemological review as a special category, namely, the epistemology of religious experience. At this point it is enough to note that we are also dealing with a form of special revelation.

If Schleiermacher and Otto represent an important articulation of appeal to religious experience as a paradigm case of divine revelation, then Kierkegaard and Karl Barth (1886-1968) represent an alternative trajectory in which events in history are taken to be the paradigm case of divine revelation. The relevant event was the appearance of the God-Man, Jesus Christ. For the early Barth, Jesus Christ was not just one more act of God in history; it constituted the sole, final, and exclusive event of divine revelation. He vehemently rejected any appeal to either religious experience or natural theology and worked out a theological rationale for this radical stance. Once he was convinced that Jesus Christ represented the sole, final, and exclusive site of divine revelation, he argued that appeal to any other norm, whether reason or experience, could only be a form of idolatry, a rejection of justification by faith, and an effort to put God in the dock to be judged by sinful human reason. Thus for Barth natural theology took us to a God other than the God revealed in Jesus Christ (idolatry), represented our efforts to climb our way up to God (the adoption of justification by works rather than faith), and put human reason above divine revelation (a way of subjecting God to human judgment). Over against all this, Barth took the concept of divine revelation and argued that the very structure of the concept of divine revelation in terms of revealer, revelation, and revealedness provided warrant for the Christian doctrine of the Trinity. The chief alternative to Barth was worked out in the massive work of Hans Urs von Balthasar (1905-1988), a Catholic theologian who conducted the debate about divine revelation and the epistemology of theology within horizon of post-Hegelian Continental philosophy. All in all the influence of Barth on reflection on divine revelation has been immense within twentieth-century Christian theology. Many if not most liberation theologians operate within his legacy; even the turn to the poor and their liberation can be traced back to him without undue strain. In this world divine revelation and issues of epistemology are barely on the radar screen as far as intrinsic interest is concerned.

A very different way to challenge the consensus that emerged in the wake of Kant and Hume was initially supplied by John Henry Newman (1801-1890). Newman essentially argued that both Hume and Kant assumed that the only way to secure theological proposals was by way of formal proof. If they met this condition, well and good; if not, then we must abandon theism, treat it as a matter of belief and faith rather than knowledge, or accept a radical tension between faith and knowledge. Newman rejected this crucial assumption and argued that many of our warranted beliefs failed to meet this prior condition of proof. Newman proposed that we can appeal to cumulative-case arguments that did not require formal calculation and that necessarily involved the use of irreducible personal judgment.[8] In developing this thesis Newman was reaching deep into the history of the Anglican tradition, which is where this line of argument was most fully developed, even though it now shows up in a variety of forms across the Christian spectrum.

The relevance of this for the debate about the epistemic status of divine revelation can be pursued by asking this question: What role might appeal to divine revelation play in a cumulative case argument for theism or Christian theism? A clue to how it might do so can be gleaned from the Humean ironic remark that rather than miracles providing warrant for this or that special revelation, prior commitment to divine action and hence of divine revelation was required if the argument from miracle was even to get off the ground. Hume defined a miracle as a violation of a law of nature brought about by a god or other invisible agent. While he was partially correct in identifying the historical and epistemic problems in any claim to have witnessed a violation of a law of nature, he implicitly recognized but did not grasp what was really at stake. Thus the crucial point to note about the resurrection of Jesus is not simply that this would be a violation of a law of nature but that it is a theological claim that God raised Jesus from the dead. Such an action would in fact provide confirmation but not proof of his being, say, a bearer of divine revelation. Moreover, the claim to have been a teacher or instantiation of special revelation would have to be considered alongside the claim that he was raised from the dead. The relevant evidence was conjunctive in nature and required good human judgment that brought to the table the full weight of relevant evidence.

In the light of this, one way to proceed is to make appeal to special revelation as one element in a cumulative-case argument for the truth of Christian theism. The other elements include such data as the contingent existence of the cosmos, the order and beauty of the universe, our commitment to a moral order, religious experience, and conspicuous sanctity. The argument takes the forms of an argument

---

8. See especially John Henry Newman, *An Essay in Aid of a Grammar of Assent* (Garden City, NY: Image Books, 1955); Newman, *Fifteen Sermons Preached before the University of Oxford between A.D. 1826 and 1843* (Notre Dame: University of Notre Dame Press, 1997).

to the best explanation. Taken together, the data as a whole are best explained by the content of traditional Christianity.[9] The case against Christian theism is a genuine one; the existence of widespread moral and natural evil does genuinely count against the rationality of Christian belief. However, in comparison to rival metaphysical alternatives represented, say, by naturalistic materialism or romantic humanism, Christian theism has much to commend it as a better alternative given the vision of informal rationality that operates as the apt epistemic framework for adjudicating the value of the alternatives. This vision rejects any attempt at special pleading by arguing that this kind of reasoning is inescapable not just in mundane affairs such as exegesis, the law, and historical investigation but also in the higher-level disputes that show up in natural science and metaphysics. Thus rather than divine revelation being isolated from reason, its data are deployed within an entirely legitimate court of reason.

A crucial assumption in play here is the assumption that special revelation in and of itself constitutes relevant evidence for the existence of God. Thus rather than first coming to believe in the existence of God and then adjudicating the evidence in favor of divine revelation, the encounter with divine revelation can itself furnish good evidence for the existence of God.[10] This is a startling rejection of the standing orthodoxy on divine revelation in philosophy and theology in the modern period. Prima facie it fits with the fact that many have come to theism or remained theists not because they were initially committed to the validity and soundness of natural theology but because they are convinced that they have encountered God through special revelation.

One obvious way to understand this is to think it of a matter of hearing a word from God or hearing the word of God and treating this along the lines in which the epistemic status of perception of the divine in religious experience has been articulated. One recognizes the action of God involved as a basic cognitive act rather than as an inferential procedure that applies explicit criteria of special revelation to this or

---

9. See Basil Mitchell, *The Justification of Religious Belief* (London: Macmillan, 1977).

10. See the argument advanced in Sandra D. Mennsen and Thomas D. Sullivan, *The Agnostic Inquirer: Revelation from a Philosophical Point of View* (Grand Rapids: Eerdmans, 2007).

that putative claim to special revelation. One way to defend what is involved would be to appeal to the principle of initial credulity. Thus if it appears to me that God has spoken to me either in a person-relative word or in hearing the word of God proclaimed, then I do hear a word from God unless I have good reason to believe otherwise. The evidence in this case would be intrinsic to the hearing. However, it could be supplemented by the content of the special revelation. Thus the special revelation could supply an illuminating account of the human condition or make available an intuitively compelling vision of the glory and beauty of God. Beyond this, the evidence could be further supplemented by other considerations that provide further confirmation for the reality and character of God. At this stage various sorts of background considerations come into play, and sorting through these is an important exercise from an epistemological point of view.

The general tendency is to construe the argument as a synchronic argument that gathers up all the relevant evidence and makes a single synthetic judgment about its strength. The fundamental logic is therefore inductive rather than deductive. Two kinds of additional developments show up in the debate. First, how might one bring the ontological argument into play in any cumulative case argument for Christian theism? One suggestion has been to bring in the ontological argument as a final move that blocks the regress to seek further explanation beyond the existence and action of God. Thus if one asks why one should not look for an explanation for the existence and action of God as a comprehensive explanatory hypothesis, the basic reply is that God exists as a necessary being who stands in no need of explanation. Clearly, the legitimacy of the ontological argument then becomes the focus of discussion, as it should be. Second, how might we eliminate the more subjective and risky element of human judgment? The obvious way to make progress on this front is to deploy the resources of Bayes' theories of probability, even though their use to date has not eliminated the need for such judgment. Whatever the merits of this approach, it has failed to win the day so that irreducible judgment remains essential to any cumulative-case argument for theism.

A very different way to make the appeal to divine revelation involves the switch to a diachronic vision of justification that allows for the natural possibility of proceeding step by step as if by means of a journey so that what matters is the end of the journey and the temporal accumulation of evidence rather than a single synchronic evaluation of all the relevant evidence. This way of thinking brings out a crucial dimension of special revelation as an epistemic concept and highlights a further important assumption on how debate about rival claims to divine revelation might be best approached.[11]

Taking the latter issue first, consider the following observation. Small "m" methodism is the thesis that before we evaluate any claim, say, to possess a genuine divine revelation, we must first have in hand the right method for adjudicating rival options. Small "m" methodism thus understood has had a long inning in epistemology as a general principle.[12] The story goes that one does not know p, to take one epistemic desideratum, unless one has already in hand the right method for knowing p, and unless one has satisfied oneself that p has passed muster according to the right method. Applied to claims about divine revelation, one needs a criterion of authenticity, say, appropriate miracles, to know whether one has a genuine revelation.

Small "m" methodism as a general thesis, however, suffers from serious objections. On the one hand, we now need a method for determining access to the right method; and this recursively leads us into an infinite regress. On the other hand, we determine in part our proposals about right method by seeing whether they include a host of particular judgments to which we are already committed. Put differently, methodism allows the skeptic to have the first and last say in epistemology. However, this already begs the question by resolving the fundamental horizon in epistemology in favor of the skeptic. We should at least allow the possibility that we begin with particular judgments as prima facie legitimate and work through to any second-order thesis about method by seeking reflective equilibrium between our judgments on particulars and our commitments on right method.

---

11. See further in William J. Abraham, *Crossing the Threshold of Divine Revelation* (Grand Rapids: Eerdmans, 2006).

12. See Roderick Chisholm, "The Problem of the Criterion," in *The Foundations of Knowing* (Minneapolis: University of Minnesota Press, 1982).

Once we give epistemic primacy to particulars, then we can reject methodism and look for an epistemic fit between the particular judgments we entertain and the relevant evidence for or against it. Thus we do not adjudicate historical proposals in the way we adjudicate mathematical proposals, or moral proposals in the way we adjudicate proposals in biology. The interesting fact about claims to special revelation is that there is no domain that is equivalent to history or biology to which we can simply turn and figure out what to say by way of rationality, justification, knowledge, and the like. What is needed is a version of particularism in which we work with the rival claims to special revelation on offer and examine in each particular case what are the apt considerations that should be consulted. Thus a claim about a book dictated by God will involve considerations that are quite different from a claim that God is revealed through the incarnation of God in Jesus Christ. One has to consult the actual content of the special revelation on offer, be prepared to hear the case made in favor of that particular divine revelation (including the case for apt evaluation), look at the conditions that may be in play for its reception, and the like, rather than dictate in advance an exclusive and precisionist criteriology of evaluation. While there may be a loose network of general criteria that apply across the board (nontriviality in content, internal consistency, explanatory power), the conditions of falsifiability and rational acceptance are necessarily revelation specific. Hence the proper approach to claims about divine revelation may well be sui generis when it comes to epistemological reflection.

A second epistemic consideration to bear in mind reflects the judgment that when we look at specific cases of appeal to divine revelation, the actual revelation on offer leads us to see such revelation as a threshold concept. Once accepted, the particular revelation is simply and totally applicable. Like the concept of legal guilt, once we accept the verdict, it is simply and totally applicable. We enter a whole new world where things change, and often change dramatically. This fits with the metaphor of threshold, for the idea of a threshold is a spatial one. Consider crossing the threshold of a building. As a first-time visitor, one does not generally know what one will encounter. Once across the threshold, the crossing is singular and absolute, and one enters a whole new world. There is now a new awareness of phenomena that were previously hidden, and the phenomena are singular; they are relative to the actual threshold crossed. It is likewise with special revelation. In the Christian tradition, the revelation and its intellectual consequences in the canonical heritage of the church are so rich that the encounter and embrace of divine revelation is a world-constituting experience. Those in other religious traditions will have their own account of what is involved. There may well be very significant over-lapping in terms of theological and moral content and religious practice, a matter that calls for cross-cultural theological reflection; but there is no escaping the need for initial revelation-relative description of what has been received.

Given these observations about how the recognition and accep-tance of special revelation actually functions, we can see immediately why adoption of special revelation in the Christian tradition is often a matter of dramatic conversion. Encountering the new world requires intellectual space, ecclesial assistance, and great patience. Further, the response to divine revelation cannot be limited in advance in terms of its depth. Thus it can foster a boldness that can easily be construed by outsiders as arrogance, not least when the recipient is prepared to die for the truth of what they have received. In addition, there is no limit to the way in which all of one's existence, including one's pre-vious intellectual and even epistemic commitments, may have to be revised. It was this consideration that led medieval theologians, rightly or wrongly, to reconceive all knowledge as requiring the concurrent action of God in divine illumination. Equally, it can lead one to enrich one's self-understanding as a cognitive agent to include belief in a *sensus divinitatis* or an *oculis contemplationis*. These developments will make no sense outside the new theological world that one has entered. Finally, all of these developments are predicated on this consideration: once one acknowledges the content of divine revelation in propositional terms, then these propositions will now be taken as knowledge rather than mere human opinion, probabilistic judgment, or ingenious speculation. Dismissing this as the appeal to the method of authority is not just a misleading account of what is at stake; it is a profound error of judg-ment. It betrays a shallow and superficial grasp of one pivotal aspect of revelation as an epistemic concept. Revelation yields knowledge of and about God.

CONCLUSION

One of the effects of the revisionist work in epistemology over the last generation has been to create space for a fresh evaluation of debates about the rationality and justification of religious belief. Options that were long thought to be dead and gone have come back with renewed vigor; a whole raft of new insights and theories has appeared that totally changed the landscape. For the most part theologians in the wake of Barth and in the aftermath of the aggressive attack from positivist and ordinary-language philosophy have deserted the field either for the more exotic shores of Continental philosophy or for the more exciting coasts of liberation and political action. Consequently, the whole topic of divine revelation has languished in the hands of conservatives at the margins of academic orthodoxy or been abandoned as a dead end where one opinion is as good as another.

In the extraordinary revival of philosophy of religion in the analytic tradition, the first responders have rightly returned to the perennial themes and challenges that have been at the core of the tradition. In epistemology, the focus has been on the merits, if any, of natural theology, the veridicality of religious experience, and the challenge of evil. Within this there has been marginal but substantial reflection on the nature and status of divine revelation. Generally, the overall disposition is to stick to the philosophy of religion in general because of fear of charges of being parochial and insufficiently inclusive. Even so, most philosophy of religion has focused on the Christian tradition with side glances to Judaism and Islam.

The current trend in philosophy more generally to become engaged, say, in philosophy of science, by paying close attention to the actual particulars of science, say, in the philosophy of biology, is not accidental or arbitrary. While philosophy has its own distinctive content, skills, and dispositions, it cannot make progress without attending to the particularities of the subject matter that show up in its deliberations. The emergence of analytic theology as a burgeoning enterprise shows that this general trend is alive and well on the borders of philosophy of religion, if not actually well within its homelands.

When it comes to epistemology, there remains enormous reluctance to step outside the contours of some kind of generic religious epistemology or epistemology of religion. The whole idea of the epistemology of theology sounds like an oxymoron. There is no sense that the epistemologist can and should attend conceptually, historically, and substantially to critical reflection to the epistemological issues thrown up by Christian theology. Such a shift in perspective need not be a narrow, parochial enterprise; the conceptual and historical materials alone, not to speak of the work of contemporary theologians, provide a massive and dense body of data for investigation. Moreover, we need, say, specifically Jewish and Islamic work that takes with radical seriousness the history and contemporary commitments of these great religions. We now need to embrace with enthusiasm and flair the epistemology of theology as a serious subdiscipline of epistemology. As we do so, conceptual, historical, and epistemological work on divine revelation will get the attention it deserves.

WORKS CITED

Abraham, William J. *Crossing the Threshold of Divine Revelation*. Grand Rapids: Eerdmans, 2006.

Bultmann, Rudolf. "The Concept of Revelation in the New Testament." In *Existence and Faith*, 58–91. New York: Meridian, 1966.

Chisholm, Roderick. "The Problem of the Criterion." In *The Foundations of Knowing*, 61–75. Minneapolis: University of Minnesota Press, 1982.

Congar, Yves M.-J., OP. *Tradition and Traditions: An Historical and a Theological Essay*. New York: Macmillan, 1967.

Levison, John R. *Of Two Minds: Ecstasy and Inspired Interpretation of the New Testament*. North Richland Hills, TX: Bibal, 1999.

Mavrodes, George. *Revelation in Religious Belief*. Philadelphia: Temple University Press, 1988.

Mennsen, Sandra D., and Thomas D. Sullivan. *The Agnostic Inquirer: Revelation from a Philosophical Point of View*. Grand Rapids: Eerdmans, 2007.

Mitchell, Basil. *The Justification of Religious Belief*. London: Macmillan, 1977.

Newman, John Henry. *An Essay in Aid of a Grammar of Assent*. Garden City, NY: Image Books, 1955.

————. *Fifteen Sermons Preached before the University of Oxford between A.D. 1826 and 1843*. Notre Dame: University of Notre Dame Press, 1997.

Rahner, Karl. *Inspiration in the Bible*. New York: Herder & Herder, 1961.

Schleiermacher, Friedrich. *On Religion: Speeches to Its Cultural Despisers*. Cambridge: Cambridge University Press, 1988.

Troeltsch, Ernst. *Writings on Theology and Religion*. London: Duckworth, 1977.

5

Ordering with Intent

Restoring Divine Order
in Isaiah and Genesis

Caroline Batchelder

THE "CREATED ORDER"

Claus Westermann argued in 1974 that the verb ברא in Genesis 1:26–28—traditionally translated "he created"—should be understood as describing "an action of God" rather than "making a general and universally valid statement about the nature of humankind."[1] That is, image-of-God language in Genesis 1 is about God's act of creating rather than humanity's mode of being. Westermann asserted that these verses have meaning only in their immediate context and that the Old Testament bears out this claim in that it goes on to say little more at all about God's image and likeness.[2] Westermann's ideas are influenced by his form-critical analysis of Genesis 1, by which he considers 1:26–30 to be part of "an independent narrative about the creation of humanity" that was only later combined with the account of the whole creation.[3] In this way he separates the story of the creation of humanity from the creation of everything else.

This essay will argue almost the opposite of Westermann's view: that Genesis 1:26–30 (and following) say something very significant about the nature of humanity in relation to God, to the cosmos, and to all its inhabitants. My argument is related to a broad hypothesis that

---

1. Thank you to Dr. Andrew Sloane (Morling College) for reading and commenting on this paper.

2. C. Westermann, *Genesis 1–11: A Commentary*, trans. J. J. Scullion (Minneapolis: Augsburg Fortress, 1984), 155–56.

3. Westermann, *Genesis 1–11*, 155–56.

the remainder of the story of humanity and God in the Old Testament—
following the desecration of God's image and likeness in Genesis 3—
may be fruitfully understood as being largely about the restoration of
humanity as God's image and likeness, in the midst of and for the sake
of God's world. This essay will approach an understanding of humanity
in the book of Isaiah through an understanding of humanity in the
first chapters of Genesis. It will then look back at Genesis through
the lens of two sections of Isaian poetry about a significant human
figure whom Yahweh calls "my servant." In doing this I will seek to
make some observations about the relationship of divine revelation
and human reason.

A succession of commentators[4] has argued in different ways that
Genesis 1 describes God's ordering of creation.[5] This ordering is the way
in which God arranges the world and its elements to bring about the
future God intends for them (e.g., "let the earth bring forth," 1:12, 24), a
future repeatedly noted as being for blessing, fruitfulness, abundance,
and fullness (1:22, 28; ברך; פרה; רבה; מלא). Thus the Genesis 1 creation
account advances to the completion (כלה) and rest (שלום) with which
it culminates (2:2).[6]

4. W. J. Dumbrell, *The Search for Order: Biblical Eschatology in Focus* (Grand
Rapids: Baker, 1994); G. J. Wenham, *Genesis 1-15*, ed. D. A. Hubbard et al., WBC (Waco,
TX: Word, 1987), 10; J. D. Levenson, "The Temple and the World," *Journal of Religion*
64, no. 3 (1984); Levenson, *Creation and the Persistence of Evil: The Jewish Drama of
Divine Omnipotence* (Princeton, NJ: Princeton University Press, 1988); J. Barr, "Was
Everything That God Created Really Good? A Question in the First Verse of the Bible,"
in *God in the Fray: A Tribute to Walter Brueggemann*, ed. T. Linafelt et al. (Minneapolis:
Augsburg Fortress, 1998), 55-65; T. E. Fretheim, *The Pentateuch*, ed. G. M. Tucker,
Interpreting Biblical Texts (Nashville: Abingdon, 1996), 73; Fretheim, *God and World
in the Old Testament: A Relational Theology of Creation* (Nashville: Abingdon, 2005),
5; E. Van Wolde, *Reframing Biblical Studies: When Language and Text Meet Culture,
Cognition, and Context* (Winona Lake, IN: Eisenbrauns, 2009); Van Wolde, "Why
the Verb ברא Does Not Mean 'to Create' in Genesis 1.1-2.4a," *JSOT* 34, no. 1 (2009);
J. H. Walton, *The Lost World of Genesis One: Ancient Cosmology and the Origins Debate*
(Downers Grove, IL: InterVarsity, 2009); Walton, *The Lost World of Adam and Eve:
Genesis 2-3 and the Human Origins Debate* (Downers Grove, IL: IVP Academic, 2015).
5. This is not to deny that creation involves God creating from nothing; see
Heb 11:3.
6. See the section that runs from Gen 1:1-2:4. The wordplay between "seven"
and "ceased" (rested) in 2:2: וישבת ביום השביעי ("and he rested on the seventh day")
may indicate editing as a temple text. See Levenson, *Creation*, 59, 85-86, 107, 109-11.

The verb ברא is only used in the Old Testament with God as subject[7] and undoubtedly depicts God's unique action. In Genesis 1 "heavens and earth" (the "totality of creation"[8]) are "created" (ברא) complete as a place in which God may rest, and their parts as well as the totality are טוב ("good" in every English translation); that is, they fulfill their assigned purpose within God's "well"ordered system.[9] The crafted literary ordering of Genesis 1 (noted from earliest scholarship)[10] reflects the craft of God's physical ordering of creation: the meticulously ordered text mirrors the meticulous ordering of heavens and earth.[11] Indeed, elements traditionally thought of as representing chaos in the ancient Near East are specifically linked with the divine verb ברא, within a balanced, harmonious design.[12] James Barr (among others) concludes that "creation out of nothing ... is not the main theme of Genesis 1." He continues, "The seven-day scheme ... is based upon separation and demarcation rather than on mere existence as against nothingness."[13]

---

7. I ברא in L. Koehler, J. Stamm, and W. Baumgartner, eds., *Hebrew and Aramaic Lexicon of the Old Testament*, 5 vols. (Leiden: Brill, 1994-2000), 1:153. The form sometimes thought to be *piel* of ברא in Josh 17:15, 18 and Ezek 23:47 (see also Ezek 21:19) may be an entirely different root; Thomas E. McComiskey in *Theological Wordbook of the Old Testament*, eds. Bruce K. Waltke, R. L. Harris, and Gleason L. Archer (Chicago: Moody, 1980), 278a.

8. Dumbrell, *Search for Order*, 16.

9. It seems likely that טוב means "functional" within God's created order; Walton, *Lost World of Adam and Eve*, 57; see Dumbrell, *Search for Order*, 20-21, "good for" "the complete correspondence between divine intention and the universe." Kreuzer cites Schmidt's comment that "'good' declares that all things have their right place and fulfil their function," S. Kreuzer, "'Behold It Was Very Good': God's Praise of the Creation (Gen 1:4, 10, 12, 18, 21, 25, 31) and Its Background," in *"My Spirit at Rest in the North Country" (Zechariah 6.8): Collected Communications to the XXth Congress of the International Organization for the Study of the Old Testament, Helsinki 2010*, ed. H. M. Niemann et al., Beiträge Zur Erforschung des Alten Testaments und des Antiken Judentums (Frankfurt: Peter Lang, 2011), 24-25.

10. See "*order* and *productivity*" in Philo, cited in J. Dickson, "The Genesis of Everything: A Historical Account of the Bible's Opening Chapter," *ISCAST* 4 (2008): 4.

11. See Dickson, "Genesis of Everything," 13.

12. E.g., sea monsters are the subject of the second of three uses of ברא, Gen 1:21. See R. Parry, *The Biblical Cosmos: A Pilgrim's Guide to the Weird and Wonderful World of the Bible* (Eugene, OR: Cascade, 2014), 37; Wenham, *Genesis 1-15*, 24. It may even be that within God's "creating" (ברא) of the whole (1:1), the elements that require a specific expression of God's ordering—perhaps because of their capacity for bringing *disorder*—appear as the objects of ברא: the sea monsters (1:21, as mentioned) and humanity (1:27).

13. Barr, "Was Everything That God Created Really Good?," 59-62.

An important implication of the proposal that God is establishing good order rather than "mere existence" in Genesis 1 is that human existence is blessed and commissioned within God's order (1:26-28). This suggests in turn that authentic humanity may be practiced best within God's good order.[14] Additionally, if Genesis 1 is understood as an explanation of physical origins only, creation "is over and done with—a historical event. Once creation is understood functionally [i.e., as ordering for a purpose], God's role as creator can be recognized as ongoing."[15]

In the book of Isaiah (as I will argue), God continues to "create" (ברא) the heavens and the earth and all they contain as God intends they will be, that is, to bring about God's order and to order even apparently chaotic elements within it.[16] God's order in Genesis 1 establishes human rule in God's image and likeness for fullness and fruitfulness and for the well-being of the earth,[17] forming an essential and basic connection between humanity and the earth within God's order.[18]

ORDERING FOR

Jon Levenson describes "a long tradition in the ancient Near East, which binds Temple building and world building,"[19] and argues that Genesis 1 may be understood as part of this tradition. So central is the Hebrew temple to biblical thought, claims Levenson, that "the Temple ... is the world *in nuce*, and the world is the temple *in extenso*."[20] So strongly are

14. See G. von Rad, *Wisdom in Israel* (London: SCM, 1972), 80. This throws light on Gal 5:19-23 and its climactic assertion, "against these things there is no law."

15. J. H. Walton, "Creation in Genesis 1:1-2:3 and the ANE: Order Out of Disorder after Chaoskampf," *CTJ* 43, no. 1 (2008): 63; my bracketed comment. See Fretheim, *Pentateuch*, 119.

16. See S. J. Grenz, *Theology for the Community of God* (Grand Rapids: Eerdmans, 2000), 110-11. This seems to be the basis of the logic of Isa 40-55 (and elsewhere), where the nations' mighty conquerors are shown to be ordered by Yahweh to bring about Yahweh's purposes and ultimately Yahweh's new creation. See Isa 41:1-3, 25; 48:7; also 65:17, 18.

17. Gen 1:26, רדה, "rule"; 1:28, כבש, "subdue," רדה; see Gen 2:15, עבד, "serve," שמר, "keep."

18. On this connection see J. R. Middleton, *The Liberating Image: The Imago Dei in Genesis 1* (Grand Rapids: Brazos, 2005), 50-55.

19. Levenson, "Temple and the World," 287; see G. K. Beale, *The Temple and the Church's Mission: A Biblical Theology of the Dwelling Place of God*, New Studies in Biblical Theology (Downers Grove, IL: InterVarsity, 2004), 60-63.

20. "In a nutshell ... in full" (Levenson, "Temple and the World," 285). See

temple and world connected that the word pair "heavens and earth"("a merism for 'the world'") may indicate a temple text wherever it is used,[21] including the Genesis 1 and Isaiah 1 creation accounts. Scholars have described verbal links between creation and the construction of successive sanctuaries, including tabernacle and temple.[22] "Tabernacle" in Hebrew is מִשְׁכָּן, cognate with the verb שָׁכַן, "to dwell, settle."[23] It is the resting place of God's presence and glory, as was Eden, as will be the temple (בֵּית יהוה/אלוהים, "the house of Yahweh/God"[24]). All three are miniatures of God's order for blessing and prospering, which humanity is commissioned to maintain and to extend.[25]

In Genesis 2 God puts אָדָם (humanity), formed in God's image, into Eden: into the rest and delight made possible by the good ordering of the world.[26] (See Gen 2:15: וַיַּנִּחֵהוּ, "and he caused [him] to rest";[27] also

---

details in Levenson, *Creation*, 86–87; J. D. Levenson, *Sinai and Zion: An Entry into the Jewish Bible*, ed. A. Y. Collins and John J. Collins, New Voices in Biblical Studies (Minneapolis: Winston, 1985), 142–45; and G. J. Wenham, "Sanctuary Symbolism in the Garden of Eden Story," in *I Studied Inscriptions before the Flood*, ed. R. Hess et al., Sources for Biblical and Theological Study (Winona Lake, IN: Eisenbrauns, 1994), 399–404.

21. In Isa 67:17, "YHWH is building a new Temple, therefore creating a new world, and vice versa." Levenson, "Temple and the World," 295.

22. E.g., Fretheim, *Pentateuch*, 119–20, Levenson, "Temple and the World," 282–289, Beale, *Temple and the Church's Mission*, 108.

23. מִשְׁכָּן in Koehler, Stamm, and Baumgartner, eds., *Hebrew and Aramaic Lexicon*, 2:646–47.

24. "House of Yahweh": see Exod 23:19 and throughout the Old Testament. "House of God" is used more rarely, e.g., Ps 42:5.

25. This does not imply a particular view of whether Gen 1 was conceived as a "temple text." It is possible that the ordering principles of creation were reflected and preserved in the sacred space of tabernacle and temple, and that the later influence of the sanctuaries resulted from exilic/postexilic editing of Genesis. See G. K. Beale and M. Kim, *God Dwells among Us: Expanding Eden to the Ends of the Earth* (Downers Grove, IL: InterVarsity, 2014). See parallels between the tabernacle and Mount Sinai (Exod 19–20) in G. J. Wenham, *The Pentateuch*, Exploring the Old Testament (London: SPCK, 2003), 68, and Beale, *Temple and the Church's Mission*, 105–7.

26. Walton has proposed that while the entire cosmos is designated as sacred space in Gen 1, its center is located in the garden of Eden in Gen 2, which resembles "the holy of holies in the tabernacle/temple"; Walton, *Lost World of Adam and Eve*, 117.

27. נוּחַ (distinct from shalom) indicates "settledness" rather than completion, i.e., conditions that enable people to get on with their lives (Waltke, Harris and Archer, eds., in *Theological Wordbook*, 1323). See the distinction in Walton, *Lost World of Genesis One*, 72–77. "Noah," whose name is cognate with the verb נוּחַ ("rest") in

Gen 2:8, 10, 15, עֵדֶן [Eden] homophonic with עֵדֶן "bliss"[28]). By extension the tasks of אָדָם in Eden, "to serve it and to keep it" (עבד and שׁמר, 2:15), function to maintain the garden as the place of God's order-for-rest. These verbs anticipate the priestly activities of serving and keeping that preserve the sanctuary's good order in Numbers 3:7–8; 8:26; and 18:5–6.[29] Humanity is surely formed as God's image and likeness for the sake of the good order of God's creation: for purposes of rest and of delight. Garden, tabernacle, and temple all echo this sovereign order.[30]

William Dumbrell has described humanity's task as being to "Edenize" the world, that is, to extend God's order from Eden out into the whole earth. He notes the "contingency and provisionality" of a future "given over into the hands of human beings."[31] But instead of serving and keeping God's order, Genesis 3 describes how אָדָם pursued knowledge of good and evil outside God's order, seeking to have its source within themselves (see the act of eating in Gen 3:6).[32] As Dumbrell comments, "Sin is not a moral lapse" but a "deliberate human assault upon the established order of creation."[33] Indeed, it may be argued that an alternative, anthropocentric way of ordering life on the earth was established

---

Gen 2:15, is righteous and obedient, and he builds at Yahweh's command an ordered, archetypal space to preserve life: a "vehicle" for the future of the earth under Yahweh's lordship. Yet the trajectory of human sin continues barely abated (see Gen 8:21). Beale, *Temple and the Church's Mission*, 104, notes in the Noah story (Gen 7–9) the first biblical distinction between clean and unclean animals, the "burnt offerings" and "soothing aroma" that are associated elsewhere with the tabernacle, as well as their mountain setting. Notably, David turned his thoughts to building the temple when "the LORD had given him rest [נוח] from all his enemies around" (2 Sam 7:1).

28. II עֵדֶן in Koehler, Stamm, and Baumgartner, eds., *Hebrew and Aramaic Lexicon*, 2:792.

29. Wenham, "Sanctuary Symbolism," 401. See the warning to Solomon if he and his sons do not "keep" and "serve," 1 Kgs 9:6–7 (Beale, *Temple and the Church's Mission*, 68).

30. See Ps 29:9, "In [Yahweh's] temple everything says 'Glory!'" Beale, *Temple and the Church's Mission*, 66, notes that the *hitpael* of הלך used for God "walking" in the garden is also used for "God's presence in the tabernacle" in Lev 26:12; Deut 23:15 (Eng. 23:14); 2 Sam 7:6–7.

31. Dumbrell, *Search for Order*, 11.

32. See Y. Avrahami, *The Senses of Scripture: Sensory Perception in the Hebrew Bible*, ed. C. V. Camp et al., Library of Hebrew Bible/Old Testament Series (New York: Bloomsbury, 2102), 95, on "the image of eating as gaining knowledge."

33. Dumbrell, *Search for Order*, 27.

through their actions.[34] Because of the essential link between human rule in God's likeness and the "good" of the earth, the rest of creation suffers as a result of human disobedience and the consequent disruption of God's order (Gen 3:14–19). While Genesis 1 describes order brought increasingly to something formerly "formless and empty"[35]— an order echoed by the Edenizing task—human action introduces an opposite tangent, where "disorder increases at the cost of order."[36] This is evidenced by the chaos that increases from Genesis 3–11.[37] In contrast to other ancient Near Eastern creation literature, evil or chaos is "not given primordial status" in the biblical accounts.[38] Instead chaos begins through the action of those charged with rule in God's likeness. Creation is unmistakably linked with God's order; conversely, disorder is frequently depicted as uncreation (see "the flood," Gen 6–8;[39] Jer 4:23–26). Instead of fullness and fruitfulness in Yahweh's image and likeness (Gen 1:28), humanity—still blessed for fullness and fruitfulness—fills the earth with corruption (see Gen 6:11–12).

Human consumption from the tree of the knowledge of good and evil in Genesis 3:6–7 is frequently represented as the loss of innocence,[40] but it was also the loss of an innocent wisdom: wisdom that was innately connected with being "like" God. Wisdom herself describes her presence at creation's ordering in Proverbs 8:23–30;[41] in the overturning of

34. See Eccl 7:29: "God made אדם upright, but they sought many schemes"; R. L. Schultz, "Unity or Diversity in Wisdom Theology? A Canonical and Covenantal Perspective," *Tyndale Bulletin* 48, no. 2 (1997): 305.

35. See the suggestion in D. T. Tsumura, *Creation and Destruction: A Reappraisal of the Chaoskampf Theory in the Old Testament* (Winona Lake, IN: Eisenbrauns, 2005), 33, that תהו ובהו describes somewhere that is not yet as it should be.

36. Dumbrell, *Search for Order*, 21.

37. See the comments on parallels with the fall and the progression of sin in subsequent chapters of Genesis in Wenham, *Genesis 1–15*, 117, 171. It is well summed up by Gen 6:12, "all flesh had ruined its way upon the earth."

38. Middleton, *Liberating Image*, 254.

39. "The story of the undoing of creation," D. J. A. Clines, *The Theme of the Pentateuch*, ed. D. J. A. Clines et al., 2nd ed., JSOTSup 10 (Sheffield: Sheffield Academic, 1997), 81; see J. Blenkinsopp, *Creation, Un-creation, Re-creation: A Discursive Commentary on Genesis 1–11* (New York: T&T Clark, 2011).

40. E.g., discussion in H. Blocher, *In the Beginning: The Opening Chapters of Genesis*, trans. D. G. Preston (Leicester, UK: Inter-Varsity, 1984), 173–75; Wenham, *Genesis 1–15*, 76.

41. On this see von Rad, *Wisdom in Israel*, 144–57.

Yahweh's order, innocent wisdom was abandoned, and the creation's fullness and fruitfulness disrupted.

REGAINING WISDOM, REGAINING GOD'S ORDER

It may be argued that over the course of the Old Testament the activity of reordering אָדָם in relation to Yahweh emerges as the key agenda of wisdom instruction.[42] Von Rad describes the force of wisdom as an "ordering power."[43] The three following examples highlight some of the ways in which Yahweh's order is restored through the getting of wisdom:

- תּוֹרָה is a means of regulating human knowledge of good and evil, enabling postfall humanity to live in God's likeness within God's order and so to regain a measure of wisdom.[44] Wisdom is directly identified with תּוֹרָה in Sirach 24:23,[45] and the תּוֹרָה has been called the "essence of wisdom" in Judaism.[46]

- Brueggemann argues that the Psalter (whose five books echo the five books of the תּוֹרָה) is intended to take its worshipers from

---

42. Von Rad, *Wisdom in Israel*, 74–96, 158–59. Cf. D. J. Treier, *Proverbs & Ecclesiastes*, ed. R. R. Reno, Brazos Theological Commentary on the Bible (Grand Rapids: Brazos, 2011), xx.

43. Von Rad, *Wisdom in Israel*, 159.

44. D. J. A. Clines, "The Tree of Knowledge and the Law of Yahweh (Psalm XIX)," *Vetus Testamentum* 24, no. 1 (1974): 1, argues that Ps 19:7-14 shows "the superiority of the law" to the tree of the knowledge of good and evil. Wenham, "Sanctuary Symbolism," 402–3, comments that in Ps 19:8-9, תּוֹרָה "is described as 'making wise the simple, rejoicing the heart and enlightening the eyes,'" evoking "*association*" with Gen 2:9 and 3:6. See Treier, *Proverbs & Ecclesiastes*, xx.

45. Von Rad, *Wisdom in Israel*, 160; R. E. Murphy, "Wisdom and Creation," *JBL* 104, no. 1 (1985): 10. In the tradition wisdom "became not only the Five Books of Moses, but the entire legal and ethical tradition of Judaism," writes B. Z. Bergman, "The Living Tree: The Roots and Growth of Jewish Law (review)," *Journal of Law and Religion*, (1989): 235 (sic); E. N. Dorff and A. Rosett, eds., *A Living Tree: The Roots and Growth of Jewish Law* (Albany: State University of New York Press, 1988), 14–15. See "The Bereshith or Genesis Rabba," in vol. 4 of *The Sacred Books and Early Literature of the East*, trans. W. W. Westcott et al. (New York: Parke, Austin and Lipscomb, 1917): "The Torah was to God, when he created the world, what the plan is to an architect when he erects a building."

46. J. Levine, "Judaism: The Written Law: Torah," in *Jewish Virtual Library* (American-Israeli Cooperative Enterprise, 2016), www.jewishvirtuallibrary.org/jsource/Judaism/The_Written_Law.html.

obedience-to-תּוֹרָה (Ps 1) to "unencumbered doxology" (Ps 150).[47] The Psalter opens with an invitation to happiness (אַשְׁרֵי־הָאִישׁ, 1:1)[48] and explores the heights and depths of human lives in the very process of their ordering under Yahweh's lordship, a process that brings worshipers at last to the unalloyed praise of the Psalter's final psalms. Worship is to be attained through the process of ordering every aspect of life under Yahweh's lordship.

- The first word of the heading of the book we know as Proverbs, מָשָׁל (מִשְׁלֵי שְׁלֹמֹה, Prov 1:1) is a homonym of two verbs, "to be like" and "to rule."[49] It may even be a wordplay,[50] suggesting that the book is about "knowing wisdom and discipline" (1:2) *in order* to rule in Yahweh's likeness; that is, that it instructs humanity how to live best by keeping and extending[51] God's good order, and so to rule as charged in Genesis 1.[52]

By its reference to the tree of life in Genesis 2–3, Proverbs 3:18 indicates that the kind of life enabled and blessed in God's creation ordering (Gen 1) may be restored by "holding fast" to wisdom:

[Wisdom] is a tree of life for those who hold fast to her,
    and the one who grasps her is happy [מְאֻשָּׁר]. (Prov 3:18)[53]

---

47. W. Brueggemann, "Bounded by Obedience and Praise: The Psalms as Canon," *JSOT* 50 (1991).

48. J. C. McCann Jr., "The Book of Psalms: Introduction, Commentary and Reflections," in *New Interpreter's Bible Commentary*, ed. L. E. Keck (Nashville: Abingdon, 2015), 304.

49. I–II מָשַׁל in Koehler, Stamm, and Baumgartner, eds., *Hebrew and Aramaic Lexicon*, 2:647-48. See "comparison" and "mastery" in R. C. Van Leeuwen, "The Book of Proverbs: Introduction, Commentary and Reflections," in *New Interpreter's Bible Commentary*, ed. Keck; also R. E. Murphy, *The Tree of Life: An Exploration of Biblical Wisdom Literature* (Grand Rapids: Eerdmans, 1996), 7. Interestingly, Ezekiel uses the same wordplay in Ezek 17:2 (see 18:2): וּמְשֹׁל מָשָׁל אֶל־בֵּית יִשְׂרָאֵל. This is addressed to בֶּן־אָדָם, suggesting a further allusion to Genesis.

50. Additionally, מָשָׁל is a phonetic play with שְׁלֹמֹה (Solomon), where the same consonants are reordered. Even in this playful use of language the act of ordering is an essential part of human "rule."

51. See "serve and keep" (Gen 2:15).

52. For further language use that supports this argument, see below.

53. All translations are my own.

This is not the tree of the knowledge of good and evil (Gen 3:6), but—
אָדָם having taken for themselves an alternative knowledge of good and
evil—wisdom is offered as a tree of life (to which the direct way is
barred) by which they may regain to some extent the fullness of life
impaired in the fall (see Gen 3:22-24; see also Prov 8:35 "for whoever
finds me [Wisdom] finds life").[54]

ORDERING IN ISAIAH

The book of Isaiah opens with Yahweh's lament over the history of Yahweh's people. It recounts how Yahweh "made great" (גדל) and "raised
up" (רום) sons,[55] who rebelled and have become estranged. They have
abandoned sonship and become like a sinful "foreign nation" to Yahweh
(הוי | גוי חטא, Isa 1:4[56]). They have less than an animal's rudimentary
knowledge of their lord (בעל) and "know not" the fundamentals of
their relation to Yahweh (1:3).[57] Isaiah's language echoes the Genesis
narratives of the formation and desecration of the human image, telling Israel and Judah's history as an echo of humanity's creation and
fall.[58] Heavens and earth, Yahweh's word, Yahweh's sons (a figure for
"image and likeness"[59]) and their rebellion, the significance of their

54. See the final chapter in W. Brueggemann, *Theology of the Old Testament:
Testimony, Dispute, Advocacy* (Minneapolis: Fortress, 1997), 747-50, titled
"Acknowledgement of Yahweh Requires Reordering of Everything Else": "Which
witnesses are believed ... will determine the shape of the world."

55. Walton, *Lost World of Adam and Eve*, 89, describes the connection of sonship with the image of God in biblical literature and in ancient Mesopotamia
more generally.

56. This is the implication of גוי in 1:4.

57. A. Berlin, *The Dynamics of Biblical Parallelism*, ed. A. Beck et al., rev. ed.,
Biblical Resources Series (Grand Rapids: Eerdmans, 2008), 97-98, translates 1:3
with "my people does not understand itself" (*hitpael* of ידע).

58. On possible relations between the texts of Genesis and Isaiah, see J.
Goldingay, "The Patriarchs in Scripture and History," in *Essays on the Patriarchal
Narratives*, ed. A. R. Millard et al. (Leicester, UK: Inter-Varsity, 1980), 34; J. Goldingay,
"'You Are Abraham's Offspring, My Friend': Abraham in Isaiah 41," in *He Swore an
Oath: Biblical Themes from Genesis 12-50*, ed. R. S. Hess et al. (Carlisle, UK: Paternoster,
1994); P. T. Willey, *Remember the Former Things: The Recollection of Previous Texts
in Second Isaiah*, ed. M. V. Fox, Society of Biblical Literature Dissertation Series
(Atlanta: Scholars Press, 1997), 32-33; M. A. Fishbane, "Inner-Biblical Exegesis," in
Hebrew Bible, Old Testament: The History of Its Interpretation, ed. M. Sæbø (Göttingen:
Vandenhoeck & Ruprecht, 1996), 45.

59. See Gen 5:3.

not knowing (Gen 3:5, 7, 22), the disordering of the earth that Yahweh's lament links to this (Isa 1:7–8; Gen 3:17–19), together with attention to "light" and "darkness," chaos, and creation,[60] suggest that Isaiah's story of Israel and Judah is written as an echo of the story of אָדָם.[61] אָדָם in Israel and Judah has followed the same path as אָדָם in Eden. "People" and "earth" increasingly "filled" with pagan practices in Isaiah 2:6, 7, and 8 are a parody of the fullness and fruitfulness intended in Genesis 1:28, and are the direct result of Yahweh's sons' *unlikeness* to Yahweh. They have become a false image, and so Yahweh "abandons" them (2:6), exiling them among the false images of the nations. Using legal language, the Isaian prophet calls for heavens and earth—the whole creation that humans were to rule and subdue, serve, and keep; the sacred space (later represented in tabernacle and temple) in which they were to be Yahweh's image and likeness—to bear witness to the sons' rebellion (1:2).

In what has been called Isaiah's "temple vision" in Isaiah 6, temple and earth merge,[62] and the see-er of the vision—along with those who read or who hear his first-person account, and so who "see" through his eyes (as it were)—is given a seraphim's eye view of Yahweh in relation to Yahweh's creation.

> Holy, Holy, Holy, Yahweh of Hosts
> The fullness of the whole earth [is] his glory! (Isa 6:3)

60. P. D. Miscall, "Isaiah: New Heavens, New Earth, New Book," in *Reading between Texts: Intertextuality and the Hebrew Bible*, ed. D. N. Fewell, Literary Currents in Biblical Interpretation (Louisville: Westminster John Knox, 1992), 47–51.

61. Blenkinsopp, *Creation, Un-creation, Re-creation*, 179, notes the presumption of Isa 40–55 that its audience was familiar with "an account of cosmic and human origins," citing 40:21, and the sixteen-fold use of ברא in 40–55. For a discussion of the textual relationship between Genesis and Isaiah, see Willey, *Remember the Former Things*. Richard Hays provides seven tests for "hearing echoes" in Scripture. These are availability, volume, recurrence, thematic coherence, historical plausibility, history of interpretation, and satisfaction; see R. B. Hays, *Echoes of Scripture in the Letters of Paul* (New Haven, CT: Yale University Press, 1989), 29–32. J. M. Leonard, "Identifying Inner-Biblical Allusions: Psalm 78 as a Test Case," *JBL* 127, no. 2 (2008): 242, 246, 258, provides another set of factors including shared words, shared phrases, rare or distinctive shared language, accumulation of these, and similar contexts, along with a series of questions about possible relations between the texts.

62. Opinion differs as to whether this vision is in the temple or in the world, and the passage reflects the tension between them. See discussion in C. Batchelder, "Undoing 'This People', Becoming 'My Servant': Purpose and Commission in Isaiah 6," *Southeastern Theological Review* 4, no. 2 (2013): 156.

This poetic couplet, distinct within a narrative section (6:1–13)[63] draws holy Yahweh into parallel with the earth's fullness and Yahweh's glory.[64] The juxtaposition of this with the earth's *unholy* fullness in the preceding chapters is striking. In 6:3 the seraphim call out about the earth in relation to Yahweh as Yahweh intends it to be and as it surely will be. What the seraphim describe is the basis of the new creation envisaged in Isaiah's final chapters (60:1–3; 65:17–25). The earth will surely be "filled" as אדם was first charged to fill it in Genesis 1:28, with humanity in God's image and likeness ruling, serving, and keeping the earth and all its parts within God's good order.

The speaker in Isaiah 6, who sees Yahweh as he truly is in relation to the earth, responds, repents (6:5), hears (6:8), and is sent as an agent of the reality he has seen. How will the vision be achieved? How does the book of Isaiah move from *here* (lost sonship, wrong fullness), to *there*, seen in the vision: the fullness of the whole earth as Yahweh's glory?

ISAIAH'S SERVANT AND YAHWEH'S ORDER IN THE EARTH

THE FIRST SERVANT SONG

The enigmatic figure of the servant emerges in Isaiah 40–55 in a series of poems traditionally called the Servant Songs as the key for the restoration of Israel, humanity, and the earth.[65] The poetry explores and develops this one, whom Yahweh calls "my servant," as both the model and the means for the formation of Yahweh's likeness again in Israel, and through Israel in humanity.

Yahweh first presents his servant in Isaiah 42:1–4[66] in direct contrast to the false images (see the "idol polemics" in 40:19; 41:5–7),[67] in

---

63. See R. Alter, *The Art of Biblical Narrative*, rev. ed. (New York: Basic Books, 2011), 31–32, on the "inset of formal verse (a common convention in biblical narrative for direct speech that has some significantly summarizing or ceremonial function)."

64. Levenson, "Temple and the World," 289.

65. The Servant Songs are (arguably) 42:1–9; 49:1–13; 50:3–11; 52:13–53:12.

66. The first Servant Song may extend to 42:9. The phrase "my servant'" has been used to address Israel in 41:8 and 9, but in 42:1 the servant is marked by a uniquely constructed relation to Yahweh. See P. Wilcox and D. Paton-Williams, "The Servant Songs in Deutero-Isaiah," *JSOT* 42 (1988): 83–85.

67. See R. J. Clifford, "The Function of Idol Passages in Second Isaiah," *CBQ* 42, no. 4 (1980); K. Holter, *Second Isaiah's Idol-Fabrication Passages*, ed. J. Becker et al., Beiträge zur biblischen Exegese und Theologie (Frankfurt am Main: Peter Lang,

response to ongoing questions about Yahweh's likeness (40:18, 25–26),[68] and in answer to Yahweh's call (41:28). Isaiah's poetic rhetoric culminates in the servant as Yahweh's true image, who may be said to be "like Yahweh" by virtue of alignment with Yahweh through obedience. "Look, my Servant! ... He will bring out מִשְׁפָּט to the nations" (Isa 42:1, see also 42:3, 4).

Hans Schmid has argued that justice in the ancient Near East (Hebrew מִשְׁפָּט) was primarily concerned with the restoration of the right order established in creation.[69] I propose that in Isaiah 40–55 the servant's task of "bringing out מִשְׁפָּט" is the human parallel to God's ordering activity in Genesis 1 and elsewhere that is expressed through the divine verb ברא.[70] It is the human imaging response to Yahweh's creation activity of ordering and fulfills the human charge of rule in God's likeness in Genesis 1:26–28.[71] The first Servant Song's reiterated line ("he will bring out/establish מִשְׁפָּט to the nations/on the earth") encapsulates the servant's recovery of the human charge. The Servant's obedience in "bringing out מִשְׁפָּט" to the earth's nations is the mark of Yahweh's image and likeness, of one who truly represents Yahweh in the earth and who "rules" obediently within—and works to extend— Yahweh's good order. The human counterpart of the divine verb ברא may be seen in the actions of the servant, who "brings out [Yahweh's] מִשְׁפָּט to the nations."[72]

The first song sketches the servant figure in a series of seven things he does not do (42:2–4; the sevenfold repetition suggests that

---

1995); H. C. Spykerboer, *The Structure and Composition of Deutero-Isaiah, with Special Reference to the Polemics against Idolatry* (Meppel: Kripps Repro B.V., 1976).

68. See F. J. Gaiser, "'To Whom Then Will You Compare Me?': Agency in Second Isaiah," *Word & World* 19, no. 2 (1999): 141–52.

69. H. H. Schmid, "Creation, Righteousness and Salvation: 'Creation Theology' as the Broad Horizon of Biblical Theology," in *Creation in the Old Testament*, ed. B. W. Anderson (Philadelphia: Fortress, 1984), 102–17. See comments in Murphy, "Wisdom and Creation," 9n19.

70. See Isa 4:5; 40:26, 28; 41:20; 42:5; 43:1, 7, 15; 45:7, 8, 12, 18; 48:7; 54:16; 57:19; 65:17, 18.

71. See the broad definition of טשׁפ, "to govern or rule," Robert D. Culver in Waltke, Harris, and Archer, eds., *Theological Wordbook*, 2443.

72. See the contrast between Yahweh's מִשְׁפָּט and humanly contrived מִשְׁפָּט ("my מִשְׁפָּט") in Isa 40:27.

he completely "does not"[73]) in order to accomplish the single task that
Israel has until now failed to do: to bring out מִשְׁפָּט to the nations. The
Servant accomplishes this first by his characteristic stance of obedience that aligns him with Yahweh and that makes him "like" Yahweh
(captured in his title "servant"). In Genesis, God sovereignly ordered the
heavens and earth and commissioned humanity to maintain God's order
and to "be fruitful" within it.[74] In Isaiah, the servant is characterized
as the one who establishes מִשְׁפָּט (Yahweh's good order). Although the
servant in Isaiah 42 is not explicitly described as Yahweh's image, the
first song presents him in contrast with the false images,[75] and the servant figure may be understood as appearing in answer to the repeated
question of God's likeness from Isaiah 40. The poetry presents the servant as Yahweh's *true* image, and as the means through which Yahweh's
order will be reestablished in the earth.

Various other elements suggest that the first Servant Song is about a
re-creation of humanity. The poetry progresses from רוח and תהו (41:29;
42:1, evoking Gen 1:2)[76] through Yahweh's act of speaking (see Gen 1:3, 6,
9, 11, 14, etc.) and culminates in the construction of the servant figure.[77]
The servant's תוֹרָה is chiastically parallel with מִשְׁפָּט in 42:4, suggesting
that "his תוֹרָה" is an expression of מִשְׁפָּט. Only Isaiah 42:4 has "his תוֹרָה"
with a human referent in the Old Testament:[78] the servant identifies so
completely with his Lord's מִשְׁפָּט, that Yahweh's תוֹרָה becomes "his תוֹרָה."

---

73. Dickson, "Genesis of Everything," 7–8, summarizes the use of the number
seven (symbolizing "wholeness") and its multiples in Hebrew thought and Gen 1.

74. See Beale and Kim, *Expanding Eden*, 37–38.

75. See 41:29 immediately preceding, and the language of construction used
both for the false images and for the servant image.

76. See B. N. Peterson, "Cosmology," in *Dictionary of the Old Testament Prophets*,
ed. M. J. Boda et al. (Downers Grove, IL: InterVarsity, 2012), 92.

77. K. Baltzer, *Deutero-Isaiah*, trans. M. Kohl, Hermenia (Minneapolis: Fortress,
2001), 20, describes the resonance of 42:1–9 with Gen 1–2, and "catchwords" from
Gen 1 as "clearly evident: 'create, heaven, firmament, earth, bring forth.'"

78. In the Old Testament, תוֹרָה is almost always Yahweh's תוֹרָה. See 2 Chr 6:16;
Ps 78:1; Jer 16:11, "my תוֹרָה" in Yahweh's mouth; in Ps 78:1, Prov 3:1, 4:2, תורתי ("my
תוֹרָה") is in a wise human mouth. (These are similar to 42:4; father speaking to son,
like the servant, embodies Yahweh's authority.) Ezekiel 43:11; 44:5, "its תוֹרָה" is the
temple's תוֹרָה. See translation solutions in NAS, NRS, and explanations in J. D. W.
Watts, *Isaiah 34–66*, WBC (Waco, TX: Word, 1987), 119; M. A. Sweeney, "The Book of
Isaiah as Prophetic Torah," in *New Visions of Isaiah*, ed. R. F. Melugin et al., JSOTSup
214 (Sheffield: Sheffield Academic, 1996), 63.

THE FOURTH SERVANT SONG

The longest of the four servant poems, the fourth Servant Song, 52:13–53:12, has a cluster of features that suggest that what the servant is doing concerns re-creation in Yahweh's likeness, not only for individuals and for Israel but for humanity more generally. While Isaiah 40–55 explicitly references Abraham (41:8, 51:2), and the fourth song's associations with Moses and the exodus are often recognized,[79] I hope to show that it intentionally echoes the fundamental human story of the fall of אָדָם. The poetry of the fourth song suggests that the Servant's task of establishing מִשְׁפָּט is fundamentally about the reversal of the fall and the re-formation of humanity as Yahweh's true likeness.

The opening verb of the fourth Servant Song, שׂכל (יַשְׂכִּיל in the *hiphil* stem) is commonly translated "will act wisely"[80] or "will prosper."[81] This causative form is used consistently in the Old Testament for those who prosper because of their obedience to Yahweh, especially through keeping תּוֹרָה.[82] They become *like Yahweh* through obedience, which results in true prospering in Yahweh's world. The Israelites (Deut 29:8 [Eng. 29:9]), Joshua (Josh 1:7, 8), Solomon (1 Kgs 2:3; 1 Chr 22:12), Hezekiah (2 Kgs 18:7), and the kings and rulers of the earth (Ps 2:10) are all pictured as prospering or are exhorted to prosper by keeping Yahweh's תּוֹרָה. The causative form of שׂכל characterizes David's success in 1 Samuel 18 (18:5, 14, 15). David not only prospered but caused others to prosper, and Yahweh was recognized as being "with him." This verb is associated with human wisdom and alignment with Yahweh through obedience, and with Yahweh's presence, which results from it. שׂכל is also used negatively about Israel's ancestors' lack of wisdom (Ps 106:7) and for human lack of wisdom in general (Job 34:27).

---

79. See especially Baltzer, *Deutero-Isaiah*; also R. E. Watts, "Echoes from the Past: Israel's Ancient Traditions and the Destiny of the Nations in Isaiah 40–55," *JSOT* 28, no. 4 (2004).

80. NIV; see "deal prudently" (KJV).

81. NIV margin; also NASB, NJB, NLT. I שׂכל in Koehler, Stamm, and Baumgartner, eds., *Hebrew and Aramaic Lexicon*, 3:1329–30.

82. There are also other kinds of alignment with Yahweh, e.g., 1 Sam 18:5, 14, 15; Neh 9:20; Ps 41:2 (Eng. 41:1); Isa 41:20. See also lack of alignment, e.g., Pss 94:8, 106:7; Job 34:27, 35; Isa 44:18.

The Bible's first use of *hiphil* שׂכל is in the story of the fall in Genesis 3, where it describes one of the attributes of the tree of the knowledge of good and evil:[83] "desirable to make one prosper" (3:6). There is a sense in which every subsequent occasion where *hiphil* שׂכל is associated with obedience or disobedience to Yahweh (codified in Yahweh's תּוֹרָה and the Decalogue) may be thought of as canonically in conversation with that first scriptural use.[84] True prospering as God intended it comes from a particular relation to God where human actions are aligned with God's actions and God is thus made present in human action. The first humans chose a forbidden means of gaining a false prosperity outside Yahweh's good order and were sent from Yahweh's presence (Gen 3:23); whenever humanity keeps תּוֹרָה, chooses obedience to Yahweh, or pursues Yahweh's wisdom, they act against the fundamental human choice to disregard Yahweh's order, and they increasingly fit themselves for Yahweh's renewed presence. As C. S. Lewis observed, "in obeying, a rational creature consciously enacts its creaturely role, reverses the act by which we fell, treads Adam's dance backwards."[85]

The causative meaning of שׂכל in the *hiphil* stem—"to bring about prospering"—is borne out in Genesis by the activation of an alternative means of prospering than that enjoyed under Yahweh's lordship, causing the fall of אָדָם and the exclusion from the sacred space of the garden. In Isaiah the causative meaning is demonstrated by the servant, who justifies many and bears their sin (53:11–12), causing the "re-Edening" of the earth, which follows Israel's active obedience in Isaiah 55:12-13. The three verbs used of the servant in the fourth song's opening verse (רום, נשׂא, גבה; "made high ... lifted up ... exalted," 52:13) have been jealously associated with Yahweh throughout the book of Isaiah (see 2:9–18), and their remarkable use for the servant at the declarative outset of the fourth song demonstrates Yahweh's recognition of the servant's full alignment with himself. The servant is *like Yahweh* by his actions and so is Yahweh's true image.

---

83. From here, "the tree of knowledge."

84. E.g., Prov 1:3 states the goal of the book of Proverbs, "to lay hold of the discipline of prospering [הַשְׂכֵּל]: righteousness and מִשְׁפָּט and uprightness."

85. C. S. Lewis, *The Problem of Pain* (London: Fontana, 1940), 56.

However, the language used to describe the servant in Isaiah 53 characterizes him as a kind of antihero, the opposite of the celebrated King David, negating every convention about one whom Yahweh prospers. How then is he aligned with Yahweh, and how does he cause prospering? The servant has no beauty or majesty; there is nothing desirable in his appearance; he is despised, rejected by people, suffering, familiar with pain, excruciating to look on (53:2–3). This contrasts absolutely with the tree of the knowledge of good and evil in Genesis 3:6, which was "good for food, a delight to the eyes, and desirable to make one prosper."[86] The tree has every appearance of beauty but is deceptive: the servant has no appearance but is truly aligned with Yahweh.

The correspondence of the subjects of the verb שכל in Genesis 3 and Isaiah 52:13—that is, the correspondence between the tree, which appears to offer prosperity in Genesis 3:6, and the servant, who actually causes prosperity in Isaiah 52:13—might be overlooked were it not that both tree and servant are also described using the verb חמד ("to desire," *niphal* participle in Gen 3:6; *qal* imperfect in Isa 53:2). The tree was wholly desirable; the servant was wholly undesirable. The tree language used to describe the servant in 53:2a affirms and extends the parallel between tree and servant: the servant is a "sapling" (יונק) that "goes up" (עלה, a verb particularly connected with plant growth[87]) before Yahweh. He is a new kind of plant, springing up "before [Yahweh]," reconfiguring what it means to prosper truly as part of Yahweh's good order.[88]

Thus the Isaian poet has drawn the servant of Isaiah 53 into parallel with the tree of knowledge in Genesis 3. The fourth song sets the servant's obedient life in contrasting parallel with the archetypal human act of disobedience in Genesis 3. It sets the life of conscious likeness to Yahweh in contrast with the first conscious act of unlikeness to Yahweh. The servant attains and makes available for "the many" (53:11–12)

86. These three characteristics meet and satisfy human needs and desires: physical sustenance, sensory delight, and intellectual/spiritual value (depending on translation of השביל).

87. J. Goldingay and D. Payne, *Isaiah 40–55*, vol. 2, *Commentary on Isaiah 44:24–55:13*, International Critical Commentary (London: T&T Clark, 2006), 298–99. See its use in 55:13.

88. See the "branch" in Isa 11:1.

prospering that was wrongfully sought in Eden. True prospering under Yahweh's lordship is offered in contrast to a form of prospering that set (and sets) aside Yahweh's lordship. The song shows that the alignment of the servant with Yahweh by obedience is what it really means to be *like Yahweh*. The servant enacts and enables prospering (ישכיל, 52:13) within God's good order as intended in Genesis 1 and as seen by seraphim, seer (and audience spectators), in Isaiah 6. The fourth song deconstructs and reorders human notions of prospering that stem from the tree of knowledge.

As noted above, in Israel's wisdom traditions, "[Wisdom] is a *tree of life* for those who hold fast to her" (Prov 3:18).[89] The servant life is lived by obedience, and those who hold it fast find the path of wisdom that will restore them in Yahweh's likeness, and that restores Yahweh to them as Lord, reordering them within Yahweh's good order and enabling them to be fruitful within it. The servant offers this realignment, re-formation, and reactivation as Yahweh's image first to Israel, whose outward "image" is unrecognizable, desecrated by the loss in the exile of all they have held to be good.[90] That it is offered beyond Israel (indeed, a restored Israel will participate in its offering) is suggested in Isaiah 52:15[91] and in subsequent chapters (see for example eunuchs and foreigners in 56:3–8; see also the vision of "days to come" in 2:2–4).

CONCLUSION

It has emerged from this reading of Isaiah and Genesis that obedience to Yahweh—the way back to being the image and likeness of God for those who have eaten from the tree of knowledge—is a form of wise knowing that redresses not only Israel's unknowing (Isa 1:3) but the foundational human acquiring of the knowledge of good and evil from a source other than God. The truly prospering life may be regained through wisdom by the alignment of human action with God through obedience. This restores the fundamental relational principles of God's

---

89. J. Richard Middleton, "What I Learned at the Evolution Conference," *Creation to Eschaton: Explorations in Biblical Theology from J. Richard Middleton* (blog), April 5, 2015, https://jrichardmiddleton.wordpress.com/2015/04/05/what-i-learned -at-the-evolution-conference/. See עץ החיים, Gen 2:9; 3:24. See also Prov 11:30.

90. See Isa 5:20.

91. "Many nations ... kings ... will see."

good order and enables the earth's restoration within that order.[92] In Genesis 3 אָדָם sought to go beyond the bounds of an obedient life by the exercise of reason in conflict with God's commands. Isaiah's reflections on the figure of the servant show that the exercise of reason for the purpose of obedience and alignment with God *is wisdom*. Wisdom is not order;[93] wisdom is what serves and keeps the sacred space of the relation to God in which all things are designed to function, which God's good order makes possible, and in which, as the seraphim saw, all things have their place (Isa 6:3; see 66:22–24).[94] Reason and revelation are essentially related: human reason is intended to be informed by the wisdom of life rightly ordered in relation to Yahweh and to be used for the purpose of furthering Yahweh's ordering work in the world. In Isaiah the servant's life sets reason in the context of relationship to Yahweh and of obedience to Yahweh. Innocent wisdom may not be regained, but conscious wisdom may be gained: "with his knowledge he will make righteous—a righteous one, my servant—the many" (53:11b).

The re-forming of the servant and of servant Israel as Yahweh's true likeness is the beginning of a reordering of humanity in relation to Yahweh that is to be extended into all the earth and that is to liberate humanity to become all that God intended (including all that humanity is gifted and intended to contribute to this becoming). This ordering is a relational sacred space that is parallel with the physical sacred space of the sanctuaries, and that likewise is to be broadened to include those who have been outsiders (see Isa 54:2–3;[95] 56:3–8). Israel (and beyond Israel, humanity in Yahweh's likeness) is also the physically enacted image restored to its place in the temple of the world, where all space will surely be sacred space (Isa 6:3).

The fractured relationships with Yahweh, one another, and the earth described in Genesis 3 are restored in the chapters immediately following the fourth song. The barren woman becomes mother of many (Isa 54 [see Gen 3:16]), Yahweh's servants receive their true heritage (54:17 [see

---

92. See Prov 4:7 (with a possible echo of Gen 1:1): "Beginning: wisdom. Get wisdom!"

93. Von Rad, *Wisdom in Israel*, 157, calls it "world reason." See objections to the identification of wisdom with order in Murphy, "Wisdom and Creation," 8–10.

94. See also Ps 119:89–91.

95. Beale and Kim, *Expanding Eden*, 68–70.

Gen 3:23]), and the earth itself is restored (55:12–13 [see Gen 3:17–19]). The servant as Yahweh's re-formed image who brings out Yahweh's good order is shown to be the key to the renewal of Israel and humanity in Yahweh's image, the Edening of the earth, and the final obedience of the nations in the book of Isaiah. The wise servant is the hinge on which the book of Isaiah moves and by which Isaiah's vision—what the seraphim see, Yahweh's divine revelation—is accomplished.

WORKS CITED

Alter, Robert. *The Art of Biblical Narrative*. Rev. ed. New York: Basic Books, 2011.

Avrahami, Yael. *The Senses of Scripture: Sensory Perception in the Hebrew Bible*. Library of Hebrew Bible/Old Testament Studies. New York: Bloomsbury, 2012.

Baltzer, Klaus. *Deutero-Isaiah*. Translated by Margaret Kohl. Hermenia. Minneapolis: Fortress, 2001.

Barr, James. "Was Everything That God Created Really Good? A Question in the First Verse of the Bible." In *God in the Fray: A Tribute to Walter Brueggemann*, edited by Tod Linafelt and Timothy K. Beal, 55–65. Minneapolis: Augsburg Fortress, 1998.

Batchelder, Caroline. "Undoing 'This People,' Becoming 'My Servant': Purpose and Commission in Isaiah 6." *Southeastern Theological Review* 4, no. 2 (2013): 155–78.

Beale, G. K. *The Temple and the Church's Mission: A Biblical Theology of the Dwelling Place of God*. New Studies in Biblical Theology. Downers Grove, IL: InterVarsity, 2004.

Beale, G. K., and Mitchell Kim. *God Dwells among Us: Expanding Eden to the Ends of the Earth*. Downers Grove, IL: InterVarsity, 2014.

"The Bereshith or Genesis Rabba." In *The Sacred Books and Early Literature of the East*. New York: Parke, Austin and Lipscomb, 1917. www.sacred-texts.com/jud/mhl/mhl05.htm.

Bergman, Ben Zion. "The Living Tree: The Roots and Growth of Jewish Law (review)." *Journal of Law and Religion* 7 (1989): 235–38.

Berlin, Adele. *The Dynamics of Biblical Parallelism*. Biblical Resources Series. Rev. ed. Grand Rapids: Eerdmans, 2008.

Blenkinsopp, Joseph. *Creation, Un-creation, Re-creation: A Discursive Commentary on Genesis 1–11*. London: T&T Clark, 2011.

Blocher, Henri. *In the Beginning: The Opening Chapters of Genesis*. Translated by David G. Preston. Leicester, UK: Inter-Varsity, 1984.

Brueggemann, Walter. "Bounded by Obedience and Praise: The Psalms as Canon." *JSOT* 50 (1991): 63–92.

———. *Theology of the Old Testament: Testimony, Dispute, Advocacy*. Minneapolis: Fortress, 1997.

Clifford, Richard J. "The Function of Idol Passages in Second Isaiah." *CBQ* 42, no. 4 (1980): 450–64.

Clines, David J. A. *The Theme of the Pentateuch*. JSOTSup 10. 2nd ed. Sheffield: Sheffield Academic, 1997.

———. "The Tree of Knowledge and the Law of Yahweh (Psalm XIX)." *Vetus Testamentum* 24, no. 1 (1974): 8–14.

Dickson, John. "The Genesis of Everything: A Historical Account of the Bible's Opening Chapter." *ISCAST* 4 (2008): 1–18.

Dorff, Elliot N., and Arthur Rosett, eds. *A Living Tree: The Roots and Growth of Jewish Law*. Albany: State University of New York Press, 1988.

Dumbrell, William J. *The Search for Order: Biblical Eschatology in Focus*. Grand Rapids: Baker, 1994.

Fishbane, Michael A. "Inner-Biblical Exegesis." In *Hebrew Bible, Old Testament: The History of Its Interpretation*, edited by M. Sæbø, 33–48. Göttingen: Vandenhoeck & Ruprecht, 1996.

Fretheim, Terence E. *God and World in the Old Testament: A Relational Theology of Creation*. Nashville: Abingdon, 2005.

———. *The Pentateuch*. Interpreting Biblical Texts. Nashville: Abingdon, 1996.

Gaiser, Frederick J. "'To Whom Then Will You Compare Me?': Agency in Second Isaiah." *Word & World* 19, no. 2 (1999): 141–52.

Goldingay, John. "The Patriarchs in Scripture and History." In *Essays on the Patriarchal Narratives*, edited by A. R. Millard and D. J. Wiseman, 1–34. Leicester, UK: Inter-Varsity, 1980.

———. "'You Are Abraham's Offspring, My Friend': Abraham in Isaiah 41." In *He Swore an Oath: Biblical Themes from Genesis 12–50*, edited by R. S. Hess, P. L. Satterthwaite, and G. J. Wenham, 29–54. Carlisle, UK: Paternoster, 1994.

Goldingay, John, and David Payne. *Isaiah 40–55*. Vol. 2, *Commentary on Isaiah 44:24–55:13*. International Critical Commentary. London: T&T Clark, 2006.

Grenz, Stanley J. *Theology for the Community of God*. Grand Rapids: Eerdmans, 2000.

Hays, Richard B. *Echoes of Scripture in the Letters of Paul*. New Haven, CT: Yale University Press, 1989.

Holter, Knut. *Second Isaiah's Idol-Fabrication Passages*. Beiträge zur biblischen Exegese und Theologie. Frankfurt am Main: Peter Lang, 1995.

Koehler, Ludwig, Johann Stamm, and Walter Baumgartner, eds. *Hebrew and Aramaic Lexicon of the Old Testament*. 5 vols. Leiden: Brill, 1994–2000.

Kreuzer, Siegfried. "'Behold It Was Very Good': God's Praise of the Creation (Gen 1:4, 10, 12, 18, 21, 25, 31) and Its Background." In *"My Spirit at Rest in the North Country" (Zechariah 6.8): Collected Communications to the XXth Congress of the International Organization for the Study of the Old Testament, Helsinki 2010*, edited by H. M. Niemann and M. Augustin, 23–31. Frankfurt: Peter Lang, 2011.

Leonard, Jeffery M. "Identifying Inner-Biblical Allusions: Psalm 78 as a Test Case." *JBL* 127, no. 2 (2008): 241–65.

Levenson, Jon D. *Creation and the Persistence of Evil: The Jewish Drama of Divine Omnipotence.* Princeton, NJ: Princeton University Press, 1988.

———. *Sinai and Zion: An Entry into the Jewish Bible.* Edited by Adela Yarbro Collins and John J. Collins. New Voices in Biblical Studies. Minneapolis: Winston, 1985.

———. "The Temple and the World." *Journal of Religion* 64, no. 3 (1984): 275–98.

Levine, Jason. "Judaism: The Written Law: Torah." In *Jewish Virtual Library.* American-Israeli Cooperative Enterprise, 2016.

Lewis, C. S. *The Problem of Pain.* London: Fontana, 1940.

McCann, J. Clinton, Jr. "The Book of Psalms: Introduction, Commentary and Reflections." In *New Interpreter's Biblical Commentary*, vol. III, edited by Leander E. Keck, 273–303. Nashville: Abingdon, 2015.

Middleton, J. Richard. *The Liberating Image: The Imago Dei in Genesis 1.* Grand Rapids: Brazos, 2005.

———. "What I Learned at the Evolution Conference." *Creation to Eschaton: Explorations in Biblical Theology from J. Richard Middleton* (blog). April 5, 2015. https://jrichardmiddleton.wordpress.com/2015/04/05/what-i-learned-at-the-evolution-conference/.

Miscall, Peter D. "Isaiah: New Heavens, New Earth, New Book." In *Reading between Texts: Intertextuality and the Hebrew Bible*, edited by Danna Nolan Fewell, 41–56. Literary Currents in Biblical Interpretation. Louisville: Westminster John Knox, 1992.

Murphy, Roland E. *The Tree of Life: An Exploration of Biblical Wisdom Literature.* Grand Rapids: Eerdmans, 1996.

———. "Wisdom and Creation." *JBL* 104, no. 1 (1985): 3–11.

Parry, Robin. *The Biblical Cosmos: A Pilgrim's Guide to the Weird and Wonderful World of the Bible.* Eugene, OR: Cascade, 2014.

Peterson, B. N. "Cosmology." In *Dictionary of the Old Testament: Prophets*, edited by Mark J. Boda and J. Gordon McConville, 90–98. Downers Grove, IL: InterVarsity, 2012.

Rad, Gerhard von. *Wisdom in Israel.* London: SCM, 1972.

Schmid, H. H. "Creation, Righteousness and Salvation: 'Creation Theology' as the Broad Horizon of Biblical Theology." Translated by B. W. Anderson and B. D. Johnson. In *Creation in the Old Testament*, edited by B. W. Anderson, 102–17. Philadelphia: Fortress, 1984.

Schultz, Richard L. "Unity or Diversity in Wisdom Theology? A Canonical and Covenantal Perspective." *Tyndale Bulletin* 48, no. 2 (1997): 271–306.

Spykerboer, Hendrik C. *The Structure and Composition of Deutero-Isaiah, with Special Reference to the Polemics against Idolatry.* Meppel: Kripps Repro B.V., 1976.

Sweeney, Marvin A. "The Book of Isaiah as Prophetic Torah." In *New Visions of Isaiah*, edited by Roy F. Melugin and Marvin A. Sweeney, 50–67. JSOTSup 214. Sheffield: Sheffield Academic, 1996.

Treier, Daniel J. *Proverbs & Ecclesiastes*. Brazos Theological Commentary on the Bible. Grand Rapids: Brazos, 2011.

Tsumura, David T. *Creation and Destruction: A Reappraisal of the Chaoskampf Theory in the Old Testament*. Winona Lake, IN: Eisenbrauns, 2005.

Van Leeuwen, Raymond C. "The Book of Proverbs: Introduction, Commentary and Reflections." In *The New Interpreter's Bible Commentary*, vol. III, edited by Leander E. Keck, 751–945. Nashville: Abingdon, 2015.

Van Wolde, Ellen. *Reframing Biblical Studies: When Language and Text Meet Culture, Cognition, and Context*. Winona Lake, IN: Eisenbrauns, 2009.

———. "Why the Verb ברא Does Not Mean 'to Create' in Genesis 1.1–2.4a." *JSOT* 34, no. 1 (2009): 3–23.

Waltke, Bruce K., R. Laird Harris, and Gleason L. Archer, eds. *Theological Wordbook of the Old Testament*. 2 vols. Chicago: Moody, 1980.

Walton, John H. "Creation in Genesis 1:1–2:3 and the ANE: Order Out of Disorder after Chaoskampf." *CTJ* 43, no. 1 (2008): 48–63.

———. *The Lost World of Adam and Eve: Genesis 2–3 and the Human Origins Debate*. Downers Grove, IL: IVP Academic, 2015.

———. *The Lost World of Genesis One: Ancient Cosmology and the Origins Debate*. Downers Grove, IL: IVP Academic, 2009.

Watts, J. D. W. *Isaiah 34–66*. WBC. Waco, TX: Word, 1987.

Watts, Rikk E. "Echoes from the Past: Israel's Ancient Traditions and the Destiny of the Nations in Isaiah 40–55." *JSOT* 28, no. 4 (2004): 481–508.

Wenham, Gordon J. *Genesis 1–15*. WBC. Waco, TX: Word, 1987.

———. *The Pentateuch*. Exploring the Old Testament. London: SPCK, 2003.

———. "Sanctuary Symbolism in the Garden of Eden Story." In *I Studied Inscriptions before the Flood*, edited by Richard Hess and David Toshio Tsumura, 399–404. Sources for Biblical and Theological Study. Winona Lake, IN: Eisenbrauns, 1994.

Westermann, Claus. *Genesis 1–11: A Commentary*. Translated by J. J. Scullion. Augsburg: Fortress, 1984.

Wilcox, Peter, and David Paton-Williams. "The Servant Songs in Deutero-Isaiah." *JSOT* 42 (1988): 79–102.

Willey, Patricia Tull. *Remember the Former Things: The Recollection of Previous Texts in Second Isaiah*. Society of Biblical Literature Dissertation Series. Atlanta: Scholars Press, 1997.

6

"As to Sensible People"

Human Reason and Divine Revelation in 1 Corinthians 8–10

David I. Starling

REVELATION, REASON, AND THE "APOCALYPTIC PAUL"

The relationship between human reason and divine revelation has been a perennial topic of discussion among philosophers and systematic theologians. In recent decades, however, due in no small part to the influence of a growing number of interpreters who have placed heavy emphasis on the apocalyptic dimensions of Paul's theology,[1] it has also come to be something of a storm center in the field of New Testament studies.

The philosophical/theological discussion and the exegetical discussion are, of course, closely interrelated. For those of us who claim that Scripture should function authoritatively or paradigmatically within the work of theological construction, a conversation about how Paul viewed the relationship between revelation and reason carries implications for the way in which we should view that relationship. The currents of influence run in the other direction, too: the most prominent figures on both sides of the "apocalyptic Paul" debate are all deeply and explicitly aware of the role that theological and philosophical precommitments play in our interpretation of the biblical texts.[2]

---

1. See the surveys in Ben C. Blackwell, John K. Goodrich, and Jason Maston, eds., *Paul and the Apocalyptic Imagination* (Minneapolis: Fortress, 2016), 3–21; R. Barry Matlock, *Unveiling the Apocalyptic Paul: Paul's Interpreters and the Rhetoric of Criticism*, JSNTSup (Sheffield: Sheffield Academic, 1996).

2. See Douglas A. Campbell, *The Deliverance of God: An Apocalyptic Rereading of Justification in Paul* (Grand Rapids: Eerdmans, 2009), 36–61; Campbell, "Apocalyptic

The last few decades' discussion of apocalyptic themes in Paul's letters has embraced a variety of intersecting concerns (including the apocalyptic dimensions of Paul's eschatology, cosmology, soteriology, politics, and epistemology) and has been plagued by a notorious lack of clarity in the use of key terms, including the word "apocalyptic" itself.[3] According to some, it should be understood principally or exclusively as a literary term, designating a particular genre of early Jewish revelatory literature;[4] others, however, make use of the term to refer to a theological viewpoint characteristically (but not exclusively) expressed in literature of that genre.[5] What constitutes an "apocalyptic" viewpoint, in this latter, theological, sense of the word, is variously understood. In this paper I will focus on the claims of those who place the accent on the epistemological implications of an apocalyptic worldview, using the word as a term for theologies that characterize God's salvific action in the world as a liberating invasion of the cosmos and emphasize the unforeseeability of that event and the impossibility of understanding and explaining it in the light of either natural reasoning or prior revelation.[6]

Epistemology: The Sine Qua Non of Valid Pauline Interpretation," in *Paul and the Apocalyptic Imagination*, ed. Blackwell, Goodrich, and Maston, 67–74; Alan Torrance, "Article Review: Douglas Campbell, *The Deliverance of God*," *SJT* 65 (2012): 82–89; N. T. Wright, *Paul and His Recent Interpreters: Some Contemporary Debates* (Minneapolis: Fortress, 2015), 216.

3. See the helpful survey of the scholarly terrain in David A. Shaw, "'Then I Proceeded to Where Things Were Chaotic' (1 Enoch 21:1): Mapping the Apocalyptic Landscape," in *Paul and the Apocalyptic Imagination*, ed. Blackwell, Goodrich, and Maston, 23–41.

4. The classic definition is that of John J. Collins, who defines apocalyptic as "a genre of revelatory literature with a narrative framework, in which a revelation is mediated by an otherworldly being to a human recipient ... envisag[ing] eschatological salvation and involv[ing] a supernatural world ... intended to interpret present earthly circumstances in light of the supernatural world and of the future, and to influence both the understanding and the behavior of the audience by means of divine authority." Collins, "Early Jewish Apocalypticism," in *Anchor Bible Dictionary*, ed. David Noel Freedman (New York: Doubleday, 1992), 282.

5. See the argument in favor of a theological definition in Richard E. Sturm, "Defining the Word 'Apocalyptic,'" in *Apocalyptic and the New Testament: Essays in Honor of J. L. Martyn*, ed. Joel Marcus and Marion Soards (Sheffield: JSOT Press, 1989), 17–48.

6. See especially J. Louis Martyn, "Apocalyptic Antinomies in Paul's Letter to the Galatians," *NTS* 31, no. 3 (1985): 410–24; Martyn, *Galatians: A New Translation with*

Those who understand Paul as an "apocalyptic" thinker in this sense of the word frequently go on to make a further, related assertion, that all of the important truth claims and exhortations contained within his letters are presented by Paul to his readers not as reasoned arguments but as proclamations and reproclamations of the singular, eschatological mystery made known by God in the gospel.

In his influential commentary on Galatians, for example, J. Louis Martyn insists that Paul's gospel "has the effect of placing at issue the nature of argument itself." Because it is a message that is, at its heart, a matter of divine revelation—"God's own utterance"—"it is not and can never be subject to ratiocinative criteria that have been developed apart from it."[7] The relevance of Martyn's claim to Paul's initial proclamation of the gospel is obvious: as Martyn puts it, "what human beings already have in their minds [e.g., their preexisting 'notions of justice, of guilt and innocence, of unrighteousness and righteousness'] cannot serve as the point of departure from which one can book a through train to the gospel."[8] But Martyn's assertion goes further than that: he considers and explicitly rejects the possibility that Paul might have "distinguishe[d] an initial and nonrhetorical proclamation of the gospel from a later and rhetorically sophisticated formulation of a written argument addressed to persons who are already Christians."[9] Even when Paul is writing to Christians, Martyn insists, his rhetoric is "more revelatory and performative than hortatory and persuasive." Paul's letter to the Galatians should thus be read, according to Martyn, not as "an argument designed to persuade the Galatians that faith is better than observance of the Law" but as "an announcement designed to wake the Galatians up to the real cosmos, made what it is by the fact that faith has now *arrived* with the advent of Christ."[10]

Introduction and Commentary, Anchor Bible (New York: Doubleday, 1997); Martyn, "Epistemology at the Turn of the Ages," in *Theological Issues in the Letters of Paul* (Nashville: Abingdon, 1997), 89–110; Campbell, *Deliverance of God*, 36–61; Campbell, "Apocalyptic Epistemology," 74–80; Campbell, "An Evangelical Paul: A Response to Francis Watson's *Paul and the Hermenutics of Faith*," *JSNT* 28 (2006): 346–50.

7. Martyn, *Galatians*, 22.
8. Martyn, *Galatians*, 146.
9. Martyn, *Galatians*, 147.
10. Martyn, *Galatians*, 23.

Martyn's writings on Galatians (along with, in more recent years, Douglas Campbell's on Romans) are certainly the most widely known and influential articulations of this interpretive approach.[11] But any adequate account of Paul's epistemology must include not only those letters but also, crucially, his letters to the Corinthian church, in which the themes of knowledge and revelation occupy such a prominent place. Among the various works that have argued for the presence of an "apocalyptic epistemology" in the Corinthian letters, Alexandra Brown makes the case most explicitly and vigorously, in her study of the epistemology and rhetoric of 1 Corinthians, *The Cross and Human Transformation*.[12]

In chapter 4 of that book, Paul's rewording of the quotation from the prophet Jeremiah in 1 Corinthians 1:31 becomes the occasion for a series of sweeping statements that Brown makes about the differences between the prophetic epistemology of Jeremiah and the apocalyptic epistemology of Paul:

> In Jeremiah, the knowledge of God is available to those who do not "refuse to know" (Jer 9:6), that is, to those who "hear the words of the covenant" and do them (Jer 11:6–8). Knowledge in Jeremiah has primarily to do with recognition and observance of the sacred tradition that defines true knowledge and wisdom. The definition is not itself foreign to the consciousness of Israel, however far astray the people may have gone. Jeremiah can appeal to sacred memory (Jer 9:7). He calls Israel back to the covenant they once knew and observed, albeit a covenant in need of mending (Jer 9:10).
>
> Paul, on the other hand, makes no appeal to the Deuteronomic past, nor even, as in the wisdom tradition, to the myth of the creation of the world (cf. Jer 9:12). For Paul, God's faithfulness (1:9) stands now on wholly new premises. While it is still Yahweh alone who rules, Yahweh is now "pleased" to save believers through means

---

11. E.g., especially Martyn, *Galatians*, 22–23, 146–47; Campbell, *Deliverance of God*, 36–61.

12. Alexandra R. Brown, *The Cross and Human Transformation: Paul's Apocalyptic Word in 1 Corinthians* (Minneapolis: Fortress, 1995). Brown's work builds on the earlier discussion in J. Louis Martyn, "Epistemology at the Turn of the Ages: 2 Corinthians 5:16," in *Christian History and Interpretation: Studies Presented to John Knox*, ed. W. R. Farmer (Cambridge: Cambridge University Press, 1967), 269–87.

other than salvation history, or the acquisition of wisdom or reason. As Paul sees it, God "in God's wisdom" has chosen to save through the *apokalypsis* of something entirely apart from history, tradition, and reason. That something new, moreover, is expressed in language that points unmistakably toward the dissolution of the world defined by sacred, social, or intellectual traditions, and toward the creation of a new world.[13]

The discontinuities between the old world and the new, according to Brown's reading of Paul, are comprehensive and radical: after the deconstructive work of the gospel is complete, all that is left of the old world is "rubble" to be cleared aside in order to create space for a new structure, which makes use of the occasional word salvaged from the linguistic rubble of the old order but gives to such words a fundamentally new meaning:

> In act 1, the Word of the Cross works to expose and "de-center" the perceptions of the hearer. This de-centering is the first step in its powerful and transformative play against what Paul calls the "wisdom of the world." At the next level of the discourse, the burden of Paul's rhetoric is to clear a path through the rubble of his hearers' now-deconstructed language, building a new framework for perception. Act 2 of the drama brings the completion of the new structure—in our text, Paul's refiguring of the terms wisdom and folly, power and emptiness, psyche and spirit—and invokes the power of the Spirit, already at work throughout act 1, to bring the hearer into the transformed mind.[14]

REVELATION AND REASON IN 1 CORINTHIANS 8-10

What are we to make of such claims? I have written elsewhere about the structure of Paul's argumentation in Galatians and the relationship between the prospective and retrospective dimensions of his hermeneutics in that letter.[15] In this essay I will concentrate on 1 Corinthians,

---

13. Brown, *Cross and Human Transformation*, 92–93.
14. Brown, *Cross and Human Transformation*, 29.
15. See especially David I. Starling, *Not My People: Gentiles as Exiles in Pauline Hermeneutics*, Beihefte zur Zeitschrift für die neutestamentliche Wissenschaft (Berlin: de Gruyter, 2011), 23–27, 40–60; Starling, "The Children of the Barren

and, more narrowly still, on the deliberative rhetoric and practical reasoning of 1 Corinthians 8–10. Here, to borrow from Alexandra Brown's categories, we find ourselves midway through act 3 of the drama of the letter; having proclaimed in act 1 the way in which God has "made foolish" the wisdom of the world (1:20) and introduced the audience in act 2 to a new and contrasting wisdom—once hidden in a mystery but now made known by the Spirit (2:6–16), Paul now applies that wisdom in a series of scenes to a succession of various issues raised by the reports Paul has received and the letter the Corinthians have sent to him, showing them in each case what it means to imagine and think and act with the mind of Christ. At this point in the letter we are therefore ideally placed to test the validity of Brown's proposal and investigate whether and to what extent the new mind thinks in the way that she proposes.

The opening verses of chapter 8 offer a neat example in support of Brown's assertions about the prominence of epistemological concerns within the letter. "We know," Paul tells the Corinthians (quoting one of their own slogans), "that 'all of us possess knowledge'" (8:1),[16] framing the particular issue of food sacrificed to idols within the larger question of what we know about what we know.

Further support for Brown's reading of the letter can be found in the way that the Corinthian slogan quoted in 8:1 meets immediately with a terse rejoinder from Paul that "knowledge puffs up, but love builds up." The language that Paul uses to prick the bubble of the Corinthian elite's pretensions is already familiar to us as readers of the letter: it falls on

Woman: Galatians 4:27 and the Hermeneutics of Justification," *Journal for the Study of Paul and His Letters* 3 (2013): 93–110; Starling, "Justifying Allegory: Scripture, Rhetoric and Reason in Gal. 4:21–5:1," *JTI* 9 (2015): 69–87.

16. The NRSV, like the majority of English versions, encloses the words at the end of v. 1a in quotation marks, representing them as a Corinthian slogan or a quotation from their letter; the same approach is generally taken to the brief maxims in v. 4 ("no idol in the world really exists" and "there is no God but one"). For arguments in support of this approach, see the comments in Roy E. Ciampa and Brian S. Rosner, *The First Letter to the Corinthians*, Pillar New Testament Commentary (Grand Rapids: Eerdmans, 2010), 373–75, 379–80; Gordon D. Fee, *The First Epistle to the Corinthians*, 2nd ed., New International Commentary on the New Testament (Grand Rapids: Eerdmans, 2014), 403–4, 409–10; Eckhard J. Schnabel, *Der Erste Brief Des Paulus an die Korinther*, Historisch-Theologische Auslegung (Wuppertal: Brockhaus, 2006), 439–40, 443–45; Wolfgang Schrage, *Der Erste Brief an die Korinther*, Evangelisch-katholischer Kommentar zum Neuen Testament (Zürich: Benziger, 1991–2001), 2:221.

the ear as an obvious echo of his earlier critique of the divisive, "puffed up" arrogance that is singled out in the concluding paragraphs of chapters 1-4 as the root problem that the preceding discourse on wisdom and leadership was designed to remedy (4:6, 18-19). Clearly the searing attack that Paul levels against "the wisdom of the world" in chapters 1-4 is not simply left behind when he turns in the succeeding chapters to the various other issues that have been brought to his attention by the reports he has received and the questions in the Corinthians' letter.[17]

As Paul's response to the issue of food sacrificed to idols unfolds across chapters 8-10, it also becomes clear (in line with Brown's reading of chaps. 1-2) that the vantage point from which he encourages the Corinthians to perceive the world is the eschatological situation of the community "on whom the ends of the ages have come" (10:11), and the mind with which he urges them to think is one that has been transformed decisively by the word of the cross. Thus, as members of a community who participate together in the body and blood of Christ (10:16), they are to regard their fellow believers as brothers and sisters "for whom Christ died" (8:11), and pattern their own actions on the servant logic modeled by Paul, in imitation of Christ (9:19; 10:31-11:1; see 4:16-17; 2 Cor 5:14-15; Rom 15:1-3; Phil 2:1-11). Scripture is to be read and appropriated through a hermeneutic that understands it as having been written "for our sake" (9:10; see 10:6, 11) and permits the kind of retrospective typological correspondences that Paul draws in 10:1-4.[18]

So far, so good for claims such as Brown's about the "apocalyptic epistemology" that Paul brings to bear on the Corinthians' thinking within this letter. But a closer reading of the content and shape of his argumentation in chapters 8-10 reveals a number of important ways in which the rhetoric of Brown's proposal overreaches and misleads.

An obvious place at which to start is with the content of the "knowledge" that the Corinthian elite appear to have been boasting in. It is certainly possible, as some commentators grant, that the introductory

---

17. See the repeated references back to the image of the "puffed up" Corinthians in 5:2 and 13:4.

18. See especially the discussion of these verses in Richard B. Hays, *The Conversion of the Imagination: Paul as Interpreter of Israel's Scripture* (Grand Rapids: Eerdmans, 2005), 8-12.

οἴδαμεν ὅτι ("We know that …") in 8:1, 4 could have been part of the Corinthian slogan or the quotation from their letter, rather than a Pauline introductory formula, but whichever way the boundaries of the quotation are delimited, the structure of Paul's argumentation across the paragraph as a whole suggests that the meaning is much the same.[19]

Regardless of whether Paul explicitly owns the content of the slogans by introducing them as something that "we know," he still goes on to make it abundantly clear in the following verses (8:5-6) that the creational monotheism expressed in the slogans of 8:4 can still (and must still) be wholeheartedly affirmed by those who have come to confess Jesus as Lord. The meaning of the claim that there is "one God … from whom are all things and for whom we exist" (with its unmistakable echoes of the Shema, and its possible additional allusions to the language of Hellenistic Judaism and Stoic natural theology)[20] must now be refracted through the prism of faith in "one Lord, Jesus Christ, through whom are all things and through whom we exist,"[21] but the function of the confession as (among other things) a repudiation of the pagan claim of "many gods and many lords" is unaltered.

Paul's quarrel, in the case of each of the slogans that he quotes in 8:1, 4, is not with the content of the Corinthian slogan but with the inferences (both theological and practical) that they draw from it and the uses to which they put it. Even when, in 8:7-13, the focus shifts from the common knowledge possessed as axiomatic by all believers (as encapsulated in the slogans of 8:4-6) to the more theologically sophisticated inferences that some but not all of the Corinthians have succeeded in drawing from them, Paul still implicitly identifies his own theological opinions with those of the "knowledgeable" Corinthians, affirming the validity of their assertions, if not their adequacy. When he returns to the subject in 10:19,[22] asking, "What do I imply then? That food sacrificed

---

19. See Ciampa and Rosner, *First Letter to the Corinthians*, 374.

20. E.g., Philo, *On the Cherubim* 125-126; *On the Special Laws* 1.208; Marcus Aurelius, *Meditations* 4.23; Pseudo-Aristotle, *On the Cosmos* 6; *Asclepius* 34; Seneca, *Epistle* 65.

21. See especially Richard Bauckham, *God Crucified: Monotheism and Christology in the New Testament* (Grand Rapids: Eerdmans, 1999), 36-40; N. T. Wright, *Paul and the Faithfulness of God* (London: SPCK, 2013), 661-70.

22. In saying that Paul "returns to the subject" in 10:19, I am not intending

to idols is anything, or that an idol is anything?" the implied answer of 8:20 is a clear (albeit qualified) "no." There is more to be said about the meaning of participation in a pagan temple meal or the ontological status of a pagan god than the glib Corinthian slogans might imply, but the truth claim at the heart of the slogans is not repudiated. Within the larger structure of the argument, the hypothetical person of 8:2 who "claims to know something" is clearly being criticized not for the content of the knowledge they claim to possess but for the arrogance with which they assume its finality and comprehensiveness (8:1b; see the reminder in 13:9 that all human knowledge, in this age at least, is "only in part"), and the lack of love for God and neighbor with which they use it (8:1b, 3).

Across the remainder of chapters 8–10, Paul's argument continues to confirm and build on elements of the knowledge that the Corinthians lay claim to, framing its appeal in rhetorical forms that imply the legitimacy of inferential reasoning from shared premises and the capacity and responsibility of the Corinthians to render judgment on its claims. Repeatedly throughout these chapters, Paul poses rhetorical questions to the Corinthians, assuming their ability to supply the correct answer,

---

to imply that the scenario in view in 10:1-22 is precisely the same as the kind of "eating in an idol's temple" that is hypothesized in 8:10. Given the wide variety of contexts in which meals could be eaten in a first-century Greco-Roman temple, there would have been ample room for Paul and his readers to imagine forms of "eating in an idol's temple" that were innocent and permissible in themselves but potentially injurious to the faith of a weaker brother or sister. The scenario envisaged in 10:1-22, however, appears to have been one that involved some form of ritual participation in the cult of the god, such that those involved were acting as "idolaters" (εἰδωλολάτραι) and "eating the sacrifices" (ἐσθίοντες τὰς θυσίας) as "participants in the altar" (κοινωνοὶ τοῦ θυσιαστηρίου). See David G. Horrell, "Theological Principle or Christological Praxis? Pauline Ethics in 1 Corinthians 8.1–11.1," *JSNT* 67 (1997): 99. For an alternative reading of the relationship between chap. 8 and chap. 10, see the argument of Gordon Fee, who proposes that the scenario hypothesized in 8:10 is the same as that envisaged in 10:1-22. On this reading, Paul chooses first (in chap. 8) to address the attitudinal issues of the Corinthians' arrogance and lack of love, tacitly assuming, for the sake of the argument, that the "knowledge" they are boasting in gives them the right to do as they please in the matter of temple meals; only subsequently, when he returns to the issue in chap. 10, does he make it clear that in his view their theological understanding is naive and inadequate, and eating at the table of a pagan god is out of the question for believers in Jesus, quite apart from its potential to cause a "weaker" brother or sister to stumble. Cf. Fee, *First Epistle to the Corinthians*, 394–401.

either from the moral intuitions that they share with their pagan neighbors (e.g., the reasoning from "human authority" [κατὰ ἄνθρωπον] that informs the questions of 9:7), by extension and analogy from the Old Testament Scriptures (e.g., 9:8–14),[23] or by reflection on the meaning embedded in the practices of the Christian community itself, interpreted against the horizon of Old Testament precedent (e.g., 10:16–18). The rhetorical question in 9:13 ("Do you not know …?") is asked ten times within the letter (see 3:16; 5:6; 6:2, 3, 9, 15, 16, 19; 9:24). Each time, no doubt, it carries a certain rhetorical sting when addressed to an audience so proud of their knowledge, but there is no reason not to take seriously its additional function as a logical appeal to the existing knowledge Paul believes that the Corinthians do in fact possess—in this case, either from common knowledge of pagan temple practices or (more likely) from the Old Testament prescriptions for the Jerusalem temple and their continuing first-century application.

Paul's appeals to Old Testament Scripture within this section of the letter include not only the arguments that he makes by analogy and extension from the Mosaic commandments; he also reminds his readers of the biblical narratives that prefigure the Corinthians' circumstances and serve as warnings not to sin as the Israelites did and risk a similar judgment (10:1–22). It is true, as we have already noted above, that the hermeneutic informing such appeals includes a retrospective figuration in which the Red Sea crossing is a baptism, the manna is "spiritual food," the water from the rock is "spiritual drink," and the rock from which it came is "Christ." But it is also true that the framework in which this sort of "apocalyptic hermeneutics" can function requires a strong sense of salvation-historical continuity, in which the gentile believers in Corinth understand the Israelites of the biblical narratives as "our ancestors" (10:1).[24]

---

23. See Fee, *First Epistle to the Corinthians*, 448–51; Ciampa and Rosner, *First Letter to the Corinthians*, 404–7; D. Instone-Brewer, "1 Corinthians 9.9–11: A Literal Interpretation of 'Do Not Muzzle the Ox,'" *NTS* 38 (1992): 554–65.

24. See the more detailed discussion in David I. Starling, *Hermeneutics as Apprenticeship: How the Bible Shapes Our Interpretive Habits and Practices* (Grand Rapids: Baker, 2016), 129–45; "'Nothing Beyond What Is Written'? First Corinthians and the Hermeneutics of Early Christian *Theologia*," *JTI* 8 (2014): 45–62.

Nor does the act of imagination that Paul requires of his readers within these paragraphs displace the kind of inferential reasoning that has characterized Paul's argument throughout the preceding chapter. Having reminded the Corinthians of the biblical stories and established the typological correspondences between their ancestors and themselves, Paul invites his readers to draw the logical conclusions that the stories imply: first, in 10:12, the general warning, expressed as a third-person imperative (ESV: "Therefore let anyone who thinks that he stands take heed lest he fall"), then, in 10:14, the more pointed and personal implication for the Corinthians ("Therefore, my dear friends, flee from the worship of idols").

Within a context of this sort, Paul's brief comment in 10:15, "I speak as to sensible people [ὡς φρονίμοις λέγω]," must surely be given its full weight. There is no need to assume that Paul expects the Corinthians to have forgotten the sharp edge of sarcasm with which the same word was used earlier in the letter, in 4:10 ("We are fools for the sake of Christ, but you are wise in Christ"); Paul's aim is not to bolster the Corinthians' delusional assurance of their own wisdom. But the function of his comment is not merely to deflate their pretensions; in choosing to frame his appeal "*as* to sensible people" Paul is simultaneously summoning them to think with the true wisdom and clear-sighted reasoning that they have hitherto failed to exercise.[25] The goal he hopes that his letter will accomplish is not only the conversion of their imaginations but also the renewal of their reasoning and the reauthorization of their judgment.

John Webster's words are apt and can serve as a fitting conclusion to this essay:

---

25. I am therefore in partial agreement with Eckhard Schnabel, who insists that Paul's designation of the Corinthians as φρόνιμοι is *nicht sarkastisch oder kritisch gemeint* and goes on to argue that its function is merely to signal that Paul is appealing to the Corinthians by means of a rational argument. There is no need to discount the likelihood that there is a sarcastic or critical edge to Paul's language here, but the context makes it clear that his intent is not *merely* sarcastic: as Schnabel rightly goes on to argue, "Er erwartet von den Christen in Korinth keinen blinden Gehorsam, sondern er will sie überzeugen und sie zum eigenen, theologisch begründeten, richtigen Urteil anzuleiten. Die folgenden Ausführungen dienen diesem Ziel" (Schnabel, *Erster Korintherbrief*, 548).

Christian theology is biblical reasoning. It is an activity of the created intellect, judged, reconciled and sanctified through the works of the Son and the Spirit.[26]

Extracted from its place in the divine economy, reason is exposed to inflammation and distortion.[27]

Nevertheless, it remains the case that

Reason is "a grace, and gift of love," and continues to be such despite our descent into depravity, because God has contradicted reason's contradiction of itself and God. The rehabilitation of reason is among the benefits that accrue to creatures from the Word's redeeming work which the Spirit is now realizing in the creaturely realm. By this unified saving action and presence of Word and Spirit, reason's vocation is retrieved from the ruins: its sterile attempt at self-direction is set aside; its dynamism is annexed to God's self-manifesting presence; it regains its function in the ordered friendship between God and creatures.[28]

The sanctifying Spirit must reorient reason to the divine Word, and only after that reorientation is reason authorized and empowered to judge and direct. Yet, as it is reoriented, reason really is authorized and empowered. And Christian theology is an instance of this redeemed intellectual judgement.[29]

WORKS CITED

Bauckham, Richard. God Crucified: Monotheism and Christology in the New Testament. Grand Rapids: Eerdmans, 1999.

Blackwell, Ben C., John K. Goodrich, and Jason Maston, eds. Paul and the Apocalyptic Imagination. Minneapolis: Fortress, 2016.

Brown, Alexandra R. The Cross and Human Transformation: Paul's Apocalyptic Word in 1 Corinthians. Minneapolis: Fortress, 1995.

Campbell, Douglas A. "Apocalyptic Epistemology: The Sine Qua Non of Valid Pauline Interpretation." In Paul and the Apocalyptic Imagination, edited by Ben C. Blackwell, John K. Goodrich, and Jason Maston, 65–86. Minneapolis: Fortress, 2016.

---

26. J. B. Webster, The Domain of the Word: Scripture and Theological Reason (London: T&T Clark, 2012), 115.
27. Webster, Domain of the Word, 116.
28. Webster, Domain of the Word, 122.
29. Webster, Domain of the Word, 123.

————. *The Deliverance of God: An Apocalyptic Rereading of Justification in Paul*. Grand Rapids: Eerdmans, 2009.

————. "An Evangelical Paul: A Response to Francis Watson's Paul and the Hermeneutics of Faith." *JSNT* 28 (2006): 337–51.

Ciampa, Roy E., and Brian S. Rosner. *The First Letter to the Corinthians*. Pillar New Testament Commentary. Grand Rapids: Eerdmans, 2010.

Collins, John J. "Early Jewish Apocalypticism." In *Anchor Bible Dictionary*, edited by David Noel Freedman, 1:282–88. New York: Doubleday, 1992.

Fee, Gordon D. *The First Epistle to the Corinthians*. New International Commentary on the New Testament. 2nd ed. Grand Rapids: Eerdmans, 2014.

Hays, Richard B. *The Conversion of the Imagination: Paul as Interpreter of Israel's Scripture*. Grand Rapids: Eerdmans, 2005.

Horrell, David G. "Theological Principle or Christological Praxis? Pauline Ethics in 1 Corinthians 8.1–11.1." *JSNT* 67 (1997): 83–114.

Instone-Brewer, D. "1 Corinthians 9.9–11: A Literal Interpretation of 'Do Not Muzzle the Ox.'" *NTS* 38 (1992): 554–65.

Martyn, J. Louis. "Apocalyptic Antinomies in Paul's Letter to the Galatians." *NTS* 31, no. 3 (1985): 410–24.

————. "Epistemology at the Turn of the Ages." In *Theological Issues in the Letters of Paul*, 89–110. Nashville: Abingdon, 1997.

————. "Epistemology at the Turn of the Ages: 2 Corinthians 5:16." In *Christian History and Interpretation: Studies Presented to John Knox*, edited by W. R. Farmer, 269–87. Cambridge: Cambridge University Press, 1967.

————. *Galatians: A New Translation with Introduction and Commentary*. Anchor Bible. New York: Doubleday, 1997.

Matlock, R. Barry. *Unveiling the Apocalyptic Paul: Paul's Interpreters and the Rhetoric of Criticism*. JSNTSup. Sheffield: Sheffield Academic, 1996.

Schnabel, Eckhard J. *Der Erste Brief Des Paulus an die Korinther*. Historisch-Theologische Auslegung. Wuppertal: Brockhaus, 2006.

Schrage, Wolfgang. *Der Erste Brief an die Korinther*. 4 vols. Evangelisch-katholischer Kommentar zum Neuen Testament. Zürich: Benziger, 1991–2001.

Shaw, David A. "'Then I Proceeded to Where Things Were Chaotic' (1 Enoch 21:1): Mapping the Apocalyptic Landscape." In *Paul and the Apocalyptic Imagination*, edited by Ben C. Blackwell, John K. Goodrich, and Jason Maston, 23–41. Minneapolis: Fortress, 2016.

Starling, David I. "The Children of the Barren Woman: Galatians 4:27 and the Hermeneutics of Justification." *Journal for the Study of Paul and His Letters* 3 (2013): 93–110.

————. *Hermeneutics as Apprenticeship: How the Bible Shapes Our Interpretive Habits and Practices*. Grand Rapids: Baker, 2016.

———. "Justifying Allegory: Scripture, Rhetoric and Reason in Gal. 4:21–5:1." *JTI* 9 (2015): 69–87.

———. *Not My People: Gentiles as Exiles in Pauline Hermeneutics*. Beihefte zur Zeitschrift für die neutestamentliche Wissenschaft. Berlin: de Gruyter, 2011.

———. "'Nothing Beyond What Is Written'? First Corinthians and the Hermeneutics of Early Christian Theologia." *JTI* 8 (2014): 45–62.

Sturm, Richard E. "Defining the Word 'Apocalyptic.'" In *Apocalyptic and the New Testament: Essays in Honor of J. L. Martyn*, edited by Joel Marcus and Marion Soards, 17–48. Sheffield: JSOT Press, 1989.

Torrance, Alan. "Article Review: Douglas Campbell, the Deliverance of God." *SJT* 65 (2012): 82–89.

Webster, J. B. *The Domain of the Word: Scripture and Theological Reason*. London: T&T Clark, 2012.

Wright, N. T. *Paul and His Recent Interpreters: Some Contemporary Debates*. Minneapolis: Fortress, 2015.

———. *Paul and the Faithfulness of God*. London: SPCK, 2013.

7

Figural Reading within Contemporary Theological Interpretation of Scripture

Problems and Parameters

Chase R. Kuhn

INTRODUCTION: THE PROBLEM

The past three decades have seen no shortage of expositions of the crisis of reason *versus* revelation.[1] Many have recognized the Enlightenment's ideology offering the promise of freedom from a "religiously troubled past." As Christopher Hall writes, "Perhaps, on the basis of reason itself, humanity could delineate a way of thinking and living religiously that could avoid past mistakes and open up new horizons for the future."[2] This offer of freedom would supposedly come from a move away from theological convictions/presuppositions (e.g., regarding the nature of the text of the Bible) and allow criticism to decide what is appropriate, worthwhile, or reasonable to believe. David Yeago is correct in his distillation of the problem: "It is assumed that a truly scholarly interpretation of the scriptural texts methodologically excludes any reference to Christian doctrine as a hermeneutical touchstone, and as a matter of historical fact, though not of logical necessity, the historical-critical

---

1. See, for example, Christopher A. Hall, *Reading Scripture with the Church Fathers* (Downers Grove, IL: InterVarsity, 1998), 22–25; David S. Yeago, "The New Testament and the Nicene Dogma: A Contribution to the Recovery of Theological Exegesis," in *The Theological Interpretation of Scripture: Classic and Contemporary Readings*, ed. Stephen E. Fowl (Oxford: Blackwell, 1997), 87–100; Fowl, "Theological and Ideological Strategies of Biblical Interpretation," in *Scripture: An Ecumenical Introduction to the Bible and Its Interpretation*, ed. Michael J. Gorman (Peabody, MA: Hendrickson, 2005), 163–69; Brevard S. Childs, "Toward Recovering Theological Exegesis," *Pro Ecclesia* 6 (1997): 16–26.

2. Hall, *Reading Scripture*, 22.

enterprise has often been understood as the liberation of rational intelligence and religious experience from the dead hand of dogma."[3] In this post-Enlightenment environment the Bible has become something to be analyzed and scrutinized rather than to be believed and enacted. Ephraim Radner expresses this as need to recognize the Scriptures are the *subject*, not the *object*; they act on the reader, not the reader on them.[4] It is false to assume this has been the environment of secular universities alone; in fact, evangelicalism has also succumbed to the pressures of modernity, even if under different dress.[5] In the face of this theologically deprived environment—that of "professional biblical scholarship"—there has been an increasing resurgence or retrieval of theologically aware and informed exegesis.[6] This movement has largely been recognized as the Theological Interpretation of Scripture (TIS), though the movement has not been uniform.

The aim of this essay is not to spell out the many different approaches to TIS (this has been attempted elsewhere)[7] but to investigate a subset of TIS that seeks to employ figural reading as an integral part of its hermeneutic. More specifically, this essay addresses the figural reading that moves beyond connecting the two Testaments, but works as a bridge for contemporary theological application. I will begin by giving

---

3. Yeago, "New Testament and the Nicene Dogma," 87.

4. Ephraim Radner, *Time and the Word: Figural Reading of the Christian Scriptures* (Grand Rapids: Eerdmans, 2016), 275.

5. Hall writes, "While one might hope that conservative Christians had escaped from the Enlightenment's crippling theological methodology, evangelical hermeneutics, particularly in the United States, has been shaped by certain key Enlightenment presuppositions. ... Evangelical scholars assented to the Enlightenment's deep suspicion of tradition and proceeded to produce a traditionless hermeneutic. The 'Bible alone' survived the Enlightenment assault against tradition, but only by becoming a timeless text filled with facts to be scientifically identified, analyzed and categorized." *Reading Scripture*, 25.

6. Kevin Vanhoozer says that we may have reached the end of the hermeneutical cold war, where exegetes and systematicians are finally able to see and hear each other again. Vanhoozer, "Four Theological Faces of Biblical Interpretation," in *Reading Scripture with the Church: Toward a Hermeneutic for Theological Interpretation of Scripture* (Grand Rapids: Baker Academic, 2006), 131.

7. See for example Daniel J. Treier, *Introducing Theological Interpretation of Scripture: Recovering a Christian Practice* (Grand Rapids: Baker Academic, 2008); Stephen E. Fowl, *Theological Interpretation of Scripture: A Short Introduction* (Milton Keynes, UK: Paternoster, 2009); Fowl, *Engaging Scripture: A Model for Theological Interpretation*, Challenges in Contemporary Theology (Oxford: Blackwell, 1998), 1–61.

a brief overview of the broader agenda of TIS in order to situate figural reading in this context. I will then briefly survey figural reading in the work of Stephen Fowl, my primary interlocutor, with some engagement with those he draws on, namely Ephraim Radner and Joseph Ratzinger. I will attempt an appreciation of this interpretive move before I take notice of several problems as I see them. I will conclude with a proposal for parameters within TIS and more specifically figural reading.

THEOLOGICAL INTERPRETATION AND MEANING

In response to the Enlightenment ideology calling for liberated reason, where there is "no imperatives to 'Believe!' only a free *credo*,"[8] some have offered a proposal for *theological* reason. John Webster puts it well when he writes,

> An account of theological reason will be Christianly deficient if it "naturalizes" reason's operations and declines to speak of reason as a sphere of God's activity. Theological reason is subject to the divine calling and the divine assistance. The notions of the calling of reason and of divine assistance of reason lift theology beyond either skepticism or retreat into apophasis. They secure for theology the basis on which it may proceed with a measure of—modest, self-distrustful yet real—confidence that rational thought and speech about God are possible because *made* possible by God.[9]

Indeed, Webster—among others—wanted to locate theology and biblical exegesis together as ecclesial practices. The Bible is *Christian* Scripture; thus it is to be read by Christians from the vantage point of faith (or confessionally). This is not naive engagement with historical texts but responsible reading within an ecclesial context, guided by the Spirit of God (Webster prefers the term "sanctified").[10] Reason and faith are not at odds, but like much else in the world, reason needs to be

---

8. Immanuel Kant, *The Conflict of the Faculties*, in *Religion and Rational Theology*, ed. A. W. Wood and G. Di Giovanni (Cambridge: Cambridge University Press, 1996), 252. Cited in John Webster, *Holy Scripture: A Dogmatic Sketch* (Cambridge: Cambridge University Press, 2003), 125.

9. Webster, *Holy Scripture*, 127.

10. Webster, *Holy Scripture*, 124.

transformed and renewed by the Holy Spirit; Christian theology need not follow "unformed or unrepentant reason."[11]

In the wake of modernity some have advocated the retrieval of pre-critical hermeneutics. Seeking to avoid the trappings of Enlightenment historical-critical methodology, various proposals have been put forward concerning how readers are to regard "meaning." Stephen Fowl has offered three categories for discerning the various approaches to meaning.[12] First he identifies "determinate interpretation," which seeks "to produce, uncover, or illuminate the meaning of the text," understanding the text as "a problem to be mastered."[13] In this hermeneutic meaning is a property of the text, and meaning of any given text is usually singular. The goal is to finish the interpretive work, even remove the necessity for interpretation, as meaning is made clear. Second, he observes an "anti-determinate interpretation," which seeks to "upset, disrupt, and deconstruct interpretive certainties."[14] This hermeneutic is heavily dependent on the philosophical work of Jacques Derrida (i.e., deconstructionism). The goal of this work is to perpetuate the interpretive task, avoiding any semblance of mastery over the text. Third and finally, Fowl points out an "underdetermined interpretation"—his own position—which "avoids using a general theory of meaning to determine interpretation." Furthermore, "Underdetermined interpretation recognizes a plurality of interpretive practices and results without necessarily granting epistemological priority to any one of these."[15] This position is articulated by Jeffrey Stout, who raises the philosophical challenges with the term "meaning" and in the end seeks to avoid the term all together by reorienting the discussion.[16] The goal, then, is less focused on knowing and more on pragmatics. In this way, this hermeneutic is utilitarian.

In raising these three categories, I am primarily interested to delve deeper into the underdetermined interpretation, as it allows us access

---

11. Webster, *Holy Scripture*, 127.
12. Fowl, *Engaging with Scripture*, 32–61.
13. Fowl, *Engaging with Scripture*, 32.
14. Fowl, *Engaging with Scripture*, 32.
15. Fowl, *Engaging with Scripture*, 33.
16. Jeffrey Stout, "What Is the Meaning of a Text?," *New Literary History* 14 (1982): 1–12. See Fowl's summary of Stout's position in *Engaging with Scripture*, 56–61.

to Fowl's disposition in his figural readings. Fowl's avoidance of meaning allows him flexibility. Rather than being epistemologically oriented (or confined), he is practically focused (e.g., politics).[17] For him the telos of interpretation is not in knowing (e.g., meaning) as much as it is in being.[18] This means that the telos is equally about a destination as it is the journey, though Fowl stresses that Christians must not get so preoccupied with the journey that they lose sight of the goal of reaching home.[19] He states the aim of interpretation as follows: "Christians are called to interpret and embody Scripture as a way of advancing towards their proper ends in God."[20] Surely Fowl envisions these "proper ends in God" as love for God and love for others, just as Augustine was concerned in interpretation to see the "establishment of the reign of love."[21] This ethical emphasis is not deprived of theology but is driven by a focus on ecclesiology, as we shall see below.

In avoiding discussion of meaning, Fowl desires to stay clear of the modernist concerns for locating some property in the text to be mined. He is not opposed to thinking of a *sensus literalis* but deploys this notion Thomistically. He argues that, from Aquinas, we can have a more dynamic understanding of a literal sense—one that allows for multiple meanings.[22] Multiple meanings are applicable within the canon but also throughout history, as God is the author of Scripture, and it is *God's* authorial intention with which readers should be primarily concerned. Movement away from human authorial intention, fixed

---

17. Kevin Vanhoozer aptly notes, "The notion that we should look 'not to the meaning but to the use' is easily traced back to Ludwig Wittgenstein, who is neither Fish nor Fowl but the philosophical presence behind both" (*First Theology: God, Scripture & Hermeneutics* [Downers Grove, IL: InterVarsity, 2002], 288).

18. D. Christopher Spinks, *The Bible and the Crisis of Meaning: Debates on the Theological Interpretation of Scripture* (London: T&T Clark, 2007), 66.

19. Fowl draws on Augustine's identification of Scripture as a vehicle to get us to our true home. Fowl, *Theological Interpretation of Scripture*, 14, 39.

20. Fowl, *Theological Interpretation of Scripture*, 39.

21. Augustine, *On Christian Teaching* 3.15, in *Nicene and Post-Nicene Fathers*, vol. 2, First Series, ed. Philip Schaff (Peabody, MA: Hendrickson: 1994), 563.

22. Fowl, *Engaging with Scripture*, 38–40. See also Fowl, *Theological Interpretation of Scripture*, 49–50. Fowl's proposal for a "working notion of the 'literal sense' of Scripture" is "the meanings that Christians conventionally ascribe to a passage in their ongoing struggles to live and worship faithfully before the Triune God" (Fowl, "Theological and Ideological Strategies," 171).

in time, allows for layers of meaning to be developed, as well as space for figural readings to be included in the literal sense. These figural readings open new opportunities for meaning(s) to be understood in contemporary contexts.

Ephraim Radner has provided a similar argument to Fowl's but moves beyond discussing the utility of figural reading to a philosophical case for the practice grounded in the relationship of time and the word. Like Fowl, Radner wishes to avoid the trappings of the modernist critical agenda. Rather than scrutinizing the text according to critical questions and apparatuses, he argues that theology demands a figural reading insomuch as God is a creative God, the world is God's creation, and the word is the living and active way in which God works in his world. Radner contends that much of modern biblical hermeneutics has decoupled dogmatic convictions from practice, retaining beliefs about God as Creator but letting go of figural reading as a mode. He decries, "Such a decoupling of fundamental dogma from figural reading has had the effect of slowly eviscerating God's creative being from our consciousness and apprehension, leaving in its place the traces that we have filled out with our dim memories, mostly of ourselves and of our fading loves."[23] His response moves from his theological conviction about the nature of reality in relationship to the Scriptures to a philosophical articulation of the relativity of time with regards to the word. Figural reading seeks to locate how current artifacts find themselves in the Scriptures, as all artifacts are indicated and included in the Scriptures.[24] For Radner this is fundamentally a christological move.[25]

Questions naturally arise around permissions with regards to interpretation of multiple meanings. Ultimately who or what is the adjudicator of appropriate practice? Fowl's answer is that it is the ecclesial community—one that is in conversation, admonishing and correcting, and one that practices forgiveness and reconciliation.[26] Like many others in TIS, Fowl advocates reading in accordance with the rule of

---

23. Radner, *Time and the Word*, 8.

24. Radner, *Time and the Word*, 103.

25. For the logic of Radner's position, see the detail of his argument set forward in sequence in *Time and the Word*, 94–106.

26. Fowl, *Theological Interpretation of Scripture*, 51–53.

faith (sometimes *regula fidei* or *analogia fidei*), represented in the creeds of the church.[27] The rule functions less like an instruction manual and more like "a moderately flexible framework within which one can order the pieces of the puzzle in order to render an image."[28]

I noted earlier that Fowl is driven by a strong ecumenical motive, as much of the application in his writings demonstrates. It is difficult to see how his ecumenical interest does not direct his avoidance of meaning in the interpretive process. It is evident that he is responding to modernism and clearly moving away from hermeneutical priorities overpowering theological interests. But is Fowl's fluidity, even in his conception of the "literal sense," actually a pathway to achieving his ecumenical aim? It most certainly is. Fowl believes the aim of theological interpretation is "faithful living and worship," and church unity is part and parcel to this faithfulness. By moving away from conversations about "meaning," much disagreement is avoided. Allowing for a plurality of interpretive practices and interpretations clears the way for more accessible grounds of unity.[29] The challenge for Fowl is that he must demonstrate how ecumenism features in the biblical vision for faithfulness, and why ecclesiology is paired evenly with theology (proper) in his hermeneutic.[30] One should not be dismissive of Fowl's ethical interests—indeed, these are admirable—but these concerns must remain secondary; that is, they are an outworking of the meaning of the text. Vanhoozer is correct that meaning must not be sidelined because of recent debates but must instead be reenvisioned theologically.[31]

The challenge I have raised above becomes more pressing when we examine how Fowl has deployed figural reading. He writes, "The primary importance of figural reading comes from the fact that there

---

27. For the historical and methodological background of this practice see John J. O'Keefe and R. R. Reno, *Sanctified Vision: An Introduction to Early Christian Interpretation of the Bible* (Baltimore: Johns Hopkins University Press, 2005), 114–39.

28. Fowl, "Theological and Ideological Strategies," 169.

29. Fowl, *Engaging with Scripture*, 58–60.

30. Fowl writes, "Theology and ecclesiology should drive scriptural hermeneutics, not the other way around" ("The Importance of a Multivoiced Literal Sense of Scripture: The Example of Thomas Aquinas," in A. K. M. Adam, Stephen E. Fowl, Kevin J. Vanhoozer, and Francis Watson, *Reading Scripture with the Church: Toward a Hermeneutic for Theological Interpretation* [Grand Rapids: Baker Academic, 2006], 37).

31. Vanhoozer, *First Theology*, 283–94.

will be times when the literal sense of Scripture may not offer us a sufficiently sharp vision to account for the world in which we live."[32] He believes that church disunity, as seen today and over many centuries, is representative of a situation necessitating a figural interpretation, as the New Testament does not envision division of the nature or scope facing Christians today. The method proposed is admirable because it seeks wisdom for Christian living from the Bible and sees the Bible as continually relevant. The challenge, however, is that it moves from a practical existential crisis—real as this *practical* concern may be—and imposes a theological conviction *on* the Bible. In other words, the held conception of the church is not present in the text and therefore must be *found*, or worse *constructed*. But here we must take caution; when the theological conviction comes from without (an interpretation of the rule of faith) we must then read *into* the text a theology. I recognize this is one way that advocates of ruled reading have operated. If my concern here is not clear, I hope it will become more evident as we turn to examine how figural reading has been utilized in TIS.

FIGURAL READING FOR CONTEMPORARY APPLICATION

Hans Frei, in his work *The Eclipse of Biblical Narrative*, most notably carries forward the work of recapturing the precritical usage of figural reading in hermeneutics.[33] Frei seeks to locate the meaning of the text, even of figures, in the narrative of the Bible. Thus significance is not given to a text based on whether it really happened, but instead based on what it contributes to the narrative. Though the trajectory of figural reading has varied within TIS, Frei's study certainly charted the course. Figural reading is once again viewed as an extension of the literal sense of the text rather than a competitor or an impostor.[34] Figural reading has been especially useful in TIS for recognizing a two-Testament canon as Christian Scripture. Reading the Old Testament figurally became a necessary and useful way of understanding it Christianly, recognizing

---

32. Fowl, "Theological and Ideological Strategies," 172.

33. Hans Frei, *The Eclipse of Biblical Narrative: A Study in Eighteenth and Nineteenth Century Hermeneutics* (New Haven, CT: Yale University Press, 1974).

34. For an interesting discussion of Frei's hermeneutic and allegory see Mark Gignilliat, "Paul, Allegory and the Plain Sense of Scripture," *JTI* 2, no. 1 (2008): 135–46.

these texts as a part of the same story of redemption carried forward by the triune God.[35]

But, as mentioned, not all figural reading has been conducted in the same manner or with the same agenda. Classic exegesis has worked to read the Old Testament in light of the New Testament and vice versa. However, in the last two decades (especially) there have been moves to read passages from across the canon with an aim towards contemporary theological application.[36] The most explicit examples of this have come from those wishing to work toward ecumenism (even if not under this named purpose). Wishing to see the currently divided church healed but unable to find New Testament texts with direct applicability to the current situation, they opt for a figural reading of Old Testament texts to address the contemporary environment.[37] Fowl suggests reading 1 Samuel 8 in this figural sense, recognizing God's granting Israel a king in their disobedience as a form of judgment. He writes, "One of the forms of God's judgment is giving us what we want. If we treat division in this light, it becomes clear that division is both a sign that we are willing to live, and even *desire* to live, separate from our brothers and sisters in Christ. ... This separation—in the form of church division—is God's judgment on our failure to live as Christ commands."[38] Further reflecting on other Old Testament passages, Fowl sees stupefaction and blindness resulting from the resistance of God's Spirit. Such a

35. Brevard Childs, *Biblical Theology of the Old and New Testaments: Theological Reflection on the Christian Bible* (Minneapolis: Fortress, 1992), 78-79.

36. I recognize this practice was alive and well in the early church, especially in the practice of allegorical reading. See O'Keefe and Reno, *Sanctified Vision*, 89-113.

37. Ephraim Radner writes, "Apart from such a figural location of the problem—one that opens up for 'instruction' the 'type' of Israel (1 Cor. 10:11)—the Church's division finds little place within the explicit ecclesial referents of the New Testament. In nonfigural terms, the New Testament simply does not envision the entrenched division of the Church; it merely points in passing to the eschatological distresses to be suffered by the Christian community at the hands of Satan, only one of which will include factions and schisms (e.g., 1 John 2:18ff.; Jude 17-19). How one understands the Church as itself a divided entity is not a topic the New Testament openly broaches." *The End of the Church: A Pneumatology of Christian Division in the West* (Grand Rapids: Eerdmans, 1998), 34. See also Fowl, "Theological and Ideological Strategies," 172.

38. Fowl, "Theological and Ideological Strategies," 173.

resistance among the church increasingly dulls the senses when reading the word.[39]

Fowl draws much of his figural reading from Ephraim Radner's example. Radner, also strongly interested in ecumenism, builds on a passing comment (or two) in Joseph Ratzinger's (Pope Benedict XVI) work *Church, Ecumenism & Politics*:[40]

> First, the separation of the churches may properly be seen in terms of "the significance of salvation history": that is, it may be caught up in the sovereign shaping of history by God in a way that must point, intrinsically, to the heart of the Gospel of Christ. Second, Ratzinger suggests that the division of the churches in this respect might be related to the division of "Israel and the Gentiles." Related, but how? It is precisely through each reality's sharing in the same divinely "disposed" significance that they are related, that is, brought together in the one Gospel of Christ. Each set of divisions plays a part in and reflects the salvation wrought in Christ in some mysterious fashion. Each set of historical episodes refers to the other—intra-Christian division and Jewish-Gentile division—through the mediating an effecting reality of Christ Jesus, to whom, in fact, each refers in a primary way. In the terms of classical hermeneutics, then, Ratzinger suggests we adopt a "figuralist" approach to assessing the significance of Christian division.[41]

Radner's understanding of a figuralist approach is distinguished from a figural reading in that it is more dynamic than static. This reading "perceives the intersignificating character of the scriptural text in a consistent and integrated (rather than merely occasional and/or limited) fashion and that, in particular, insists that the context for such intersignification lies primarily in the temporal reality of God's 'economy,' which links Israel to the Church via the central 'figurating' form

---

39. Fowl, "Theological and Ideological Strategies," 173.

40. "Perhaps institutional separation has some share in the significance of salvation history which St Paul attributes to the division between Israel and the Gentiles—namely that they should make 'each other envious,' vying with each other in coming closer to the Lord (Rom 11:11)." Joseph Ratzinger, *Church, Ecumenism and Politics* (Middlegreen: St Paul Publications, 1987), 87.

41. Radner, *End of the Church*, 28.

of Jesus Christ."[42] Radner seeks to demonstrate how this interpretive method was utilized by Calvin and Owen as well as by Bellarmine and the Jansenists.[43]

Radner's (and Fowl's) location of the church figurally with Israel requires a supersessionist ecclesiology.[44] In relating the church with Israel, he expresses continuity with warnings of divine judgment. His logic follows: (1) the division of Israel was integrally related to the people's sin and punishment; (2) disunity was characterized by increased sin; (3) the nation grew increasingly deaf, dumb, and blind (spiritually speaking) to God's warnings and calls to repentance; and (4) this ultimately led to divine "abandonment" in sin, namely, exilic or other punishment. Finally, Radner argues, "Partitioned Israel is 'abandoned' Israel; and this Israel, separated among its members, is separated too from the Holy Spirit. This equation between sinfulness, abandonment, and 'resistance' to the Spirit is the burden of Stephen's speech in Acts 7 (cf. vv. 42 and 51), and it stands as an explicator to the large number of texts from the prophets where the condition of divided Israel is described in the explicit terms of pneumatic absence or antagonism."[45] Fowl'is less willing to concede Radner's point about the Spirit's absence but stresses a certain resistance to the Spirit and the peril of this resistance, especially for hearing the Word.[46]

Building on Radner's and Ratzinger's proposal, Fowl identifies relevant implications from figural readings of Romans 9–11 and Ephesians 2–3.[47] First, division is a form of resistance to the Spirit of God (Rom 9–11). As he argued before from 1 Samuel 8, this resistance leads to a dulling of believers' abilities to hear and respond to the Word. In this

---

42. Radner, *End of the Church*, 29–30n48.

43. Radner's parallels fail, however, because where Owen, for example, identifies the church with a divided Israel, it is more simile than "figuralist."

44. Ephraim Radner, "The Absence of the Comforter: Scripture and the Divided Church," in *Theological Exegesis: Essays in Honor of Brevard S. Childs*, ed. Chris Seitz and Kathryn Greene-McCreight (Grand Rapids: Eerdmans, 1999), 374–75.

45. Radner, *End of the Church*, 37–38.

46. Stephen E. Fowl, "Scripture and the Divided Church," in *Horizons in Hermeneutics: A Festschrift in Honor of Anthony C. Thiselton*, ed. Stanley E. Porter and Matthew R. Malcom (Grand Rapids: Eerdmans, 2013), 220. Fowl indicates his agreement with Ephraim Radner on this point. See Radner, *End of the Church*, 230.

47. Fowl, *Theological Interpretation of Scripture*, 58–63.

context believers should be provoking others to faith. In his application, Fowl is careful to reserve judgment of which part of the church is the natural vine, the grafted vine, and who is in danger of being lopped off. Second, God is bringing all things together in Christ (Eph 1), including divided Israel, the gentiles, and even the cosmos. This work of reunion is part of God's glorious plan to make his wisdom known to powers and principalities. In the church's divided state, this witness is hindered and frustrated.

Before moving to an evaluation of this method, I want to offer brief remarks about the exegesis of these texts mentioned above. By forcing an ecumenical ecclesiological reading of these texts, the application precedes and even becomes the meaning of the text. In the instance of Jew and gentile relations in Romans 9–11 the concern is far more about God's redemptive work in history. Thus, doctrinally speaking, it is soteriology rather than ecclesiology that is in view. Ephesians 2–3 is certainly ecclesiological, but perhaps in a different sense than is taken up by Fowl. Once again, it is *soteriology* that is in view, especially in a way that is fundamentally oriented to the work of the triune God. Ecclesiology features in Ephesians 2–3 insomuch as it highlights the wisdom of God demonstrated in his salvific achievement in Christ. But in Ephesians disunity is not something rebuked; instead, it is unity that is to be maintained as a reality belonging to the church fundamentally in Christ by the Spirit (Eph 4:3). By imposing an ecumenical agenda on the text figurally, theological riches are easily overlooked, and textual meaning misconstrued and misapplied.[48]

APPRAISAL AND PROPOSAL

Having considered some of the practices of figural reading in contemporary TIS, we shall now move to a brief appraisal and offer suggestions for interpretive parameters moving forward. As we move to this section, it should be noted that Stephen Fowl and Ephraim Radner write with deep care and concern for the church and truly model the ethos they advocate, demonstrating admirable charity and love toward others working at interpretation. My hope is that in what I have presented

---

48. I recognize that I am using the word "meaning" here in a way that Fowl himself would not. This, of course, is part of my contention with his method.

here and in what I critique below, I will represent them fairly and in the same manner.

It is praiseworthy that efforts are being made to uphold the witness of Scripture as divine revelation and understand that word as significant and relevant for Christians through the ages, even today. Current problems are not seen as too difficult, or the Bible—or worse, God—being out of touch with our situation. Fowl takes aim at interpretation in a very commendable direction: to see people living faithfully in worship to God. Indeed, the retrieval of figural reading, and with it the belief that the Bible speaks literally in multiple ways (e.g., typologically), demonstrates helpful gains for our engagement with the Scriptures. I believe the end result of this will be a Christocentric reading of the Bible that will better appreciate the triune God's self-revelation to us.

However, I have four concerns with the sort of figural reading exemplified by Fowl. First, the dismissal of meaning appears to treat the Bible in a utilitarian fashion. Relocation of "meaning" to the too-hard box, or perhaps more appropriately "too divisive" box, makes Fowl's underdetermined interpretation *appear* more capricious. Spinks is accurate in his critique of Fowl when he writes, "Fowl describes theological interpretation as the mutual influence of the readers' reading of Scripture and the readers' interpretive interests. In practice, however, it is not clear how the reader is influenced by the text itself. This leaves Fowl open to the charge that an 'underdetermined approach invites manipulation of the text to affirm whatever the community wants to affirm.'"[49] Fowl would surely respond that the avoidance of manipulation comes through the regulation of the rule of faith, as it is the rule that sets the boundaries for interpretation in the community. But we must ask, is this enough? Because a belief is orthodox, does this mean that any interpolation of meaning is permissible, so long as it is agreeable to the rule?

Second, neither the rule of faith nor the interpretive community should be the arbiter of truth. Fowl, in an admirable (from the perspective of agreement/compromise) but fatal move (from the perspective

---

49. Spinks, *Bible and the Crisis of Meaning*, 66. Spinks depends on Klyne Snodgrass for this critique. See Snodgrass, "Reading to Hear: A Hermeneutics of Hearing," *Horizons in Biblical Theology* 24, no. 1 (June 2002): 1–32 (esp. 6).

of conviction), turns away from allowing Scripture to be the judge of truth (Scripture interpreting Scripture) and moves instead to give place to the rule of faith as arbiter. The ecclesial community carries out the adjudication of this interpretation, but the notion of this community is elusive. What and where is this community? Is this a public reading, and where, when, and how does it happen? Carson is right in noting that many in the TIS community advocate such a locale for interpretation, all while working in academic contexts.[50] I believe that Fowl understands his work with and within the rule being in accordance with the truth of Scripture. However, there is a de facto elevation of the rule to the level of scriptural authority. Fowl likely sees this as *the* common ground—the catholic faith—on which all can agree. But this elevation of the rule's authority is actually equally divisive. Indeed, it is contrary to Fowl's own tradition (Anglican/Episcopalian), standing against Articles 10 and 11 of the Thirty-nine Articles of Religion. Within his proposal, as exemplified in his figural reading, there is a danger of subjugating the biblical text to the rule, as it (the rule) is interpreted contextually. Fowl's figural reading depends on an extratextual (that is, extrabiblical) sign (divided church) and grid (rule of faith). D. A. Carson helpfully notes that it will not do "to argue that the *analogia fidei* might be a legitimate extratextual grid, for the *analogia fidei* itself must be shown to be grounded in the text of Scripture."[51]

Third, ecclesiology must not be the tail that wags the dog. Fowl's commitments in his hermeneutics is the primary place where he fails. Ecclesiology must not supplant or even parallel theology proper. Ecclesiology is a derivative doctrine, by dogmatic necessity—the church is *creatura verbi*. If we locate Scripture as part of the divine self-communicative acts, then it belongs with theology in a place of dogmatic priority.[52] This is not to diminish the significance of ecclesiology

---

50. D. A. Carson, "Theological Interpretation of Scripture: Yes, But …," in *Theological Commentary: Evangelical Perspectives*, ed. R. Michael Allen (London: T&T Clark, 2011), 203–4.

51. Carson, "Theological Interpretation of Scripture," 199.

52. I believe Ephraim Radner would agree with this dogmatic ordering. He stresses the christological constraint of figural reading. I do not agree with the totality of his method, but I am appreciative of his theological authenticity. I would encourage more nuance than Radner provides, particularly a clearer delineation

but to give proper attention to its systematic place. I appreciate that the priority of ecclesiology in Fowl's hermeneutics is the means by which he upholds the ethical end to which he works. However, this can be done, and even be done *better*, when ecclesiology is not given primacy.

The advocacy for figural or figurating interpretation relating to church disunity begins with the presumption of ecumenical theology. This is not argued for but rather surmised as the dominant conviction. Citation of a creed—Nicene, Apostles', or simply the rule of faith—is presumed to be evidence enough for such argumentation. However, there are many divergent ecclesiologies, even within creedal and confessional heritages. The position contended for, associating the church with Israel, demands a supersessionist ecclesiology—one of the major causes of divergence today.[53] Furthermore, the locus of unity is another source of tension. Many ecumenists seek an institutional unity that nearly (if not overtly) overlooks the local church. But what if catholicity and unity are not forsaken, even in the current "divided" context?

Finally, and following on from the last point, much of the aim of figural reading seems noble, but the vision of unity is very underdeveloped. Harmony sounds like a very wonderful ideal. In fact, it is difficult to think about who would argue against love and unity or how they would do so if they did. However, it is difficult to envision many of the proposals pragmatically. I will give two examples of what I mean. First, where and how will unity be manifested? It is one thing to speak of unity as an ideal, but what would it actually look like? Practicalities of authority, polity, location, identification, and the like seem intangible.[54] If there are to be serious efforts toward this end, then there will need to be proposals of what unity might actually entail both practically and theologically. It seems that earthly union and catholicity of a corpus of *churches* is difficult to establish biblically. I cannot think of

---

between Christ and all of reality. Christology orders reality—both in design and telos—but Christ remains distinct from his creation, even if he has entered creation in the incarnation. So, though he may serve as a type, we need not force Christ to be typical of all reality. See Radner, *Time and the Word*, 100–106.

53. As noted above, Radner addresses supersessionism and its relationship to this discussion. Radner, "Absence of the Comforter," 374–75.

54. I appreciate Fowl's attempts at naming some of the ethical demands of a move toward unity. Fowl, "Scripture and the Divided Church," 220–24.

any biblical texts that are persuasive proofs for such a position, and Fowl and Radner have demonstrated the same. Fowl takes notice that the local church is the place where unity is most clearly worked out but that each local and individual context is already consciously or unconsciously shaped by disunity.[55] But what constitutes this disunity? Theological factionalism? Surely it cannot be location, as a plurality of congregations is essential geographically. Arguments for the locus of ecclesial unity must be saved for another time, but a preliminary statement may be offered that unity/singularity may more appropriately be established for the heavenly and eschatological church (Eph 2-3; Heb 12:18-29).[56] Within such a proposal unity is an ecclesial concern at the level of the local (earthly) church, and general Christian love toward other Christians takes a different place theologically and ethically.[57]

In conclusion, I will propose parameters for TIS broadly but figural reading more specifically. I have demonstrated that the shortcomings of some recent attempts at theological application via figural readings have in large part stemmed from an evasion of "meaning" and an employment of the Bible according to the rule of faith. I do not believe that all of these efforts lack merit, but I do believe they are largely problematic. The heart of my concern is this: figural reading should not begin with an extratextual (especially extrabiblical) sign or theology and then find a way to make the text support or accommodate that agenda or sign.[58] In other words, the text of Scripture cannot be approached in such a utilitarian manner, a *carte blanche* reading subject to the reading/interpretive community's desires.[59] Ruled reading

---

55. Fowl, "Scripture and the Divided Church," 224-25.

56. Chase R. Kuhn, *The Ecclesiology of Donald Robinson and D. Broughton Knox: Exposition, Analysis, and Theological Evaluation* (Eugene, OR: Wipf & Stock, 2017), 72-83, 114-20, 157-62.

57. I would advocate a broader notion of Christian fellowship belonging to the redeemed community (i.e., people of God), allowing for ecclesiology to be a subset (activity) of this broader community. Kuhn, *Ecclesiology of Donald Robinson and D. Broughton Knox*, 98-105.

58. Fowl anticipates this critique, but I am not sure he has persuasively overcome it. Fowl, *Engaging with Scripture*, 26.

59. I do not think what I am arguing here is guilty of a "slippery slope fallacy." My concerns are shared in the cautions of others. Vanhoozer writes, "While it is true that Fowl and Jones refer to the importance of critical biblical scholarship and to 'virtuous' interpretation in the context of reading the Bible 'over-against

is surely useful, but it must be regulated. My proposal is that the rule should serve theological application in guarding what goes out from the text rather than give license for what goes into a text. We may therefore find agreement with the doctrinal tradition of the church but still recognize the ultimate authority of the Scriptures in the life of the church—an authority that comes from our dogmatically primary conviction that the triune God has spoken.

WORKS CITED

Augustine. *On Christian Teaching. Nicene and Post-Nicene Fathers*. Vol. 2. First Series. Edited by Philip Schaff. Peabody, MA: Hendrickson, 1994.

Carson, D. A. "Theological Interpretation of Scripture: Yes, But …," in *Theological Commentary: Evangelical Perspectives*, edited by R. Michael Allen, 187–207. London: T&T Clark, 2011.

Childs, Brevard S. *Biblical Theology of the Old and New Testaments: Theological Reflection on the Christian Bible*. Minneapolis: Fortress, 1992.

———. "Toward Recovering Theological Exegesis," in *Pro Ecclesia* 6 (1997): 16–26.

Fowl, Stephen E. *Engaging Scripture: A Model for Theological Interpretation*. Challenges in Contemporary Theology. Oxford: Blackwell, 1998.

———. "The Importance of a Multivoiced Literal Sense of Scripture: The Example of Thomas Aquinas." In *Reading Scripture with the Church: Toward a Hermeneutic for Theological Interpretation*, edited by A. K. M. Adam, Stephen E. Fowl, Kevin J. Vanhoozer, and Francis Watson, 35–50. Grand Rapids: Baker Academic, 2006.

———. "Scripture and the Divided Church," in *Horizons in Hermeneutics: A Festschrift in Honor of Anthony C. Thiselton*, edited by Stanley E. Porter and Matthew R. Malcolm, 217–33. Grand Rapids: Eerdmans, 2013.

———. "Theological and Ideological Strategies of Biblical Interpretation." In *Scripture: An Ecumenical Introduction to the Bible and Its Interpretation*, edited by Michael J. Gorman, 163–76. Peabody, MA: Hendrickson, 2005.

———. *Theological Interpretation of Scripture: A Short Introduction*. Milton Keynes, UK: Paternoster, 2009.

Fowl, Stephen, and Gregory Jones. *Reading in Communion: Scripture and Ethics in Christian Life*. Grand Rapids: Eerdmans, 1991.

---

ourselves,' it is not altogether clear how this can be done in the absence of any stable or determinate textual meaning (the natural sense)." *First Theology*, 289. Vanhoozer refers to Stephen Fowl and Gregory Jones, *Reading in Communion: Scripture and Ethics in Christian Life* (Grand Rapids: Eerdmans, 1991), 39–42. See also Daniel J. Treier, "Typology," in *Dictionary of Theological Interpretation*, ed. Kevin Vanhoozer (Grand Rapids: Baker Academic, 2005), 826.

Frei, Hans. *The Eclipse of Biblical Narrative: A Study in Eighteenth and Nineteenth Century Hermeneutics.* New Haven, CT: Yale University Press, 1974.

Gignilliat, Mark. "Paul, Allegory and the Plain Sense of Scripture." *JTI* 2, no. 1 (2008): 135–46.

Hall, Christopher A. *Reading Scripture with the Church Fathers.* Downers Grove, IL: InterVarsity, 1998.

Kant, Immanuel. *The Conflict of the Faculties.* In *Religion and Rational Theology*, edited by A. W. Wood and G. Di Giovanni. Cambridge: Cambridge University Press, 1996.

Kuhn, Chase R. *The Ecclesiology of Donald Robinson and D. Broughton Knox: Exposition, Analysis, and Theological Evaluation.* Eugene, OR: Wipf & Stock, 2017.

O'Keefe, John J., and R. R. Reno. *Sanctified Vision: An Introduction to Early Christian Interpretation of the Bible.* Baltimore: Johns Hopkins University Press, 2005.

Radner, Ephraim. "The Absence of the Comforter: Scripture and the Divided Church." In *Theological Exegesis: Essays in Honor of Brevard S. Childs*, edited by Chris Seitz and Kathryn Greene-McCreight, 355–94. Grand Rapids: Eerdmans, 1999.

———. *The End of the Church: A Pneumatology of Christian Division in the West.* Grand Rapids: Eerdmans, 1998.

———. *Time and the Word: Figural Reading of the Christian Scriptures.* Grand Rapids: Eerdmans, 2016.

Ratzinger, Joseph. *Church, Ecumenism and Politics.* Middlegreen: St Paul, 1987.

Snodgrass, Klyne. "Reading to Hear: A Hermeneutics of Hearing." *Horizons in Biblical Theology* 24, no. 1 (June 2002): 1–32.

Spinks, D. Christopher. *The Bible and the Crisis of Meaning: Debates on the Theological Interpretation of Scripture.* London: T&T Clark, 2007.

Stout, Jeffrey. "What Is the Meaning of a Text?" *New Literary History* 14 (1982): 1–12.

Treier, Daniel J. *Introducing Theological Interpretation of Scripture: Recovering a Christian Practice.* Grand Rapids: Baker Academic, 2008.

———. "Typology." In *Dictionary of Theological Interpretation*, edited by Kevin J. Vanhoozer, 823–27. Grand Rapids: Baker Academic, 2005.

Vanhoozer, Kevin J. *First Theology: God, Scripture & Hermeneutics.* Downers Grove, IL: InterVarsity, 2002.

———. "Four Theological Faces of Biblical Interpretation." In *Reading Scripture with the Church: Toward a Hermeneutic for Theological Interpretation*, edited by A. K. M. Adam, Stephen E. Fowl, Kevin J. Vanhoozer, and Francis Watson, 131–42. Grand Rapids: Baker Academic, 2006.

Webster, John. *Holy Scripture: A Dogmatic Sketch.* Cambridge: Cambridge University Press, 2003.

Yeago, David S. "The New Testament and the Nicene Dogma: A Contribution to the Recovery of Theological Exegesis." In *The Theological Interpretation of Scripture: Classic and Contemporary Readings*, edited by Stephen E. Fowl, 87–100. Oxford: Blackwell, 1997.

8

Meditation and Reason

Some Reflections on the Right Way to Happiness in God

Christopher R. J. Holmes

INTRODUCTION

"The happiness of humanity is in God," writes Thomas Aquinas, commenting on Psalm 1.[1] If Thomas is correct, humanity's beatitude is extrinsic to itself, being found in God and in God alone. We are created by God and for God, indeed for seeing God "face to face" (1 Cor 13:12). It is in God that we as human beings find supreme fulfillment. Theological knowledge has a destiny, "the perfect possession of God."[2] Our end as creatures is also our beginning, the magnanimous and blessed Trinity, Father, Son, and Holy Spirit.

It is fitting to begin a paper on the relationship between meditation and reason in Christian theology by appealing directly to Holy Scripture. Theology has to do with God, and the theologian receives God's testimony to his person and works through Scripture. Scripture, especially the Psalter, provides us with a divine pedagogy. Scripture instructs us in God and seeing all things in relation to God. For example, Psalm 143:5:

---

1. Thomas Aquinas, "Psalm 1," in *St. Thomas's Commentary on the Psalms*, trans. Hugh McDonald, Stephen Loughlin, et al. Note that Thomas only commented on the first fifty-four psalms. An English-language translation is available, but only electronically. Hugh McDonald et al., trans., The Aquinas Translation Project, www4.desales.edu/~philtheo/loughlin/ATP/index.html (last modified September 4, 2012).

2. Thomas Joseph White, OP, *The Incarnate Lord: A Thomistic Study in Christology* (Washington, DC: Catholic University of America Press, 2015), 507.

> I remember the days of old,
>> I think about all your deeds,
>> I meditate on the works of your hands.

The key to understanding God's presence and activity is to meditate on God's past works.

"The way to happiness," argues Thomas, following Psalm 143:5, is twofold. First, "we should submit ourselves to God," remembering and thinking about God's deeds. Second, happiness involves "the understanding, by always meditating." Understanding's highest form is meditation. Thomas avers that only that which is meditated on is truly understood. Complete happiness is a matter of submission to God and meditation on God.

Where does Jesus fit into this? Commenting on Psalm 1, Thomas notes, "Christ is first among the blessed ones."[3] Christ's blessedness, his immediate vision of God, is manifest in his submission to his Father and in his filial understanding as the Father's Son. We become blessed in Jesus and in his Spirit, coming to know the Father, Son, and Holy Spirit. Christ is the one who takes us on a journey toward submission to God, and who drastically reorients our understanding in such a way that we come to know and enjoy the Trinity "as the first and final end of the science of Christ."[4] These two words, "submission" and "meditation," are key to understanding the way to our true happiness in God the Trinity.

In this paper I make two points about reason's relationship to God. First, reason cannot make us happy with respect to divine teaching and truth. Reason cannot lead us to God. Reason cannot evoke the revealed principles that sacred doctrine accepts as its own. Nonetheless, reason has an important function with respect to sacred teaching. When reason is mortified and vivified by the light of divine revelation, it is a most useful tool for helping us know things via the revelation of God. Reason's happiness, I shall argue, is found in submitting itself to God, in being ordered to God. Second, reason is a catalyst by which we understand holy teaching. When treated as an end in itself, reason is a hard master; it enslaves. However, when reason is in the service of

---

3. Aquinas, *Commentary on the Psalms*, Psalm 1.
4. White, *Incarnate Lord*, 507.

understanding, which itself serves meditation, reason is made happy. When the human submits to God through understanding by meditation, then reason is able to fulfill its role in facilitating reception of divine truth.

SUBMISSION AND MEDITATION

Reason is not an end in itself. It is, rather, a God-given means by which creatures, created in God's image and thus blessed with intellect and will, consider truth. Reason does not consider itself. When rightly ordered, it considers what lies outside itself, that is, truth. Consideration of divine truth is what Thomas calls "the chief occupation of wisdom."[5] Such consideration involves reason, not of course understood as an end in itself but in service of apprehending the truth.

It is the wise person who remembers, thinks, and meditates. She does these things, however, not as if they were self-contained enterprises. The truth, Thomas argues, must be published.[6] Wisdom meditates on and publishes the divine truth, and in so doing it "refutes the error[s] contrary to truth."[7] In the case of reason, divine truth refutes reason's autonomy. Reason, on this side of the fall, seeks autonomy due to its captivity to the "cosmic powers of this present darkness" (Eph 6:12). Reason is not simply "deficient in the things of God"; reason is, as is the case with our intellect and will, hostile to the things of God.[8] Accordingly, reason does not want to "remember," "think about," and "meditate on the works" of God's hand. And yet, reason's deficiency, and I would add its antagonism toward God, does not diminish its intrinsic value.

Recourse to "natural reason" is not a bad thing, theologically speaking, for what is natural is "caused," and caused indeed by God "as the highest cause."[9] Revealed principles do not abolish natural reason, for what God causes is good. Reason, as that which is caused, participates in its cause, which is of course uncaused. Reason is surpassed by revealed

5. SCG I, I.
6. SCG I, I.
7. SCG I, I.
8. SCG I, II.
9. ST I, q. 1, a. 6.

truth but not abolished. Its deficiencies are healed by truths that utterly exceed it. The chief deficiency I have in mind is reason's propensity to reject as false that which it cannot investigate. Natural reason of course can investigate some things about God and speak about them with a degree of clarity. Think, for example, of Calvin's "sense of divinity."[10] Such a sense, of course, is deeply wounded and corrupted by the fall, but not entirely. Reason that accepts its place in God's economy must not reject as false those things it cannot investigate, indeed things that can only be known and understood by divine revelation and in faith.

To put this differently, the way of reason cannot compete with what Thomas calls "the way of faith," nor should it.[11] The way of faith is supernatural, whereas the way of reason is natural. Reason can arrive at certainty and truth when it comes to divine things, but not "definite certainty" and "pure truth."[12] The latter are gifts "offered to man by the way of faith." The way of faith does not compete with reason, but it does exceed it because faith mediates on works of God's grace, works of salvation.

If we follow Thomas's line of thought on these matters, we see that "the divine clemency has made this salutary commandment, that even some things which reason is able to investigate must be held by faith."[13] Accordingly, reason gives us the hard way of investigating truth. Reason's way is hard insofar as it investigates things without or apart from the divine light. This is not to denigrate reason but rather is a matter of pastoral urgency. The easy way of knowing God is a matter of remembering, thinking about, and meditating on, the much harder way that of investigating truths that are most naturally held by faith. Knowledge of God that is free of doubt and error flees from investigating anything

---

10. So Calvin: "Men of sound judgment will always be sure that a sense of divinity which can never be effaced is engraved upon men's minds. Indeed, the perversity of the impious, who though they struggle furiously are unable to extricate themselves from the fear of God, is abundant testimony that this conviction, namely, that there is some God, is naturally inborn in all, and is fixed deep within, as it were in the very marrow." See *Calvin's Institutes: Abridged Edition*, ed. Donald K. McKim (Louisville: Westminster John Knox, 2001), 1.3.3.

11. *SCG* I, IV.

12. *SCG* I, IV.

13. *SCG* I, IV.

without faith. Such knowledge reasons in faith. Stated differently, it is a matter of reason being perfected by faith.

The things of God far surpass our intellect. God asks us to believe truths that are above us. We cannot believe these truths, for example, truths such as that of the Trinity of persons in God, if we are not born from above. Think Nicodemus. As Thomas notes, "certain things far surpassing his intellect should be proposed to man by God."[14] God is not a respecter of limits we think of as natural. Instead, God delights in stretching our intellect, or pushing our thinking to beyond the breaking point, so as to form us into the kinds of people who are at peace with receiving truth that far surpasses us. Indeed, what Thomas, following many of the church's great teachers, wants us to appreciate is the difference between apprehending and comprehending.[15] Through the light of grace are we able to apprehend via remembering, thinking, and meditating, but not comprehend.

In what is perhaps the most important statement on reason that he makes in the *Summa Contra Gentiles*, Thomas writes that "although human reason is unable to grasp fully things that are above reason, it nevertheless acquires much perfection, if at least it hold things, in any way whatever, by faith."[16] Reason has its limits; many truths are inaccessible to it, though they do not contradict it. Reason is subject, moreover, to the perfecting work of God insofar as it holds truths in faith. Faith fulfills reason. Faith does not abolish reason; faith does not mortify reason. Faith fulfills reason, raising reason above itself in such a way that it can hold to truths that surpass it.

Thomas's construal is quite felicitous because of the way he distinguishes between grasping and holding. Reason, when it sets out to grasp, defeats itself; reason, when it sets out to hold to divine things,

---

14. *SCG* I, V.

15. For a judicious unfolding of the difference between comprehending and apprehending, see *St. John Chrysostom on the Incomprehensible Nature of God*, trans. Paul W. Harkins (Washington, DC: Catholic University of American Press, 1982). Chrysostom's opponents, the Anomoeans, contend, "God's essence is comprehensible to human nature." Chrysostom argues that God, "even by the accommodation of condescension, cannot be seen" or comprehended, only apprehended. See *Homily* III.13; 24.

16. *SCG* I, V.

acquires perfection. Holding, rather than grasping, is reason's most appropriate posture via divine truth. Expressed in the idiom of Psalm 143:5, when the saints remember, thinking, and meditate they find the desire to grasp being mortified, and the desire to hold in faith being vivified. Regenerate intelligence finds its apogee in faith.

If such is the case, is there any place for what Thomas calls "naturally known principles"?[17] In short, yes: we naturally know God. What Thomas means is that it is natural to us to know that God authors our nature. Knowledge of ourselves as authored is not alien to us but natural. God authors us in such a way that it is entirely natural to us to know that we are caused and not our own cause, that God is our refuge and not we ourselves. What is not natural to us, however, are "those things which are received by faith from divine revelation."[18] For example, the command to be born again is not naturally known to us; similarly, knowledge of the consubstantiality of the Father, Son, and Spirit is not natural to us; and more, the knowledge of the works of God's hand in terms of Exodus and the giving of the law, these things, too, are not natural to us. Indeed, we cannot know God's great works of liberation and of law giving without scriptural revelation and meditation on the same. Meditation expands our hearts and minds in such a way that we come to see how natural it is to live in light of God's promises and commands. The upshot of Thomas's account, at least in part, is that it encourages a profoundly noncompetitive account of natural knowledge in relation to the knowledge received by faith from divine revelation. The latter, Thomas writes, "cannot be contrary to our natural knowledge."[19] To be sure, knowledge received by faith transcends and surpasses the natural, and is utterly inaccessible to it; however, knowledge received in faith does not contradict natural knowledge. As we remember, think, and meditate, we come to see how natural it is to know God as our God and to live as his covenant partner.

Where I would suggest a slight expansion to Thomas's account is in terms of the ascetics of receiving by faith from divine revelation. I am not an expert in Thomas and am sure that there are parts of the

---

17. *SCG* I, VII.
18. *SCG* I, VII.
19. *SCG* I, VII.

corpus that unfold just this point, but at least in terms of his account
as contained in *Summa Contra Gentiles* and the *prima pars* of the *Summa
Theologica*, there is a need to supplement it with talk derived from the
Psalter. As we noted earlier, Thomas, when commenting on Psalm 1,
writes that happiness in God comes about via submission to God and
through "the understanding, by always meditating."[20] The degree to
which we are able to receive by revelation things that are not contrary
to our natural knowledge is the degree to which we desire God's stat-
utes. The rigor with which we meditate on God's works and sing God's
praises determines the extent to which we can receive holy teaching.
This needs to be emphasized.

Faith represents a higher way of knowing. Faith does not work from
sensible things; instead, faith sees with the eyes of the heart truths
inaccessible to sense perception. Reason works, however, with simili-
tudes that "retain a certain trace of likeness to God."[21] Goodness, unity,
truth, and reality, these are sensible things that "retain a certain trace
of likeness to God."[22] Goodness, unity, truth, and existence itself, these
things we know of, indeed apprehend sensibly, but we do not know
them as they are in God. To know of goodness as it is in God and indeed
as coexistent with God himself, we need faith. The knowledge of God's
goodness that we have from sensible things is, as Thomas notes, "so
imperfect that it proves altogether inadequate to manifest the substance
itself of God."[23] The one substance of God in which three persons subsist
cannot be known apart from faith. Even then, God's substance will be
known only in faith, never without faith and apart from Christ.

I think that the above account, largely derived from Thomas, about
reason in relationship to mediation serves an important purpose for
the faithful. I am not under any illusions that the above account would
make sense for those whom Thomas calls "our opponents," by which he
means unbelievers.[24] The truths of Christian faith are only intelligible
as truths held by faith. Faith, as St. Paul reminds us, comes, on the one

---

20. Aquinas, *Commentary on the Psalms*, Psalm 1.
21. *SCG* I, VIII.
22. *SCG* I, VIII.
23. *SCG* I, VIII.
24. *SCG* I, IX.

hand, "from what is heard" or, on the other hand, following the idiom of the Psalter, by meditating on the works of God's hands (Rom 10:17). The faithful are those who by grace are learning that their happiness lies in God. Submission to God is the way to happiness. Meditation on God is the way to understanding. Such truths are deeply participatory truths. Reason, when it receives its perfection in faith, will help us to hold to them but will never supply us with them. Reason does not supply faith with its content. Faith's content is God and all things in relationship to God. Reason betrays its God-given function when it tries to grasp what may only be held.

CONCLUSION

In sum, Christ as "the first among the blessed ones" declares us blessed and makes us blessed in him.[25] We learn to see through him and in his Spirit. As Thomas notes in his *Compendium*, "the more one sees God, who is the essence of goodness, the more necessary it is to love him, and so also the more one will desire to enjoy him."[26] We see in this life through the eyes of the heart by faith. By faith we see what reason cannot, simply because what "we see in a mirror, dimly" far surpasses reason's capacity to investigate (1 Cor 13:12). God, in his clemency and essential goodness, knows our infirmities and heals them from within, providing us with a much easier way, that is, the way of faith.

The Spirit gifts us with sight through faith, sight that ultimately leads to love. The more one sees in faith with the eyes of the heart, the more one loves the one unseen. The more one loves him who is invisible, the more one desires to enjoy him. You see the progression: sight, love, then enjoyment, the latter being I think synonymous with happiness. The human's happiness is in God. Remembering, thinking about, and meditating on: these acts that the faithful undertake are but the means by which they begin to see and in turn love with a view to enjoying. We cannot enjoy God via reason as reason works only with "sensible things."[27] Instead, if we receive in faith from divine revelation,

---

25. *Commentary on the Psalms*, Psalm 1.

26. Thomas Aquinas, *Compendium of Theology*, trans. Richard J. Regan (New York: Oxford University Press, 2009), II, §9.

27. *SCG* I, VIII.

we start to see the one who is the essence of goodness. In seeing, we realize just how much the one seen is worthy of love, and in loving God, we move toward the ultimate goal, happiness. "The happiness of man is in God."[28] Thanks be to God.

WORKS CITED

Aquinas, Thomas. *Basic Writings of Saint Thomas Aquinas*. Vol. 1, *God and Creation*. Edited by Anton C. Pegis. Indianapolis: Hackett, 1997.

———. *Compendium of Theology*. Translated by Richard J. Regan. New York: Oxford University Press, 2009.

———. *St. Thomas's Commentary on the Psalms*. The Aquinas Translation Project. Translated by Hugh McDonald et al. Last modified September 4, 2012. http://hosted.desales.edu/w4/philtheo/loughlin/ATP/index.html.

———. *The Summa Contra Gentiles of Saint Thomas Aquinas*. Translated by English Dominican Fathers. London: Burns, Oates and Washbourne, 1924.

Calvin, John. *Calvin's Institutes: Abridged Edition*. Edited by Donald K. McKim. Louisville: Westminster John Knox, 2001.

Harkins, Paul W., trans. *St. John Chrysostom on the Incomprehensible Nature of God*. Washington, DC: Catholic University of America Press, 1982.

White, Thomas Joseph, OP. *The Incarnate Lord: A Thomistic Study in Christology*. Washington, DC: Catholic University of America Press, 2015.

---

28. *Commentary on the Psalms*, Psalm 1.

9

A Mysterious Relationship?

Herman Bavinck on Revelation and Reason

Bruce R. Pass

REVELATION AND REASON: PARADOX OR PROBLEM?

Although the relation of revelation and reason has attracted the attention of Christian thinkers from the earliest times, it is only with the advent of modernity that the notion of an unknowable God making himself known has been cast as a problem. Modern solutions to this problem generally have involved either a denial of revelation at the expense of reason or a denial of reason at the expense of revelation; however, within modernity a stream of theologians have regarded such solutions as fundamentally misguided, insisting rather that the notion of an unknowable God making himself known is not a problem that must be solved but a paradox to be preserved.

Herman Bavinck (1854–1921) was one such theologian. For Bavinck the notion that the God who is unknowable in himself can make himself known to his creatures is not a problem to be solved but a mystery to be adored.[1] In fact, for Bavinck the quest to "solve" the relation of revelation and reason is idolatrous, for such an attempt seeks to supplant the reality that renders all our knowing worshipful, namely, mystery. For Bavinck, the whole of life is λογικὴ λατρεία, yet the seat of reason especially is to be a sanctuary of praise. The task of knowing is irreducibly doxological, and its doxological character is grounded in mystery. Mystery elicits worship, and for that reason mystery constitutes an essential

---

1. Hence, "agnosticism sees here an irresolvable contradiction in what Christian theology regards as an adorable mystery." Herman Bavinck, *Reformed Dogmatics*, ed. John Bolt (Grand Rapids: Baker Academic, 2003–2008), 2:49.

element of Bavinck's theological and general epistemology. To rightly understand this emphasis on mystery, however, it must be situated in the context of late nineteenth-century Protestantism. Only from this vantage point can the significance of mystery in Bavinck's construal of the relation of revelation and reason be properly appreciated.

MYSTERY, THE LIFEBLOOD OF DOGMATICS

If one were to sum up Herman Bavinck's theological rationale in as few words as possible, one might say that Bavinck sought to be Reformed yet modern.[2] Bavinck's writings consistently evidence an attempt to bring Reformed theological commitments into conversation with modernity and to rehabilitate modern thought to its origins in the Western Christian tradition. This can be readily seen in the recurring motifs that function as bridging concepts between modernity and Bavinck's Reformed Orthodox heritage.[3]

The concept of mystery is to be numbered among these motifs. The significance of mystery as a bridging concept can be seen in Richard Grützmacher's claim that late nineteenth-century Protestantism had replaced a transcendent theology of revelation with an immanent theology of mystery.[4] Grützmacher, a Lutheran contemporary of Bavinck, regarded theologians such as Albrecht Ritschl and Adolf Von Harnack as having eliminated the concept of divine revelation from Christian theology, ironically, by means of a term that had for centuries been taken as synonymous with divine transcendence. "Mystery," according to Grützmacher, had been redefined by late nineteenth-century Protestantism

---

2. Naturally, this attracted criticism from the side of both orthodoxy and modernity. See Herman Bavinck, *Modernisme en orthodoxie* (Kampen: J. H. Kok, 1911).

3. Prominent among these motifs is "organism." James Eglinton has provided an excellent analysis of the close relationship between the doctrine of the Trinity and the concept of the organic in *Trinity and Organism: Towards a New Reading of Herman Bavinck's Organic Motif* (London: T&T Clark, 2012). Elsewhere I have explored the significance of self-consciousness and the subject-object dichotomy. Cf. Bruce Pass, "Herman Bavinck and the Cogito," *RTR* 74, no. 1 (2015): 15–33; Pass, "Herman Bavinck and the Problem of New Wine in Old Wineskins," *IJST* 17, no. 4 (2015): 432–49.

4. Richard Grützmacher, "Die Theologie der Offenbarung und die Theologie des Geheimnisses," in *Modern—Positive Vorträge* (Leipzig: Deichert, 1906), 38–39. Bavinck cites this lecture in his direct treatment of the term "mystery" toward the end of the prolegomena to Reformed dogmatics; see *Reformed Dogmatics*, 1:621n55.

in such a way that it now opposed, rather than affirmed, the reality of divine revelation. "Therewith a position is marked out, which stands in the sharpest contrast to that recommended by Scripture and Luther. ... Precisely there, where the one identifies revelation, the disclosure of an other-worldly, transcendent, eternal world, the other identifies only the indication of a mysterious, temporary, this-worldly profundity. ... The supernatural notion of revelation is [thus] replaced by a natural notion of mystery."[5] The term "mystery" predominates to such an extent that, for Grützmacher at least, "mystery" could be regarded as the central motif of modern theology.[6] The prevalence of the word "mystery" in Bavinck's writings therefore, would have made his writings sound very modern. For Bavinck the Trinity is a mystery,[7] the incarnation is a mystery,[8] the life of the church is a mystery,[9] the means of grace are a mystery.[10] Faith, grace, atonement, reconciliation, and prayer are all mysteries.[11] "Mystery," in fact, "is the lifeblood of dogmatics."[12] When Bavinck says this, however, he means something very different from what Ritschl, or Von Harnack, or any of the other modern theologians Grützmacher had in mind.

---

5. "Damit ist eine Stellungnahme gekennzeichnet, die sowohl in schärftster Distanz zu der von Schrift und Luther empfohlenen steht. ... Dort nämlich, wo die einen Offenbarung, die Erschliessung einer jenseitigen oberen, ewigen Welt finden, finden die anderen nur die Andeutung einer geheimnissvollen, zeitlichen, innerweltichen Tiefe. ... Der supranaturale Offenbarungsbegriff wird durch einen naturalistischen Geheimnisbegriff ersetzt" (Grützmacher, "Die Theologie der Offenbarung und die Theologie des Geheimnisses," 41).

6. Grützmacher, "Die Theologie der Offenbarung und die Theologie des Geheimnisses," 38–39. Alister McGrath notes that in a reminiscence Theophil Wurm (1868–1953) recalled Harnack suggesting a two-part structure under which everything usually covered in a work of dogmatic theology would be assigned to the rubric of "mysteries." Alister E. McGrath, *The Making of Modern German Christology 1750–1990* (Grand Rapids: Zondervan, 1994), 97–98.

7. Bavinck, *Reformed Dogmatics*, 4:452.

8. Bavinck, *Reformed Dogmatics*, 3:274, 301, 304.

9. Bavinck, *Reformed Dogmatics*, 1:384.

10. Bavinck, *Reformed Dogmatics*, 4:484, 532.

11. Bavinck, *Reformed Dogmatics*, 2:618; see also Herman Bavinck, *The Philosophy of Revelation: The Stone Lectures for 1908–09, Princeton Theological Seminary*, trans. Henry E. Dosker, Nicholas M. Steffens, and Geerhardus Vos (New York: Longmans, Green, 1909), 198.

12. Bavinck, *Reformed Dogmatics*, 2:29.

With the claim that mystery constitutes the lifeblood of dogmatics, Bavinck sounds an echo of what Luther and Calvin before him affirmed when they spoke of human beings being able to apprehend yet never able to comprehend divine revelation. For example, in the *Bondage of the Will* we hear Luther state, "[This] touches on the secrets of His Majesty. ... It is not for us to inquire into these mysteries, but to adore them."[13] Similarly, John Calvin in his *Institutes of the Christian Religion* writes, "It is, indeed, true that in the law and the gospel are comprehended mysteries which tower far above the reach of our senses. ... His wonderful method of governing the universe is rightly called an abyss, because while it is hidden from us, we ought reverently to adore it."[14] Thus, Bavinck may sound quite modern with his regular insistence that so much of Christian doctrine is a mystery, but he is in fact affirming something very premodern. Because God reveals himself, we may know him, yet this knowledge never attains to comprehension. In every respect divine self-revelation is circumscribed by mystery.

Mystery, therefore, represents a prime example of the way Bavinck brings orthodox theological commitments into conversation with modernity. With the term "mystery" we see Bavinck using the language of modernity to rehabilitate modern thought to its origins in the Western Christian tradition. This is important in approaching Bavinck's construal of the relation of revelation and reason; it also illuminates two distinct ways in which the concept of mystery functions within this relation. First, mystery functions as a limiting concept for Bavinck's appropriation of the doctrine of divine ideas, and second, like Luther and Calvin before him, mystery conditions the worshipful character of creaturely knowing.

MYSTERY AS A LIMITING CONCEPT

The doctrine of divine ideas is a doctrine largely mediated to Protestant orthodoxy by William Ames (1576–1633)[15] but ultimately finds its origins

---

13. John Dillenberger, ed., *Martin Luther: Selections from His Writings* (Garden City, NY: Doubleday, 1961), 195.

14. Calvin, *Institutes* 1:213.

15. Richard A. Muller, "Calvinist Thomism Revisited: William Ames (1576–1633) and the Divine Ideas," in *From Rome to Zurich—Between Ignatius and Vermigli: Essays*

in early Christian Neoplatonism.[16] The doctrine of divine ideas traces creation to an exemplar in the divine mind and thus views creation as an instantiation and embodiment of divine thought. For the relation of revelation and reason this holds two important implications. First, the entirety of creation is regarded as revelatory. Bavinck writes, "The entire world is a revelation of God, a mirror of his attributes and perfections. Every creature in its own way and degree is the embodiment of a divine thought."[17] Second, the doctrine of divine ideas furnishes Bavinck with a means of maintaining an absolute distinction between God and the world against the pantheistic tendencies of German idealism, while simultaneously opposing the kind of epistemological separation of God from the world enshrined by Immanuel Kant. Like many before him, Bavinck accounts for the creaturely intelligibility of divine ideas by means of a Logos metaphysic. It is the divine Logos who forges the correspondence between divine and human thought and the correspondence between the knowing subject and known object. In a passage redolent with allusions to Augustine, Victorinus, and Thomas Aquinas, Bavinck writes,

> But the conviction can, therefore, rest only in the belief that it is the same Logos who created both the reality outside of us and the laws of thought within us and who produced an organic connection and correspondence between the two. ... But insofar as things also exist logically, have come forth from thought, and are based in thought (John 1:3; Col. 1:15), they are also apprehensible and conceivable by the human mind. ... Just as we look into the natural world, not by being in the sun ourselves, but by the light of the sun that shines on us, so neither do we see things in the divine being but by the light that, originating in God shines in our own intellect. Reason in us is that divine light; it is not itself the divine logos, but it participates in it.[18]

---

in *Honor of John Patrick Donnelly, S.J.*, ed. Kathleen Comerford, Gary Jenkins, and W. J. Torrance Kirby (Leiden: E. J. Brill, 2017), 103–20.

16. In particular, Augustine's exposition of this theme was especially influential. Augustine, *Eighty-Three Different Questions*, trans. David L. Mosher (Washington, DC: Catholic University of America Press, 1982), 79–81.

17. Bavinck, *Reformed Dogmatics*, 2:530–31.

18. Bavinck, *Reformed Dogmatics*, 1:231–32.

The doctrine of divine ideas thus allows Bavinck to posit a very close relationship between revelation and reason. The whole of creation bears the impress of the Logos because it constitutes the instantiation of divine thought, and the impress of the Logos is recognizable to us because the laws of thought also bear the impress of the Logos. Yet over against the doctrine of divine ideas, Bavinck posits another Augustinian category to prevent the coalescence of revelation and reason, namely, mystery. The category of mystery ensures that this Logos metaphysic does not offer reason untrammeled access to the divine mind. Mystery guards against any notion that we may know God as God knows himself, or for that matter, that we may know creation as God knows creation. The function of mystery as a limiting concept in Bavinck has been overlooked in the secondary literature and has precipitated notable interpretative problems in connection with the relation of revelation and reason in Bavinck.[19] The likely reason for this is that Bavinck draws specific attention to the fact that the New Testament does not use mystery to limit what we can know of God. Bavinck writes, "The New Testament term μυστήριον, accordingly, does not denote an intellectually uncomprehended and incomprehensible truth of faith but a matter that was formerly hidden in God, was then made known in the gospel, and is now understood by believers."[20] Bavinck upholds the integrity of New Testament's use of the term "mystery," as an unveiling of something that was previously unknown, but this New Testament sense of the term does not exhaust or limit the ways in which Bavinck uses it. In fact most commonly Bavinck uses mystery in two quite different ways. Beyond the New Testament idea of mystery as something that is both knowable and known, Bavinck also uses the term "mystery" to denote that which is knowable yet unknown and that which defies human reason altogether.

The second sense of the term "mystery" concerns that which is presently unknown and bears specific reference to the asymptotic of human

---

19. For example, Eugene Heideman makes the claim that in Bavinck reason knows no limits other than the limits of revelation. Eugene P. Heideman, *The Relationship of Revelation and Reason in E. Brunner and H. Bavinck* (Assen: Van Gorcum, 1959), 236. For a detailed analysis of the misleading character of this claim see Bruce Pass, "Revelation and Reason in Herman Bavinck," *WTJ* (forthcoming).

20. Bavinck, *Reformed Dogmatics*, 1:620.

knowing. It most often comes into play in connection with Bavinck's commentary on the rapid expansion of the natural sciences at the dawn of the twentieth century. For example, "Even if we knew all the laws of motion and of change to which matter is subject, its essence would still remain a mystery,"[21] or even more strongly, "The intelligibility of nature, which was so long believed in by science, is therefore more and more giving place to the confession of its unknowableness."[22] While this second sense of the term "mystery" concerns matters that are as yet beyond the reach of the human intellect, Bavinck also uses "mystery" to describe matters that defy human reason altogether. Characteristically, "mystery" in this third sense of the term is used in connection with the point at which the infinite touches the finite. Bavinck writes, "In all that God reveals, we finally encounter an impenetrable mystery at the point where the eternal touches the temporal, the infinite the finite, the Creator the creature."[23]

What is particularly important to note about this third sense of the term is that it bears simultaneous reference to many of the same realities to which the New Testament sense of the term also applies. In other words, much of special revelation is a mystery in both the first and the third senses of the word. The reason for this is precisely that much of special revelation concerns "the eternal touch[ing] the temporal, the infinite the finite, and the Creator the creature." Mysteries such as the incarnation and the indwelling of the Holy Spirit are prime examples of mysteries that belong to both the first and third categories, mysteries that can be believed and known yet remain indemonstrable to reason.

Mystery according to the second and third senses of the term, therefore, functions as a limiting concept over against the doctrine of divine ideas. While the doctrine of divine ideas secures the ontological intelligibility of revelation, the category of mystery secures certain epistemological parameters for the creaturely knowing subject. As regards

---

21. Bavinck, *Philosophy of Revelation*, 91.

22. Bavinck, *Philosophy of Revelation*, 104. Care needs to be taken, nonetheless, with Bavinck's language of "unknowableness" here. Bavinck does not mean that creation is ontologically unintelligible but is simply confessing that we will never exhaustively fathom the mysteries of science. Cf. Herman Bavinck, *Kennis en leven* (Kampen: J. H. Kok, 1922), 208.

23. Bavinck, *Reformed Dogmatics*, 4:93.

the intelligibility of creation generally, it not only gives expression to the incomplete character of our knowledge but also guards any pretension on the part of creaturely knowers to a divine knowledge of the creation. As regards the intelligibility of the Creator, it likewise secures the ectypal character of our knowledge of God. There is, however, a further role played by mystery in Bavinck's account of knowing that proceeds from its function as a limiting concept.

MYSTERY AS THE GROUND OF WORSHIPFUL KNOWING

Mystery, according to Bavinck, is what conditions the properly doxological character of creaturely knowing. For Bavinck the provisional and incomplete character of creaturely knowing is neither a lamentable consequence of the fall nor an aspect of our human condition to be rescinded in the future glory. Although faith will pass over into sight, our creaturely appropriation of divine revelation will remain in glory a finite appropriation of divine revelation, not passing over into comprehension. "'Vision as to essence' and 'comprehension' are completely synonymous. God, moreover, is infinite, and human beings are finite and remain so also in the state of glory. ... Moreover, were human beings to comprehend God in the state of glory, it would amount to the deification of humanity and the erasure of the boundary between the Creator and the creature."[24] For Bavinck provisional and incomplete knowledge is the knowledge that is proper to creatures. Comprehension, as opposed to apprehension, is the prerogative only of a Creator.[25] Comprehension concerns the knowledge of an object's inner possibility; it is the knowledge that surpasses "knowing that" and "knowing what," penetrating to "knowing how." Knowing how entails a certain relation between knowing subject and known object, and it is the relation of Creator to creature. Bavinck states: "We comprehend only the things that

---

24. Bavinck, *Reformed Dogmatics*, 2:190–91. Also compare the discussion of knowledge in this age and the next in Bavinck, *Kennis en leven*, 224–25.

25. Ultimately this is to be linked to Bavinck's appropriation of the doctrine of divine ideas. Comprehension is the prerogative of the Creator because all things have their origin in the divine mind and because God's knowledge is coextensive with his being. Were one to comprehend even the external instantiation of divine thought, it would suggest an immediacy to divine self-knowledge. Comprehension, strictly speaking, is a prerogative of the divine mind.

are totally in our power, the things we can make or break."[26] Hence, in a restricted sense the engineer might be said to comprehend his design and the composer said to comprehend his symphony, but ultimately creatures do not comprehend anything, because their creative powers are entirely derivative. Creatures do not create anything *ex nihilo*, and so their comprehension of objects is always subject to epistemological regress. It is for this reason that Bavinck writes, "There are few things we comprehend. … I comprehend, or think I comprehend, the things that are self-evident and perfectly natural. Often comprehension ceases to the degree a person digs deeper into a subject. That which seemed self-evident proves to be absolutely extraordinary and amazing. The farther a science penetrates its object, the more it approaches mystery. Even if on its journey it encountered no other object it would still always be faced with the mystery of being."[27]

Comprehension, even of this-worldly realities, is metaphysically beyond creatures. Even the most thoroughgoing apprehension, when faced with the mystery of existence, must capitulate any claim to comprehension because such knowledge, unlike God's, does not instantiate the existence of its object. It remains posterior to its object, unable to account for its existence. Thus, scientific inquiry, whether natural or theological, will never deify its practitioners. Even were science to arrive at the most extensive knowledge of its object, such knowledge would remain incomplete.[28] This very incompletion, however, is what

---

26. Bavinck, *Reformed Dogmatics*, 1:619.

27. Bavinck, *Reformed Dogmatics*, 1:619.

28. One might perhaps question in what sense the knowledge of analytic propositions such as "triangles have three sides" remain incomplete. To a certain degree Bavinck reserves a special place for the purely formal sciences but often proceeds to minimize the significance of such knowledge. Thus, properly "scientific knowledge exists only when we see the cause and essence, the purpose and destiny of things, when we know not only the *that* (ὅτι) but also the *wherefore* (διότι) and thus discern the causes of all things (*rerum dignoscimus causas*)." Presumably therefore, mathematical truths such as 1+1=2, like the truths of faith, are complete in the sense that they are certain, yet if isolated from their significance within the whole, the truth they convey remains very incomplete. In this respect Bavinck qualifies the epistemologically privileged position he assigns the formal sciences with the words of Schopenhauer, "People never stop praising the reliability and certainty of mathematics. However, what benefit is there for me in knowing with ever so much certainty and reliability something which I do not in the least care about?" (Bavinck, *Reformed Dogmatics*, 1:221).

lends creaturely knowing its profoundly moral character. Confronted by the limits of their understanding, creatures are reminded of the surpassing wisdom of the Creator. Reminded of this complete knowledge that summoned all that exists into being and that sustains all that exists from moment to moment, the creature is moved to awe, amazement, and wonder. Hence, Bavinck writes: "Comprehension excludes amazement and admiration. ... Where comprehension ceases, however, there remains room for knowledge and wonder. ... Faith turns into wonder; knowledge terminates in adoration; and their confession becomes a song of praise and thanksgiving."[29]

Mystery therefore, shapes the life of the knowing subject into a life of worship, and in that capacity it becomes a life of profound joy. Adoration, wonder, and praise are the joyous noetic experiences God ordains for his children, yet they are experiences open only to those who acknowledge mystery. To those who, like Adam, strive after a knowledge that is improper to creatures, there is a very different set of noetic experiences, experiences darkened by sin and its sorrowful consequences. That human beings do not comprehend anything is therefore no lamentable outcome for Bavinck. Comprehension would be improper to creatures, precisely because it precludes worship.

THE RELATION OF REVELATION AND
REASON: AN ADORABLE MYSTERY

The relation of revelation and reason in Bavinck, therefore, is best accounted for as a *mysterious* relationship.[30] Through divine revelation the creature comes to know the God who is unknowable in himself, yet precisely *how* this obtains remains a mystery to the knowing subject. It remains a mystery because this inner possibility of the knowledge of God is something that surpasses "knowing that" and "knowing

---

29. Bavinck, *Reformed Dogmatics*, 1:619, 621.

30. Here it must be acknowledged, however, that the relation of revelation and reason has a specific focus in Bavinck. Bavinck does not use the term "reason" as an inclusive term that embraces the activity of the mind generally. For the most part, "reason" in Bavinck refers to the discursive and inferential process of acquiring knowledge. Thus, the relation between revelation and reason, strictly speaking, concerns dogmatic science rather than the capacity of the mind to appropriate divine revelation. For a more extensive treatment of these issues, see also Pass, "Revelation and Reason in Herman Bavinck."

what" and penetrates to "knowing how." Because it penetrates to the knowing how, the relation of revelation and reason, strictly speaking, is something known only to the Creator. In this relation is comprehended mysteries which tower far above the reach of the human mind and touch on the secrets of God's majesty, and for Bavinck, it is good for creaturely knowers not to inquire into such mysteries but to adore them. To approach the relation of revelation and reason in such terms, as a paradox to be preserved rather than as a problem to be solved, does not, however, compromise the integrity of either term. It simply acknowledges mystery as proper to creaturely knowing. In fact, in circumscribing all our knowing, mystery preserves its doxological character. It both chastens our pretensions as knowers and by evoking wonder and adoration, guides all our knowing to its ultimate goal in praise. For Bavinck, mystery is the wellspring of worship. This is why Bavinck, like Luther and Calvin before him, regarded the paradox of the unknowable God revealing himself in such a way that he may be known by finite and even sinful creaturely knowers not as a contradiction that must be overcome or an antimony that must be resolved, but as a mystery to be adored.

WORKS CITED

Augustine. *Eighty-Three Different Questions.* Translated by David L. Mosher. Washington, DC: Catholic University of America Press, 1982.

Bavinck, Herman. *Kennis en leven.* Kampen: J. H. Kok, 1922.

———. *Modernisme en orthodoxie.* Kampen: J. H. Kok, 1911.

———. *The Philosophy of Revelation: The Stone Lectures for 1908–09, Princeton Theological Seminary.* Translated by Henry E. Dosker, Nicholas M. Steffens, and Geerhardus Vos. New York: Longmans, Green, 1909.

———. *Reformed Dogmatics.* Edited by John Bolt. 4 vols. Grand Rapids: Baker Academic, 2003-2008.

Calvin, John. *Institutes of the Christian Religion.* Edited by John T. McNeill. Translated by Ford Lewis Battles. 1536 ed. Philadelphia: Westminster, 1970.

Dillenberger, John, ed. *Martin Luther: Selections from His Writings.* Garden City, NY: Doubleday, 1961.

Eglinton, James. *Trinity and Organism: Towards a New Reading of Herman Bavinck's Organic Motif.* London: T&T Clark, 2012.

Grützmacher, Richard. "Die Theologie der Offenbarung und die Theologie des Geheimnisses." In *Modern-Positive Vorträge,* 38–39. Leipzig: Deichert, 1906.

Heideman, Eugene P. *The Relationship of Revelation and Reason in E. Brunner and H. Bavinck.* Assen: Van Gorcum, 1959.

McGrath, Alister E. *The Making of Modern German Christology 1750-1990.* Grand Rapids: Zondervan, 1994.

Muller, Richard A. "Calvinist Thomism Revisited: William Ames (1576-1633) and the Divine Ideas." In *From Rome to Zurich—Between Ignatius and Vermigli: Essays in Honor of John Patrick Donnelly, S.J.,* edited by Kathleen Comerford, Gary Jenkins, and W. J. Torrance Kirby, 103-20. Leiden: E. J. Brill, 2017.

Pass, Bruce. "Herman Bavinck and the Cogito." *RTR* 74, no. 1 (2015): 15-33.

———. "Herman Bavinck and the Problem of New Wine in Old Wineskins." *International Journal of Systematic Theology* 17, no. 4 (2015): 432-49.

——— "Revelation and Reason in Herman Bavinck." *WTJ* (forthcoming, 2018).

10

Discipleship on the Level of Thought

The Case of Karl Barth's Critique
of the Religion of Revelation

Chris Swann

The relationship between revelation and reason in Karl Barth's theology is vexed. On the one hand, Barth is frequently portrayed as being opposed to reason. His infamous *Nein!* to any form of natural theology is only the most notorious example of Barth's unyielding commitment to the primacy of revelation. Divine self-revelation in Christ is so magnified, its scope so all-encompassing, that no room appears left for human reason—or any form of human agency—to play a significant role in accessing truth about God or God's world. The late John Webster sums up this line of criticism: "the logic of Barth's thought ... make[s] serious consideration of human action superfluous, even, perhaps, a trespass on the sovereignty of grace."[1] On this view, humanity remains silent because God's self-revelation takes up all the airtime. On the other hand, Barth is sometimes censured not so much for his opposition to reason as for his imprisonment to it. Some critics have argued that Barth's thinking is corrupted by a kind of rationalism that tends toward abstraction and speculation. For instance, Alister McGrath scathingly lumps Barth in with the Enlightenment as well as with the more speculative strain of Reformed scholasticism.[2] According to McGrath, Barth veers away from the Bible's story of the concrete achievement of salvation in Christ toward a more rationalistic focus on overcoming our ignorance of

---

1. John Webster, *Barth's Ethics of Reconciliation* (Cambridge: Cambridge University Press, 1995), 1.

2. Alister E. McGrath, *Iustitia Dei: A History of the Christian Doctrine of Justification*, 2nd ed. (Cambridge: Cambridge University Press, 1998), 357–71.

God's true and perpetual stance toward us. As a result, Barth allegedly transposes the drama of redemption into an interior struggle to wake up to reality.

This chapter is conceived as a contribution toward the dismantling of this self-contradictory image of Barth as at once hostile to reason and taken hostage by it. Examinations of Barth's configuration of the relationship between revelation and reason typically (and understandably) focus on his explicit discussion of this nexus in *Church Dogmatics* I/1.[3] I follow a different route, however, taking Barth's critique of the religion of revelation in *Church Dogmatics* IV/2 §66.3 as a case study in his theological method. Eberhard Busch characterizes Barth's theology as "discipleship on the level of thought."[4] Beyond this there are also important formal, material, and methodological reasons for focusing on this subsection. These will emerge in due course as I examine its context, describe its content, and evaluate its contribution toward a reassessment of the relationship between revelation and reason in Barth.

THE CONTEXT OF BARTH'S CRITIQUE
OF THE RELIGION OF REVELATION

The context of Barth's critique of the religion of revelation in *CD* IV/2 §66.3 ought to be registered. To begin with, two aspects of the dogmatic location of Barth's critique of the religion of revelation in §66.3 highlight the way in which it is anchored in the overall theme of *CD* IV/2—namely, the exaltation of humanity in the person and work of Christ. First, in keeping with Barth's programmatic "correction" of the doctrine of election in *CD* II/2, his vision of humanity here is far more consistently governed by his Christology than in earlier treatments of the religion of revelation (e.g., in *CD* I/2 §17).[5] As Joseph Mangina highlights, Barth's thick description of the identity and action of the

---

3. See, e.g., Trevor Hart, "Revelation," in *The Cambridge Companion to Karl Barth*, ed. John Webster (Cambridge: Cambridge University Press, 2000), 37–55.

4. Eberhard Busch, *The Great Passion: An Introduction to Karl Barth's Theology*, trans. G. Bromiley (Grand Rapids: Eerdmans, 2010), 27.

5. Bruce McCormack has comprehensively documented the pivotal role of *CD* II/2 in Barth's thought; see Bruce L. McCormack, *Karl Barth's Critically Realistic Dialectical Theology: Its Genesis and Development, 1909–1936* (Oxford: Clarendon, 1995), especially chap. 11.

human covenant partner in CD IV "echoes" his description of Christ in a carefully circumscribed relation of analogy.[6] Since the exaltation of humanity is the focus of the Christology of IV/2, Barth's corresponding account of human agency in general and reason in particular therefore reaches something of a high-water mark at this point.

Second, in keeping with the "narrative turn" that George Hunsinger has detected in Barth's Christology, beginning with CD IV/1,[7] the critique of the religion of revelation in this context is not freestanding but an integral part of his wider project of thinking together the two natures, two states, and three offices of Christ. So CD IV/1 presents Christ's divine identity with the God of Israel in terms of his humiliation—"the way of the Son of God into the far country"—climaxing in his priestly work of self-offering on the cross, whereas CD IV/2 presents Christ's representative humanity in terms of his glorification (or lifting up), climaxing in his kingly designation as Lord and Christ in his resurrection. As a result, the critique of religion of revelation is presented as part of a sanctified response to and correspondence with God's revelation of true humanity in Christ.

The more immediate context of Barth's critique of the religion of revelation is also worth noting. Section 66.3 occurs within Barth's discipleship-shaped revision of the doctrine of sanctification. Significantly, Barth resists viewing sanctification as the continuous and progressive application of the accomplishment announced in justification. In place of this more or less traditional view of the relationship between justification and sanctification, Barth "actualises" both.[8] What this means is that he follows John Calvin's insistence that justification and sanctification are both "benefits" simultaneously bestowed on the basis of the believer's participation in Christ. But Barth radicalizes Calvin's

---

6. Joseph L. Mangina, "Bearing the Marks of Jesus: The Church in the Economy of Salvation in Barth and Hauerwas," *SJT* 52, no. 3 (1999): 273.

7. George Hunsinger, "Karl Barth and the Politics of Sectarian Protestantism: A Dialogue with John Howard Yoder," in *Disruptive Grace: Studies in the Theology of Karl Barth* (Grand Rapids: Eerdmans, 2000), 120n19.

8. His treatment of sanctification parallels the way Paul Nimmo argues that Barth "actualises" justification in "Reforming *simul iustus et peccator*: Karl Barth and the 'Actualisation' of the Doctrine of Justification," *Zeitschrift für dialektiche Theologie* Supplement Series 6 (2014): 91–104.

classic Reformed approach in two related ways. On the one hand, he draws together the accomplishment of reconciliation and its application in sanctification (and justification). Sanctification is therefore located properly and truly in Christ. Christ is *the* Holy One. As the electing God and the elect human being, Christ is uniquely sanctified in his incarnate person and his work. Holiness is never infused or imparted to Christians. It always remains "alien," belonging to Christ alone. At most, Christians become "creaturely reflections" of the singular holiness with which Christ stands over against them along with all others. On the other hand, where Calvin made participation depend on faith, Barth claims that *all* are representatively included in the definitive work of sanctification in Christ *de iure*. While not all human beings are "active participants" in Christ and his holiness, all are "passive participants."[9] By rights all may anticipate the full experience of sanctification as God's own treasured possession. Nevertheless, only those whom the Spirit awakens experience de facto and ahead of time the telos of all disclosed in Christ.[10]

The resulting "christological determination" of Barth's vision of sanctification does not so much render Christian holiness unnecessary or unreal as give it a distinctive shape—the shape of discipleship. As John Webster points out, "Sanctification is not only the holiness that the gospel *declares* but also the holiness that the gospel *commands*, to which the creaturely counterpart is *action*."[11] Barth develops a similar insight in §66.3, where he explicitly mobilizes the New Testament discipleship language.

---

9. George Hunsinger gives a good account of this "active participation" as opposed to "passive participation" in Christ; see "Sanctification," in *The Westminster Handbook to Karl Barth*, ed. R. E. Burnett (Louisville: Westminster John Knox, 2013), 193–98.

10. It is worth noting that in both of these revisions Barth draws extensively on biblical resources, along with his (in)famous "correction" to the doctrine of election from *CD* II/2. And so, even as he complicates and contests Calvin's picture, he regards himself as faithfully carrying forward its best insights—that is, those that are most biblically true and most transparently proclaim the glad tidings of the gospel.

11. John Webster, *Holiness* (London: SCM, 2003), 87.

"Follow me" is the substance of the call in the power of which Jesus
makes men his saints. ... The lifting up of themselves for which
He gives them freedom is not a movement which is formless, or
to which they themselves have to give the necessary form. It takes
place in a definite form and direction. Similarly, their looking to
Jesus as their Lord is not an idle gaping. It is a vision which stimu-
lates those to whom it is given to a definite action. The call issued
by Jesus is a call to discipleship.[12]

The definite action taken in responding to Christ's call to discipleship is the only action that truly corresponds to the recognition of Jesus
as Lord that sanctification requires. Sanctification only "lives" insofar
as it keeps Jesus central. The holiness of the Christian life exists only in
the presence of its living and active Lord. Sanctification is therefore discipleship shaped. In giving shape to sanctification like this, discipleship
displays in practice what Kimlyn Bender has dubbed the "christological
determination" of the church and Christian life in Barth's thought.[13]
Here as elsewhere, God's revelation in Christ rather than secular reason
(or any other factor) governs Barth's thinking—including his thinking
about the limitations of the religion of revelation. In this sense his critique of religion is "unreasonable." The religion of revelation comes in
for critique because of Christ, not Kant.

THE CONTENT OF BARTH'S CRITIQUE
OF THE RELIGION OF REVELATION

I have located Barth's critique of the religion of revelation in §66 in the
context of his actualized and therefore discipleship-shaped account
of sanctification. I must therefore turn now to describe its content.
In doing so the first thing to observe is that it appears at the climax of
Barth's extended treatment of the call to discipleship. Responsiveness
to Christ's call is the practical as well as theoretical occasion for the
critique of the religion of revelation Barth offers in this context. There
are four key aspects of this call as Barth presents it, each taking its cue

---

12. *CD* IV/2, §66.3, 533.
13. See Kimlyn J. Bender, *Karl Barth's Christological Ecclesiology* (Burlington, VT:
Ashgate, 2005).

from and developing Bonhoeffer's landmark treatment in *The Cost of Discipleship*.[14]

First, the call to discipleship manifests the sovereign freedom and authority of Christ: "The call to discipleship is the particular form of the summons by which Jesus discloses and reveals Himself ... in order to claim and sanctify [someone] as his own, and as His witness in the world."[15] Summarizing the call narratives of the Gospels as instances of Christ's commanding grace, Barth observes that Christ's call to follow him is issued to those he has chosen. In this way Christ's call attests his freedom and lordship in election. John Webster has parsed this in relation to the first call narrative in Mark's Gospel: Mark 1:14-20. According to Webster, the otherwise inexplicable responsiveness of the first disciples to Christ's summons is rendered coherent by the emphasis of the preceding narrative on the identity and mission of Jesus: "The one who calls is Jesus, the Father's beloved Son; his call is supremely authoritative and lawful because it is the call of the one who is in person the saving rule of God and who brings help and blessing to sinners."[16] This is the deepest reason why discipleship is the normative New Testament way in which people become "active participants" in their *de iure* sanctification in Christ. The call to discipleship points back to the one issuing it. And it sets people free because it manifests the Lord in whom humanity itself is representatively exalted to the freedom of covenant partnership with God.

Second, the call to discipleship functions as the concrete instance and expression of Christ's demand for faith. As such Barth insists that it is the personal, active, authoritative, and free means by which Christ binds people to himself, thus sanctifying them. As a result, it is

---

14. Barth does not disguise his admiration for Bonhoeffer's handling—and living—of the theme of discipleship (533-34): "Easily the best that has been written on this subject is to be found in *The Cost of Discipleship*, by Dietrich Bonhoeffer. ... In [this text] the matter has been handled with such depth and precision that I am almost tempted to reproduce [it] in an extended quotation. For I cannot hope to say anything better on the subject than what is said here by a man who, having written of discipleship, was ready to achieve it in his own life, and did in his own way achieve it even to the point of death."

15. *CD* IV/2, §66.3, 534.

16. John Webster, "Discipleship and Calling," *Scottish Bulletin of Evangelical Theology* 23, no. 2 (2005): 135-36.

always concrete and never general or abstract. It always enacts a person's union with and allegiance to Jesus: "in practice the command to follow Jesus is identical with the command to believe in Him."[17] At the climactic moment in the covenant history narrated in Scripture, Jesus calls people to discipleship. This call encounters people in freedom, cutting through all prior determinations. And in binding these people to Jesus himself, it sets them free. The restoration of the demoniac in Mark 5 could be seen as emblematic of this dynamic. After Jesus drives the legion of demons out of the man, his humanity is restored. He is set free. But this freedom finds expression not only in gratitude to Jesus but in the desire to accompany him. In this way, discipleship unites faith and obedience as the active form of trust in the living Lord.

The third aspect of the call to discipleship as Barth presents it is that it essentially demands a twofold turning—turning from oneself in self-denial and turning to Jesus in active, definite, and specific "simple obedience" to his command.[18] Discipleship cannot remain hanging in midair as a matter of private attitude change or inner reform, with no visible concrete manifestation in obedience. Barth clearly envisages something far more radical than gradualist step-wise progress in sanctification here. Viewed in terms of the call, discipleship is always a matter of changing sides, making a clean break, dying to the old self in order to live to God in Christ. As Barth goes on to say in §66.4, the biblical vision of sanctification involves a "falling out with oneself."[19] For the old self, condemned in Christ, is pitted against the new, called by and to Christ. This emphasis on the total rather than the partial in sanctification is the sense in which Hunsinger is right to identify an affinity with Luther's *simul iustus et peccator* in Barth's thinking. However, far from a pessimistic concession, Barth's vision of the intense conflict between a person's identity in Christ and their old identity as enacted in discipleship is the necessary outworking of their Spirit-bestowed experience of Christ's victory.

The fourth and final aspect of the call to discipleship that Barth singles out follows on from this picture of struggle as participation

---

17. *CD* IV/2, §66.3, 536.

18. *CD* IV/2, §66.3, 538–40.

19. *CD* IV/2, §66.4, 563.

in Christ's victory. For discipleship means freedom. The call is nothing short of the unveiling of God's kingdom, which confronts and opposes all other kingdoms, unmasking their false claims, disarming them, and triumphing over them so that people—and ultimately all of God's world—can be set free. In this light, the human response to the call of discipleship simply witnesses and corresponds to the prior and determinative "onslaught" of God's liberating kingdom in Christ: "In this onslaught it is a matter of God's destruction, accomplished in the existence of the Son of Man, of all the so-called 'given factors,' all the supposed natural orders, all the historical forces, which with the claim of absolute validity and worth have obtruded themselves as authorities—mythologically but very realistically described as 'gods'—between God and man, but also between man and his fellows; or rather which inventive man has himself obtruded between God and himself and himself and his fellows."[20] These idolatrous forces—themselves merely projections of self-deluded humanity—distort human life and relationships as they lay perverse claim to our worship and allegiance. But it is these forces that Christ's call exposes and from which it liberates people. As a result, the freedom granted disciples of Jesus with respect to these "given factors" becomes a tangible sign and public attestation of the triumph of God's kingdom, and a foretaste of the telos of creation. Discipleship unifies resistance to idolatry with the freedom for which humanity is restored.

Barth introduces his critique of the religion of revelation in the context of the discursive material elaborating on this fourth aspect of the call to discipleship. A number of biblical texts provide the backbone for this critique. But Barth's main focus is the Sermon on the Mount (Matt 5–7). Following the Sermon's sequence and logic, Barth sets religion alongside possessions, reputation, violence, and tribalism—that "impulsive intensity with which man allows himself to be enfolded by, and thinks that he himself should enfold" those connected by the physical bonds of family.[21] He identifies each of these among the "given factors" of the world. Such given factors are good gifts from God

20. *CD* IV/2, §66.3, 543.
21. *CD* IV/2, §66.3, 547–51.

that are elevated to that status of false gods, becoming disfigured and disfiguring versions of themselves in the process.

Two things are worth noting here—one methodological, the other material. Methodologically, Barth's critique of the religion of revelation is grounded in a kind of attention to Scripture in which human reason operates in its proper mode as reflection on the living Subject and Lord of revelation attested in the Bible. George Hunsinger identifies the way in which, informed and governed by his attentive, "post-critical" biblical exegesis, Barth elaborates the cognitive content of this exegesis "beyond the surface content of scripture as a way of understanding scripture's deeper conceptual implications and underlying unity."[22] Ultimately the living Lord Jesus himself gives coherence to the biblical witness for Barth. As a result, human reason operates properly when it listens to Jesus and heeds his living direction. Along with the rest of human life, reason must be shaped in response to the call to discipleship. In this sense, the critique of the religion of revelation here is both "unreasonable" and "reasonable." It is "unreasonable" in taking its cues from God's self-revelation in Christ. But at the same time it is thoroughly "reasonable," for responding to Christ in the power of the Spirit is the way anyone becomes aligned "with the way things really are," as Christopher Holmes puts it.[23]

Materially the target of Barth's critique here is not religion in general. When Barth explicitly turns to religion, he points out that "what Jesus has in mind was not the piety of heathen religion, but that of the Israelite religion of revelation."[24] Again, the Sermon on the Mount dictates this—specifically Matthew 6:1–18. There Jesus attacks the self-aggrandizing tendency of even the strictest Jewish piety. With utter perversity, the sinful tendency to practice our "piety before others in order to be seen by them" (Matt 6:1) transforms worship of the one true God into self-worship. As a result, Barth says, "the kingdom knocks

---

22. George Hunsinger, *How to Read Karl Barth: The Shape of His Theology* (Oxford: Oxford University Press, 1991), 5.

23. Christopher R. J. Holmes, "The Spirit and the Promise: On Becoming Aligned with the Way Things Really Are," in *Apocalyptic and the Future of Theology: With and beyond J. Louis Martyn*, eds. Douglas Harink and Joshua B. Davis (Eugene, OR: Cascade, 2012), 221–37.

24. *CD* IV/2, §66.3, 551.

at the door of the sanctuary of supreme human worship." The call to discipleship cuts across the tendency evident even in the religion of revelation to treat God's self-revelation as something that may be boasted of and paraded before others. Against this, the kingdom exerts itself in the concrete summons to disciples of Jesus to practice their piety in secret. This cuts off the air supply of self-worship, as it were.

Discipleship that attends to Christ's critique of the religion of revelation, therefore, does not merely recognize that revelation is essentially dynamic—for it is a miraculous "event" in which God remains the free Lord, establishing his liberating kingdom. It also attests this kingdom by striving to restrain our self-aggrandizing tendency to twist responsiveness to revelation into a performance. Ultimately, Barth contends, "This restraint will be a witness to the pious world with its continual need to publicize itself, and perhaps even to the secular world."[25] Tom Greggs therefore exaggerates only slightly when he claims to detect in moments like this a movement in Scripture "from religious to non-religious or anti-religious expression of God."[26] Barth's critique does join hands with the kind of antireligious Enlightenment critique of religion frequently associated with secular reason. But it goes beyond it. For it is an exposé of sin's ability to hijack even God's revelation itself, twisting it into an imprisoning idolatry. As such, discipleship takes the form (at least in part) of self-suspicion—especially when approaching revelation, that most sacred of gifts from God. And it does this in the name of freedom. As Ernst Käsemann puts it: "Discipleship of the Crucified leads necessarily to resistance to idolatry on every front. This resistance is and must be the most important mark of Christian Freedom."[27]

THE CONTRIBUTION OF BARTH'S CRITIQUE OF THE RELIGION OF REVELATION

I have located and described Barth's critique of the religion of revelation. The time has come to consider what it discloses about his method—and

25. CD IV/2, §66.3, 552.
26. Tom Greggs, *Theology against Religion: Constructive Dialogues with Bonhoeffer and Barth* (London: T&T Clark, 2011), 4.
27. Ernst Käsemann, "The Freedom to Resist Idolatry," in *Theologians in Their Own Words*, ed. D. R. Nelson, J. M. Moritz, and Ted Peters (Minneapolis: Fortress, 2013), 103–11.

particularly how he relates reason and revelation—and to briefly gesture toward some possible contemporary implications.

In terms of content, Barth's critique of the religion of revelation
exemplifies the way Christology functions to give it shape, overall and
in the details. Some have described this in terms of a basic "Chalcedonian pattern" in Barth's thought. Others dispute the felicity of this,
given Barth's revisionism with respect to the metaphysics of Chalcedon.[28] Potentially more helpful is W. Travis McMaken's account of the
"paradoxical identity" between divine and human freedom, which
structures Barth's thinking about a wide range of topics. To offer an
all-too-brief summary of McMaken's argument, Barth attempts to do
justice to the historicized, active "narrative unity" of divine and human
agencies beginning with Christology and moving out from there. He
does this by insisting on the closest possible unity (indeed *identity*) of
the two, while paradoxically refusing to compromise the integrity of
either by thinking of them as somehow reversible or interchangeable.[29]

As a whole, the vision of discipleship Barth develops in *CD* IV/2 §66.3
displays this pattern of "paradoxical identity." For Christ's lordly and
free activity in calling disciples is identified with the active human
response of freedom in such a paradoxical way as to uphold the integrity and noninterchangeability of both. The first two aspects of Barth's
recasting of sanctification in terms of discipleship emphasize God's
freedom. In the call of discipleship, Christ exerts his commanding
grace. He reveals himself as Lord at the same time as he personally
and actively binds people to himself. The third and fourth aspects of
Barth's presentation of discipleship emphasize the human freedom
this underwrites. For the call of discipleship effects a concrete break
with the past and an eschatologically oriented participation in the

---

28. George Hunsinger, "Karl Barth's Christology: Its Basic Chalcedonian
Character," in *Cambridge Companion to Karl Barth*, ed. Webster, 127–42; Bruce
McCormack, "Karl Barth's Historicized Christology: Just How 'Chalcedonian' Is
It?," in *Orthodox and Modern: Studies in the Theology of Karl Barth* (Grand Rapids:
Baker Academic, 2008), 201–34; Paul T. Nimmo, "Karl Barth and the *Concursus Dei*—A
Chalcedonianism Too Far?," *IJST* 9 (2007): 58–72.

29. W. Travis McMaken, "Definitive, Defective or Deft? Reassessing Barth's
Doctrine of Baptism in *Church Dogmatics* IV/4," *IJST* 17, no. 1 (2015): 89–114, especially 98–107.

kingdom onslaught against the idolatrous "given factors" that distort and imprison God's creation.

The "paradoxical identity" of divine and human agency is evident in the critique of the religion of revelation. On the one hand, Christ's call cuts across the "given factor" of biblical piety. Jesus claims human allegiance even over against adherence to the religion authorized in revelation. He is the Lord, calling his disciples to him with sovereign divine agency. In doing so, however, Christ's call engenders human agency. Such agency is expressed in radical self-suspicion—although this is merely the underside of a radical freedom. As we have seen, sin persistently perverts even the religion of revelation into a self-aggrandizing performance that enslaves us to publicizing ourselves. So the self-suspicion engendered by Christ's call does not only suffocate the idolatrous tendency to turn piety into a performance; it positively frees us for the struggle to worship and witness to Christ, loving others.[30]

In addition, in terms of method, Barth's critique of the religion of revelation exemplifies the kind of postcritical attention to Scripture that animates his mature theological project. Paul Dafydd Jones remarks: "Barth's interpretation of the New Testament plays a pivotal role in his mature christology."[31] And Hunsinger has shown how for Barth more generally this grounds a kind of "rationalism" in the sense of faith seeking understanding. The Christology emerging from the crucible of Barth's postcritical theological exegesis of Scripture determines the twin reality that there is "no knowledge without faith" at the same time as there is "no faith without knowledge."[32] According to Hunsinger, there is "no knowledge without faith" for Barth because theology must make constant recourse to its living center in Christ. It is therefore neither neutral nor speculative. Instead, it is "self-involving,

---

30. Although Barth does not develop the ethical side of this insight here, it is not too difficult to extrapolate his awareness of the way self-regard poisons even the religion of revelation. As Luther saw, self-regard sabotages the ethical impulse by installing the pernicious *incurvatus in se* at the heart of all attempts to love others. See, e.g., Michael Banner, *A Brief History of Christian Ethics* (Chichester, UK: Wiley-Blackwell, 2009), chap. 4.

31. Paul Dafydd Jones, "The Heart of the Matter: Karl Barth's Christological Exegesis," in *Thy Word Is Truth: Barth on Scripture*, ed. George Hunsinger (Grand Rapids: Eerdmans, 2012), 173.

32. Hunsinger, *How to Read Karl Barth*, 49–64.

self-grounded, self-commending, and self-interpreting."[33] In the terms
of this paper, it is an exercise in *discipleship*. That is, it is a matter of the
disciple's attentiveness to the call of Christ and of trusting obedience
to his concrete "direction" in his or her specific circumstances.

At the same time, Hunsinger establishes that there is "no faith without knowledge" for Barth. That is to say, Christian revelation is intrinsically rational—it inexorably presses toward reflection, articulation,
and explication. Jesus frees people for a kind of rational self-reflection,
the basic mode of which is partisan (indeed, *confessional*) attention to
the text of Scripture. As Hunsinger puts it, "the ordinary language of
faith, as displayed normatively in scripture" is for Barth "the direct and
fitting object" of theological reason.[34] While Barth was by no means
ignorant of the methods and results of biblical criticism, his approach
is postcritical. Hans Frei summarizes Barth's approach well: "you must
always be a theological exegete, and then in particular cases ... you
will find an *ad hoc* relation, maybe negative, but maybe positive, with
the always tentative results of historical criticism."[35] Such postcritical
attention to the biblical witness to revelation is the form of reason most
congruent with the free Lord at its center.

As I have shown, Barth's critique of the religion of revelation in
§66.3 is grounded in Matthew 6:1–18 and the living Lord attested there.
Far from being hostage to reason, Barth is clearly striving to make revelation programmatic for this critique. It is therefore an "unreasonable" critique in the sense that it takes its bearings from revelation,
not reason—in Kantian or any other mode. At the same time, reason
is exercised in response to Christ's call to discipleship. This is why it
results in radical self-suspicion. Although it is obviously differently
motivated from the revelation-denying hermeneutic of suspicion associated with Feuerbach and others, at this point Barth's critique of the
religion of revelation joins hands with and even outpaces it. According
to Barth, Christ calls on his disciples to embrace freedom from the idolatrous "given factors" as an extension of their self-denial. The old self

---

33. Hunsinger, *How to Read Karl Barth*, 54.

34. Hunsinger, *How to Read Karl Barth*, 55.

35. Hans W. Frei, "Scripture as Realistic Narrative: Karl Barth as Critic of
Historical Criticism," in *Thy Word Is Truth*, ed. Hunsinger, 55.

entangled with sin must be decisively broken with, and the new self in Christ embraced. To do so is thoroughly "reasonable." For it lines up with the reality disclosed in Christ. By the power of his Spirit, Christ frees his disciples to correspond to reality—becoming truly and fully themselves in covenant partnership and anticipating "the freedom of the glory of the children of God" (Rom 8:21), in which all creation is destined to share. Such is the rational freedom of discipleship.

Contemporary systematic theology and ethics would do well to learn from Barth's discipleship-shaped critique of the religion of revelation. In terms of the content of Barth's vision, we must learn to do justice first and foremost to the free lordship of Christ. Revelation rather than secular reason must set our agenda. But in doing this, we must uphold the "paradoxical identity" between the sovereign divine agency enacted in Christ's self-revealing call and the liberation of genuine human agency from the "given factors" that imprison it. In terms of Barth's method of attending to the witness of Scripture, we must learn that allegiance to the living Lord attested there cannot close us off in principle from the critical deliveries of reason—either in the form of biblical criticism or a Feuerbachian hermeneutic of suspicion. Although we need not put secular reason in first place, our discipleship may at points require us to work with and even go beyond it, dying to ourselves in self-criticism and other-centered freedom.

If we learn from Barth in these ways, contemporary Christian systematics and ethics may well come to answer the "somewhat inchoate" objection Michael Banner identifies in the supposed inability of "dogmatic ethics ... to maintain a Christian voice in the [public] arena of debate and discussion."[36] Following Barth, contemporary Christian systematics and ethics may not conform to the publicly accepted canons of secular reason—indeed, it may even explicitly question or contradict them from time to time. Yet in learning from Barth's vision of discipleship—and especially his critique of the religion of revelation—contemporary systematics and ethics may learn to display an appealing reasonableness in trenchant self-criticism and commitment to the good of others, without shifting from their center in God's revelation in Christ.

36. Michael Banner, *Christian Ethics and Contemporary Moral Problems* (Cambridge: Cambridge University Press, 1999), 26-27.

WORKS CITED

Banner, Michael. *A Brief History of Christian Ethics*. Chichester, UK: Wiley-Blackwell, 2009.

———. *Christian Ethics and Contemporary Moral Problems*. Cambridge: Cambridge University Press, 1999.

Barth, Karl. *Church Dogmatics* IV/2. Translated by Geoffrey W. Bromiley. Edited by Geoffrey W. Bromiley and T. F. Torrance. London: T&T Clark, 1958.

Bender, Kimlyn J. *Karl Barth's Christological Ecclesiology*. Burlington, VT: Ashgate, 2005.

Busch, Eberhard. *The Great Passion: An Introduction to Karl Barth's Theology*. Translated by G. Bromiley. Kindle ed. Grand Rapids: Eerdmans, 2004.

Frei, Hans W. "Scripture as Realistic Narrative: Karl Barth as Critic of Historical Criticism." In *Thy Word Is Truth: Barth on Scripture*, edited by George Hunsinger, 49–59. Grand Rapids: Eerdmans, 2012.

Greggs, Tom. *Theology against Religion: Constructive Dialogues with Bonhoeffer and Barth*. London: T&T Clark, 2011.

Hart, Trevor. "Revelation." In *The Cambridge Companion to Karl Barth*, edited by John Webster, 37–55. Cambridge: Cambridge University Press, 2000.

Holmes, Christopher R. J. "The Spirit and the Promise: On Becoming Aligned with the Way Things Really Are." In *Apocalyptic and the Future of Theology: With and beyond J. Louis Martyn*, edited by Douglas Harink and Joshua B. Davis, 221–37. Eugene, OR: Cascade, 2012.

Hunsinger, George. *How to Read Karl Barth: The Shape of His Theology*. Oxford: Oxford University Press, 1991.

———. "Karl Barth and the Politics of Sectarian Protestantism: A Dialogue with John Howard Yoder." In *Disruptive Grace: Studies in the Theology of Karl Barth*, 114–28. Grand Rapids: Eerdmans, 2000.

———. "Karl Barth's Christology: Its Basic Chalcedonian Character." In *The Cambridge Companion to Karl Barth*, edited by John Webster, 127–42. Cambridge: Cambridge University Press, 2000.

———. "Sanctification." In *The Westminster Handbook to Karl Barth*, edited by Richard E. Burnett, 193–98. Louisville: Westminster John Knox, 2013.

Jones, Paul Dafydd. "The Heart of the Matter: Karl Barth's Christological Exegesis." In *Thy Word Is Truth: Barth on Scripture*, edited by George Hunsinger, 173–95. Grand Rapids: Eerdmans, 2012.

Käsemann, Ernst. "The Freedom to Resist Idolatry." In *Theologians in Their Own Words*, edited by Derek R. Nelson, Joshua M. Moritz, and Ted Peters, 103–11. Minneapolis: Fortress, 2013.

Mangina, Joseph L. "Bearing the Marks of Jesus: The Church in the Economy of Salvation in Barth and Hauerwas." *SJT* 52, no. 3 (1999): 269–305.

McCormack, Bruce L. *Karl Barth's Critically Realistic Dialectical Theology: Its Genesis and Development, 1909–1936*. Oxford: Clarendon, 1995.

———. "Karl Barth's Historicized Christology: Just How 'Chalcedonian' Is It?" In *Orthodox and Modern: Studies in the Theology of Karl Barth*, 201–34. Grand Rapids: Baker Academic, 2008.

McGrath, Alister E. *Iustitia Dei: A History of the Christian Doctrine of Justification*. 2nd ed. Cambridge: Cambridge University Press, 1998.

McMaken, W. Travis. "Definitive, Defective or Deft? Reassessing Barth's Doctrine of Baptism in Church Dogmatics IV/4." *IJST* 17, no. 1 (2015): 89–114.

Nimmo, Paul T. "Karl Barth and the *Concursus Dei*—A Chalcedonianism Too Far?" *IJST* 9 (2007): 58–72.

———. "Reforming *simul iustus et peccator*: Karl Barth and the 'Actualisation' of the Doctrine of Justification." *Zeitschrift für dialektiche Theologie* Supplement Series 6 (2014): 91–104.

Webster, John. *Barth's Ethics of Reconciliation*. Cambridge: Cambridge University Press, 1995.

———. "Discipleship and Calling." *Scottish Bulletin of Evangelical Theology* 23, no. 2 (2005): 133–47.

———. *Holiness*. London: SCM, 2003.

11

Revelation and Reason

A Christological Reflection

John McClean

This chapter defends an account of reason consistent with that held by the Reformed orthodox thinkers of the seventeenth century and their successors such as Herman Bavinck. I will give a brief outline of this position and then turn to the main point of the discussion—some christological reasons for holding this view.

Sebastian Rehnman observes that John Owen is neither "a straightforward evidentialist nor a straightforward fideist." For Owen, faith comes from God's grace and is based on revelation or supernatural evidence. In that sense he is fideist. He writes that "we believe the Scripture to be the word of God with divine faith for its own sake only." He explains that Christian faith rests on the authority and truthfulness of God's revelation, and these features are grasped by faith, or by our minds in the exercise of faith. He asserts that "'Thus saith the Lord' is the reason why we ought to believe, and why we do so."[1] This sounds to be straightforward fideism. Yet Owen also holds that Christian faith ought to have rational or cognitive support. So he is in a certain way an evidentialist. He says that "there are sundry cogent arguments, which are taken from external considerations of the Scripture, that evince it on rational grounds to be from God ... motives of credibility, or effectual persuasives to account and esteem it to be the word of God."[2] These, he says, "may in their proper place be insisted on," and they provide

---

1. John Owen, *The Reason of Faith*, ed. William H. Goold, vol. 4 of *The Works of John Owen* (London: Johnstone & Hunter, 1850–1855 [1677]), 70.
2. Owen, *Reason of Faith*, 20.

defenses against attacks on Scripture and may be "inducements into believing, or concomitant means of strengthening faith in them that do believe."[3] For Owen, "no one can come to faith merely by rational evidence, but rational evidence contributes significantly to whether or not one has faith."[4]

Francis Turretin, probably the preeminent expositor of the position of Reformed orthodox on this question, similarly carefully prescribes the place of reason for theology.[5] He claims that the Reformed position holds "a middle ground" neither confounding theology with philosophy "as the parts of a whole" nor setting them against each other.[6] Reason has a role in theology, and so philosophy may aid theology but must not be viewed as part of theology. He carefully distinguishes between revelation as the "foundation of faith" and reason as the "instrument of faith."[7] Reason has "a ministerial and organic relation" to theology, and faith should use reason "as an instrument of application and mode of knowledge."[8] It has a role to "illustrate" and "collate" scriptural passages or arguments, to draw out "inferences," and to help assess whether various positions agree or disagree with what has been revealed.[9] He holds that reason, considered abstractly, is in perfect harmony with revelation, but that following the fall reason is corrupt, and unregenerate reason cannot grasp the truths of faith, and in fact it can be properly employed in reference of truths about God only by the regenerate.[10]

---

3. Owen, *Reason of Faith*, 71.

4. Sebastian Rehnman, "Graced Response: John Owen on Faith and Reason," *Neue Zeitschrift Für Systematische Theologie Und Religionsphilosophie* 53, no. 4 (2011): 448.

5. Sebastian Rehnman, "Alleged Rationalism: Francis Turretin on Reason," *CTJ* 37, no. 2 (November 2002): 259, suggests that he probably gives "the best statement" about the place of reason in theology in the Reformed orthodox.

6. Francis Turretin, *Institutes of Elenctic Theology* (Phillipsburg, NJ: P&R, 1992–1997), 1:13.2. See Stephen J. Grabill, "Natural Law and the Noetic Effects of Sin: The Faculty of Reason in Francis Turretin's Theological Anthropology," *WTJ* 67, no. 2 (September 2005): 261–79.

7. Turretin, *Institutes of Elenctic Theology*, 1:8.7.

8. Turretin, *Institutes of Elenctic Theology*, 1:8.6, 12.15.

9. Turretin, *Institutes of Elenctic Theology*, 1:8.3.

10. Turretin, *Institutes of Elenctic Theology*, 1:8.4, 10.1. For discussion of the similar position held by Petrus van Mastricht and noting the views of Owen and Turretin, see Andrew Leslie, "The Reformation a Century Later: Did the Reformation Get Lost Two Generations Later?," in *Celebrating the Reformation, Its*

This approach insists both that revelation must rule reason and that reason must be put to use to defend, analyze, and apply revelation. It places a tighter limitation on natural theology than did mainstream medieval theology. As Richard Muller explains, the Reformation applied its soteriology to its view of reason more fully than had medieval theology. "Whereas the medieval doctors had assumed that the fall affected primarily the will and its affections and not the reason, the Reformers assumed also the fallenness of the rational faculty."[11] This means that for whatever extent the Reformed orthodox allow a natural theology, they will set stricter limits compared to the mainstream medieval view, which held that sin touches the will and desires more than cognition.

As a theological position that asserts the primacy of Scripture, this position has been based in biblical revelation and grounded in theological reason. After a couple of necessary definitions, I will show how a classic Christology, developed from Scripture, supports the Reformed position. My discussion comes under two simple headings: "revelation in Christ chastens reason" and "revelation in Christ establishes reason"; under each heading I explore several complementary aspects of revelation in Christ as they cast light on the place of reason.

DEFINING REASON AND REVELATION

This discussion does not need to settle on a precise view of reason. It will be enough to take reason as the capacity to self-consciously understand and to apply such understanding to respond appropriately to ourselves and our environment. To be rational is to be someone who is accountable to have reasons for what one understands and what one does, and who is responsible for and able to test those reasons. Rationality cannot be reduced to a particular set of rules, not least because one element of rational thought is the task of determining which set of rules are best applied for a particular case.[12] Reasoning is not strictly separable

---

Legacy and Continuing Relevance, ed. Mark D. Thompson, C. Bale, and Ed Loane (London: Apollos, 2017), 297–304.

11. Richard A. Muller, *Post-Reformation Reformed Dogmatics: The Rise and Development of Reformed Orthodoxy, ca. 1520 to ca. 1725*, vol. 3, *The Divine Essence and Attributes* (Grand Rapids: Baker, 2002), 108.

12. See Harold I. Brown, "Rationality," in *The Oxford Companion to Philosophy*, 2nd ed., ed. Ted Honderich (Oxford: Oxford University Press, 2005), www.oxford

from other human activities such as trusting or feeling, even though it is somewhat distinguishable from them.[13]

Revelation is God's work to bring people to know him. It consists of all that God does that he intends to terminate in human knowledge of himself. It includes both general and special revelation, namely, the objective revelation of God in prophetic words, theophanies, and deeds, all three as they occur climactically in Christ and the apostolic gospel and the teachings that come from him and have him as their content. It includes the written Scriptures, which flow from this revelatory work and the work of the Spirit, by which believers receive objective revelation and so come to enjoy communion with God. For this discussion I will consider revelation in Christ. I will do so because while Christ is not the only locus of revelation, he is the focus of revelation and the substance of Christian revelation. If we are going to think *in concreto* about revelation and reason, then to think in close engagement with Christology is appropriate.

REVELATION IN CHRIST CHASTENS REASON

The Incarnation Demonstrates the Failure of Human Resources, Including Rational Resources

Why the incarnation? Anselm's answer is that only in the incarnation could the debt of honor due to God be repaid in such a way that humanity could be redeemed and not destroyed.[14] That is, the redemption of humanity requires someone who can make a sufficient payment to God, "but the obligation rests with man, and no one else, to make the payment."[15] His solution, or rather God's solution, is that the God-Man pays

---

reference.com.ezproxy.sl.nsw.gov.au/view/10.1093/acref/9780199264797.001.0001/acref-9780199264797-e-2127.

13. Alan G. Padgett, "Faith Seeking Understanding: Collegiality and Difference in Theology and Philosophy," in *Faith and Reason: Three Views*, ed. S. Wilkens (Downers Grove, IL: InterVarsity, 2014), 89–91. Donald G. Bloesch, *A Theology of Word and Spirit: Authority and Method in Theology* (Downers Grove, IL: InterVarsity, 2005), 37, defines reason as "any human cognitive faculty or capability" and so includes "mystical intuition" as much as "philosophical insight and intellectual comprehension." My usage is somewhat tighter than that.

14. Anselm, *Cur Deus Homo* 2.5-15, in *The Major Works: Anselm of Canterbury*, ed. Brian Davies and Gillian R. Evans (Oxford: Oxford University Press, 1998), 318-25.

15. Anselm, *Cur Deus Homo* 2.6, p. 320.

the price to restores God's honor. So, God comes from beyond and saves from within. The incarnation through virgin conception underscores the inadequacy of all human resources for our communion with God. Redemption requires a whole new start, the second Adam, who comes from outside us to be one of us. God does not build on what we are able to do. No, the incarnation is God doing for us what we are *unable* to do for ourselves.

What Anselm argued with regard to our debt paid in our stead can also be said about the gift of revelation. Knowledge of God had to be provided to us, mediated by and accommodated to our fallen humanity, but cannot arise from our fallen state. The very fact of the incarnation underlines the failure of our resources.

HUMANITY UNDERSTOOD IN THE LIGHT OF REDEMPTION IN CHRIST IS SHOWN TO NOT KNOW GOD

Consider the Pauline theme that people do "not know God" (Gal 4:8; 1 Thess 4:5; 2 Thess 1:8). Romans 1:21-25 is a dark portrait of humanity suppressing the knowledge of God, refusing to glorify or thank him and turning to idolatry. Paul spells out the implications of human thought and knowledge: they "became futile in their thinking, and their senseless minds were darkened," they became "fools" and "exchanged the truth about God for a lie" (1:21, 22, 25). Paul describes gentiles "in the futility of their minds ... darkened in their understanding, alienated from the life of God because of their ignorance and hardness of heart" (Eph 4:17-18).

This description includes Jews as much as gentiles. A key argument in Romans is that Jews as much as gentiles are not only guilty but also fail to know God. In Romans 2 Paul takes Israel's claims to know and turns them back as accusations. The claims in view are all about knowledge—to "know his will and determine what is best" from the law, to be "a guide to the blind, a light to those who are in darkness, a corrector of the foolish, a teacher of children, having in the law the embodiment of knowledge and truth" (2:18-19). Paul challenges his Jewish interlocutor: "You, then, that teach others, will you not teach yourself? While you preach against stealing, do you steal? You that forbid adultery, do you commit adultery? You that abhor idols, do you rob temples? You that boast in the law, do you dishonor God by breaking the law?" (Rom 2:21-23). He is pointing to moral failures that belie the claim to *know* God and his will. So the series of texts in Romans 3:10-18 are applied to Jews and gentiles: "There is no one who is righteous ... no one who has understanding ... no one who seeks God. ... There is no fear of God before their eyes" (3:11, 18).[16] Paul takes the prophetic condemnations of the blindness of idolatry and totalizes them both, applying them to all Jews and gentiles, and radicalizes them, leaving not a hint of true knowledge of God.

How did Paul come to this conviction? I suggest that it was along the same path by which he came to the conviction that no one could be justified apart from Christ. That the crucified Jesus of Nazareth was the risen Messiah showed that salvation requires the death of the Messiah; and if that was so, then no one was able to justify themselves. In the same way, knowledge of God comes only from the revelation of God in Christ. Just as Israel cannot justify itself, so it is blind and idolatrous. He must have first discovered this in himself when he was struck blind by his encounter with Christ before he had his eyes opened and was sent to bring God's name to the gentiles and Israel (Acts 9:15). He told Agrippa that after a vision of "light from heaven, brighter than the sun" his task was to open eyes and turn people "from darkness to light" (26:13, 18).[17] Paul realized, in light of revelation in Christ, that human reason, our capacity to know, understand, and interpret, does not establish us in the knowledge of God.

THE THEOLOGY OF THE CROSS SHOWS THE FAILURE OF HUMAN REASON

I turn, then, to Martin Luther, who perhaps more than anyone grasped the implication of this Pauline theme and the christological focus of

---

16. This verdict is repeated in Rom 11:8-10, where Paul applies other Old Testament texts (Isa 29:10; Deut 29:4; Ps 69:22-23 [LXX]). Even when Moses is read there is a veil over the minds of Israel because their minds are hardened (2 Cor 3:13-15).

17. See further the discussion of the gospel itself as a "revelation" in Klyne Snodgrass, "The Gospel in Romans: A Theology of Revelation," in *Gospel in Paul: Studies on Corinthians, Galatians and Romans for Richard N. Longenecker* (Sheffield: Sheffield Academic, 1994), 288-314.

revelation. His "theology of the cross" insisted that God's wisdom and power contradict human norms of wisdom and power.[18] A theologian of glory assumes that God's ways fit our expectations and that his wisdom and power impress us, on our terms. Luther objects that such a person "does not deserve to be called a theologian."[19] In contrast, a theologian of the cross has discovered, by God's grace, that God saves through the suffering and death of Christ on the cross. The theology of the cross has soteriological roots and is intimately linked to Luther's view of justification by faith. It builds from the fact that God justifies the ungodly (Rom 4:5). Righteousness *coram Deo* (before God) subverts our presumed understanding of righteousness *coram hominibus* (before man).

Robert Kolb describes Luther's theology as "a new conceptual framework for thinking about God and the human creature."[20] Luther applied this trenchantly to the claims of reason, declaring it a "blind, wild fool," "the devil's whore," and "the devil's bride." He wrote that "faith slaughters reason" since reason demands that God comply with its standards and expectations and that God refuses to do so. Gerhard Forde summarizes: "Theologians of glory operate on the assumption that creation and history are transparent to the human intellect, that one can see through what is made and what happens so as to peer into the 'invisible things of God.'"[21] The theology of the cross says that reason not only fails to grasp revelation, but it refuses and opposes revelation in Christ. It sets up its own categories and standards and demands that God's truth should fit those to be counted as true. But God will not comply.

---

18. See Robert Kolb, "Luther in an Age of Confessionalization," in *The Cambridge Companion to Martin Luther*, ed. Donald K. McKim (Cambridge: Cambridge University Press, 2003), 223. Alister E. McGrath, *The Genesis of Doctrine: A Study in the Foundation of Doctrinal Criticism* (Grand Rapids: Eerdmans, 1997), 25, appeals to Luther's theology of the cross to argue that Christian theology should know that "experience and reality are, at least potentially, to be radically opposed."

19. Martin Luther, *Heidelberg Disputation* 19; *LW* 31:40.

20. Robert Kolb, "Luther on the Theology of the Cross," *Lutheran Quarterly* 16, no. 1 (2002): 443-44.

21. Gerhard Forde, *On Being a Theologian of the Cross: Reflections on Luther's Heidelberg Disputation, 1518* (Grand Rapids: Eerdmans, 1997), 72-73.

THE CHALCEDONIAN FORMULATION IS NOT RATIONALLY COMPREHENSIBLE

The content of orthodox Christology also demonstrates the inability of reason to comprehend revelation. John Hick sparked much of the modern debate about the rationality of the incarnation with his words in *The Myth of God Incarnate*, "to say, without explanation, that the historical Jesus of Nazareth was also God is as devoid of meaning as to say that this circle drawn with a pencil on paper is also a square."[22] James Anderson has argued persuasively that classical Christology is not irrational but is genuinely paradoxical; its affirmations appear to be logically contradictory, and every attempt to show that there is no real contradiction ends up moving away from classical Christology.[23] Attempts to remove such paradoxes to produce a rationally consistent Christology always fall short of Chalcedonian orthodoxy.[24]

---

22. John Hick, "Jesus and the World Religions," in *The Myth of God Incarnate* (London: SCM, 1977), 178. Hick has since clarified that he recognizes that the concepts of humanity and deity are so open that it is possible to "adjust them in relation to each other to make a literal understanding of the incarnation possible." His question is "whether it is possible to do so in a way that satisfies the religious concerns which give point to the doctrine." John Hick, *The Metaphor of God Incarnate: Christology in a Pluralistic Age*, 2nd ed. (Louisville: Westminster John Knox, 2006), 4.

23. James Anderson, *Paradox in Christian Theology: An Analysis of Its Presence, Character, and Epistemic Status* (London: Paternoster, 2007), 60–106.

24. Anderson reviews several recent attempts to produce a rationally coherent Christology and shows that they fail to retain all the important elements of classical orthodoxy. We could add to his discussion William Lane Craig's "modified Apollinarianism," which seeks to provide a rational coherence for Christology by holding that "the Logos already possessed in His pre-incarnate state all the properties necessary for being a human self," apart from possessing a body. So, "in Christ the one self-conscious subject who is the Logos possessed divine and human natures which were both complete." See J. P. Moreland and William L. Craig, *Philosophical Foundations for a Christian Worldview* (Downers Grove, IL: InterVarsity, 2003), 606–13, and William L. Craig "The Coherence of the Incarnation," *Ankara Üniversitesi İlahiyat Fakültesi Dergisi* 50, no. 2 (2009): 195, http://dergiler.ankara.edu.tr/dergiler/37/1146/13444.pdf. See also the critique by Richard A. Ostella, "The Revived Apollinarianism of Moreland and Craig in *Philosophical Foundations for a Christian Worldview* (IVP, 2003)," presented to Evangelical Theological Society Midwest, March 28, 2014, available at www.westminsterreformedchurch.org/True%20Humanity%20and%20Deity%20of%20Christ/ETS2014FinalDraft.Apollinarianism .pdf. Richard Swinburne, "The Coherence of the Chalcedonian Definition of the Incarnation," in *The Metaphysics of the Incarnation*, ed. Anna Marmodoro and Jonathan Hill (Oxford: Oxford University Press, 2011), 153–67, suggests a similar solution, appealing to Freud's view that "a person can have two systems of belief

Norman Geisler and W. D. Watkins seem at first glance to hold a position that rebuts Anderson's claim. They argue that it "would be contradictory to affirm of any person either of the following at the same time and in the same sense: one person yet two persons, or one nature yet two natures," but it is not contradictory "to affirm one person in two natures" because, by distinguishing between persons and natures, classic Christology avoids claiming that one entity is both human and divine at the same time in the same respect.[25] Having argued that the claim is rationally coherent, they add the caveat that "we are unable to conceive ... how ... the two natures are united in the one person of Christ. ... We can ... know that to affirm two natures in one person is not contradictory. But none of these contentions entail that we know exactly how the natures are conjoined."[26] "The incarnation is not fully comprehensible nor fully explainable by finite beings."[27] This is precisely the way in which the material claims of classical Christology chasten reason. Reason seeks to understand and explain, yet it cannot understand or explain Christ.

Anderson argues for a "rational affirmation of paradoxical theology" because we should "anticipate paradox in some of our theological knowledge" since God is "incomprehensible."[28] We expect true statements about God and his relation to humanity to contain apparent contradictions. Anderson argues that the paradoxes in certain Christian doctrines, "rather than threatening the rationality of Christian belief in these doctrines, actually helps to explain their rationality."[29]

In a similar vein, Sarah Coakley identifies an "oddness" in the Chalcedonian definition that she compares to a riddle in which "we express

---

to some extent independent of each other," though Swinburne also refers to his proposal as a "two minds" view.

25. Norman L. Geisler and W. D. Watkins, "The Incarnation and Logic: Their Compatibility Defended," *Trinity Journal* 6 (1985): 194.

26. Geisler and Watkins, "Incarnation and Logic," 195.

27. Geisler and Watkins, "Incarnation and Logic," 196.

28. Anderson, *Paradox in Christian Theology*, 218, 237–41.

29. Anderson, *Paradox in Christian Theology*, 242. He asserts that paradox should be allowed in Christian thought only when the elements of the paradox are warranted by God's revelation and cannot be understood nonparadoxically, and "if the appearance of contradiction can be plausibly attributed to divine incomprehensibility," 266.

and do not express a thing, see and do not see a thing."[30] She argues
that while Chalcedon intends to be referential and to describe "the
ontological reality" of the incarnation, it is deliberately not striving for
precision of language and in that sense is not "literal":[31] "It does not ...
intend to provide a full systematic account of Christology, and even less
a complete and precise metaphysics of Christ's makeup. Rather, it sets
a 'boundary' on what can, and cannot, be said ... and then leaves us at
that 'boundary,' understood as the place now to which those salvific
acts must be brought to avoid doctrinal error, but without any suppo-
sition that this linguistic regulation thereby *explains* or *grasps* the reality towards which it points."[32] Anderson and Coakely both affirm that
christological formulations show the incapacity of reason to grasp the
revelation of God in Christ. Yet neither of them suggest that Christology
is irrational. That directs us to the second element of the discussion.
Revelation in Christ chastens reason but then establishes it.

REVELATION IN CHRIST ESTABLISHES REASON

CHRIST IS THE INCARNATE LOGOS

The incarnation is the act in which the Logos takes on human nature.
The term "Logos," so prominent in early christological discussion,
comes from John's prologue, with its clear allusion to Genesis 1. The title
alludes to the creative word and wisdom of God portrayed in the Old
Testament (Pss 33:6, 9; 148:5; Prov 3:19; 8:30; Jer 10:12; Heb 11:3; 2 Pet 3:5).[33]

The connection between God's creative wisdom and the title of Logos
was developed in the exegesis of Philo of Alexandria. It is not that Philo
provides the most significant background to John's prologue, but he
provides an important precursor.[34] For Philo, *logos* named God's own

---

30. Sarah Coakley, "What Chalcedon Solved and Didn't Solve," in *The Incarnation:
An Interdisciplinary Symposium on the Incarnation of the Son of God*, ed. Stephen T.
Davis, Daniel Kendall, and Gerald O'Collins (Oxford: Oxford University Press, 2002),
152–56; quote from Cora Diamond, *The Realistic Spirit: Wittgenstein, Philosophy, and
the Mind* (Cambridge, MA: MIT Press, 1995), 267.

31. Coakley, "What Chalcedon Solved and Didn't Solve," 156–59.

32. Coakley, "What Chalcedon Solved and Didn't Solve," 161.

33. Ben Witherington III, *John's Wisdom: A Commentary on the Fourth Gospel*
(Louisville: Westminster John Knox, 1995), 52.

34. Craig A. Evans, *Word and Glory: On the Exegetical and Theological Background*

rationality, which was the template for the cosmos and also for the human mind. Because the human mind, the cosmos, and God all participated in the same *logos*, then it was possible for humans to understand the world and God, and this is the ontological foundation of every discipline and means that all knowledge is referred, finally, to God. The *logos* was inherently rational, so to say that God reveals himself by his word is not only to refer to God's self-expression or his covenantal word of promise but also to mean that God's self revelation is rational. Jiří Hoblík summarizes Philo's view: "The relationship between God and humankind is thus more than a relationship between creator and creation, for they are brought together by the agency of the Logos and the spirit, and their relationship is governed by the analogy between divine and human reason, which can be talked about only on the basis of the intermediary level that is rational faculty and that unconditional refers to its Creator."[35]

Ben Witherington III suggests that one of the reasons John chose the title Logos is that it unites creation and salvation history.[36] It does so very explicitly by affirming the place of created human reason. The divine Logos, who is the source of all human enlightenment, has become flesh and entered into the human situation (John 1:1–14). Philo could never have affirmed this, but his thought provided the conceptual vocabulary that enabled John to not only affirm that the Creator has come to be a creature but that the one who has made the world understandable and has given humanity understanding is the agent of redemptive revelation in the incarnation.

The Chalcedonian Rejection of Apollinarianism Affirms the Place of Human Reason

The possibility of human reason knowing God is affirmed by classic Christology in its rejection of Apollinarianism. Apollinarius of Laodicea (ca. 310–ca. 390) held that the Logos (and not human nature) provides the mind of Christ. So the debate his thought engendered was

---

of John's Prologue (Sheffield: JSOT Press, 1993), 100–114; David T. Runia, *Philo in Early Christian Literature: A Survey* (Minneapolis: Fortress, 1993), 83.

35. Jiří Hoblík, "The Holy Logos in the Writings of Philo of Alexandria," *Communio Viatorum* 56, no. 3 (2014): 260.

36. Witherington, *John's Wisdom*, 53.

concerned with the relationship between the Logos and human mind and rationality.[37] In Apollinarius' account of salvation, "God predominates over Christ's human flesh; God acts in Christ as a single, divine agent, and the flesh is ... a passive instrument of the divine activity."[38] The result was that Christ is the mediator as a *mean*, a *tertium quid* neither wholly human nor wholly God but a mixture of God and humanity. Frances Young explains that "it is this new creation, the divine mixture, God and flesh perfected in one nature, that bring divinization and salvation."[39]

Apollinarius took this view because of his understanding of the makeup of a human person and also perhaps because of his view of Christ's heavenly body.[40] His Christology was also shaped by his view of sin as the triumph of the desires of the flesh over the mind.[41] Redemption required that the rule of desire be reversed; he writes that "what was needed was unchangeable intellect that did not fall under the domination of the flesh."[42] This is to claim that salvation is grounded in the divine Word and not the human mind. For him, Christ is not the God-man who works for our salvation from the inside, but Christ remains outside, in the likeness of humanity but not consubstantial with humanity. This view flows on to his theology of grace. As the Word divinizes flesh, so we come to salvation by divinization, which means the replacement and destruction of the human mind. True knowledge of God, in the Apollinarian scheme, must bypass human reason.[43]

The reply of Gregory of Nazianzus was that Christ must have a human mind if he is to save us with our minds: "If anyone has put his

---

37. Robert L. Calhoun, *Scripture, Creed, Theology: Lectures on the History of Christian Doctrine in the First Centuries* (Eugene, OR: Cascade, 2011), 279–84.

38. Christopher A. Beeley, "The Early Christological Controversy: Apollinarius, Diodore, and Gregory Nazianzen," *Vigiliae Christianae* 65, no. 4 (2011): 382.

39. Frances M. Young and Andrew Teal, *From Nicaea to Chalcedon: A Guide to the Literature and Its Background*, 2nd ed. (London: SCM, 1983), 251.

40. Lewis Ayres, "Shine, Jesus, Shine: On Locating Apollinarianism," *Studia Patristica* 40 (2006): 143–58.

41. Beeley, "Early Christological Controversy," 384.

42. Apollinarius, *Fragment 76*, quoted in Beeley, "Early Christological Controversy," 385.

43. See C. FitzSimons Allison, *The Cruelty of Heresy: An Affirmation of Christian Orthodoxy* (Harrisburg, PA: Morehouse, 1994), 105–18.

trust in Him as a Man without a human mind, he is really bereft of mind, and quite unworthy of salvation. For *that which He has not assumed He has not healed; but that which is united to His Godhead is also saved*. ... But if He has a soul, and yet is without a mind, how is He man, for man is not a mindless animal?"[44] The Council of Chalcedon reached a sagacious and elegant solution to the problem of Christ and the human mind. It affirmed that the Lord Jesus Christ is "truly God and truly man, consisting also of a reasonable [or rational] soul and body." To affirm Christ's "rational soul" is crucial, for that is a soul that operates with human reason. Jesus is "of one substance with us as regards his manhood" and "like us in all respects, apart from sin." He has all the human capacities, to suffer and to reason as a human. So, in the series of privatives, the formula states that he has two natures "without confusion, without change, without division, without separation ... the characteristics of each nature being preserved."

Developments after Chalcedon helped to further clarify the relationship of humanity and divinity in the hypostatic union.[45] Leontius of Jerusalem (ca. 485–ca. 543), followed by John of Damascus (ca. 660–ca. 750), described Christ's humanity as anhypostatic and enhypostasic. That is, Christ is without a human personal center (avoiding the Nestorian view that there are two persons in Christ). Alone, this denial leaves us wondering about the true humanity in the incarnation. What do we make of a human who does not have a personal center? The positive statement of *enhypostasia* affirms that the humanity of Jesus has personal existence in union with the person of the Son.[46]

---

44. Epistle 51 of St. Gregory the Theologian, "To Cledonius, against Apollinarius," www.monachos.net/content/patristics/texts/158-gregory-to-cledonius.

45. These debates continue, with modern thinkers expressing the view that Chalcedon fails to affirm genuine humanity for Christ; see Wolfhart Pannenberg, *Jesus—God and Man*, 2nd English ed., trans. Lewis L. Wilkins and Duane A. Priebe (Philadelphia: Westminster, 1977), 338–40; Karl Rahner, "Current Problems in Christology," in *Theological Investigations* (Baltimore: Helicon, 1965), 1:161. See also John P. Galvin, "From the Humanity of Christ to the Jesus of History: A Paradigm Shift in Catholic Christology," *TS* 55 (1994): 252–73; John McIntyre, *The Shape of Christology: Studies in the Doctrine of the Person of Christ*, 2nd ed. (Edinburgh: T&T Clark, 1998), 97–99.

46. See Dennis Michael Ferrara, "Hypostatized in the Logos: Leontius of Byzantium, Leontius of Jerusalem and the Unfinished Business of the Council of Chalcedon," *Louvain Studies* 22, no. 4 (1997): 312–27; and Fred Sanders, "Chalcedonian

As an exposition of Chalcedon, the affirmation that Christ's humanity is enhypostasic in union with the Son makes a crucial point for
anthropology and for our reflections on rationality. God is not the
antithesis of creaturely existence, nor the opposite of humanity, nor
the denial of humanity. In his works God provides the foundation and
ground for creation. They come from him as his gifts. We are created
through him, in him all things hold together, and we live and move
and have our being in him. Humanity is made in his image, not as his
opposite. We are made to enter into communion with him. So while
humanity cannot be transformed into God, neither is humanity lost in
union with God. As the Reformed affirmed, the finite cannot bear the
infinite (*finitum non capax infiniti*), but the whole of existence rests on
the fact that the infinite can bear and sustain the finite (*infinitum capax
finiti*). Humanity can never reach to God, but just as God condescends to
create and continues to sustain, so in his grace he can assume humanity,
and in that union humanity finds its perfect expression.

Thus, revelation in Christ establishes reason, not by displaying it as
a general principle but by bringing humanity back to its proper relationship of communion with God in which our reason can operate as
it should.

Christ's Mediatorial Knowledge of God Is Key to His Work of Revelation

One final claim adds depth to the significance of Christ's human knowledge. In opposition to Apollinarianism, we should insist that Christ
mediates revelation because he has a full and fully human knowledge
of God. He is the revealer because he receives revelation.

It is sometimes assumed that Christ's humanity obscures God's self-
revelation and so we must penetrate through the veil of his humanity to
know God.[47] Against such a view, we should rather see that revelation

---

Categories of the Gospel Narrative," in *Jesus in Trinitarian Perspective*, ed. Fred
Sanders and Klaus Issler (Nashville: B&H, 2007), 25–36.

47. Richard Bauckham, "Jesus as the Revelation of God," in *Divine Revelation*, ed.
Paul Avis (London: Darton, Longman & Todd, 1997), 174, raises the question clearly
and argues that the eschatological hope of revelation of Christ (1 John 3:2) reminds
us that his revelation in his first coming had an aspect of hiddenness about it. Barth,
similarly, sees a paradox in Christ's revelation of God in his humanity. He is the

through the Incarnate One is accommodated for us through his humanity rather than being veiled by it. Christ's redemptive revelation comes
through the whole of his life, leading to the climax in his second appearing, when we shall not only see him as he is (1 John 3:2) but be con-
formed to his glorified humanity (Phil 3:21), and so, in and through
his humanity, we shall see God's face (Rev 22:4). In all of this, Christ's
humanity mediates knowledge of God. Such a claim is coherent with
the place of Christ's humanity in his all work. His humanity serves
his mission and does limit it. The Westminster Confession (8:3) puts
it admirably when it states that the Lord Jesus as very God and very
man "was sanctified, and anointed with the Holy Spirit, above measure,
having in Him all the treasures of wisdom and knowledge." Christ as
God and Man is perfectly fitted for his work, and this applies as much
to his work as prophet as to priest and king. At the heart of Christ's
prophetic work is his own knowledge of God, received in his humanity
as revelation. The Westminster formulation reflects this when it refers
to Christ as having "all the treasures of wisdom and knowledge" and
being "full of grace and truth."

In the incarnation the Son who from eternity knows the Father perfectly also has a human life, in which by the Spirit he comes to know
the Father in perfect, human obedience. He is both the Word of God
and a prophet who received the word. In his humanity Christ grew in
knowledge and wisdom (Luke 2:40, 52) given by the Spirit. He rejoiced
at visions and insights from God (10:18) and refreshed himself in prayer
(Matt 14:23; Mark 1:35; 3:21; 6:46; Luke 5:16; 6:12; 9:18, 28; 11:1). He ago-
nized in Gethsemane and on the cross and looked forward to his return
to the glory of the Father (John 12:23; 13:31, 32; 14:28). Michael Allen,
arguing for the significance of Christ's human faith, concludes that
the "assumption of true humanity necessarily involves the embrace of
certain limitations, specifically intellectual and developmental ones."[48]

---

humanity of God, and yet this humanity veils God. Trevor Hart, "Revelation," in
The Cambridge Companion to Karl Barth, ed. John B. Webster (Cambridge: Cambridge
University Press, 2000), 59, explains Barth's view that "in apprehending the man
Jesus, we do not as such and without further ado lay hold of God. We are, after all,
beholding his humanity which serves as a created veil for the divinity as well as a
door which, at God's own behest, may open for us."

48. R. Michael Allen, *The Christ's Faith: A Dogmatic Account* (New York: T&T

The human pilgrim knowledge of God possessed by Christ is a deep, abiding, intimate, and constant fellowship with the Father. It is analogous to the ectypal knowledge of the Father enjoyed by the Son in all eternity, but it is always a human knowledge of God.

Jesus' human knowledge of the Father is mediated by the Spirit as he is formed, led, and empowered by the Spirit (Matt 1:18, 20; 3:10; 12:28, 32-33; Luke 1:35; 2:40; 3:21-22; 4:1, 14; 12:10; John 1:33; Heb 9:14; Rom 1:1-4; 1 Tim 3:16; 1 Pet 3:18).[49] In the context of the ministry of the Spirit it is developed through meditation on Scripture. He knows his task through his contemplation of Scripture in light of his call (Matt 3:17; Mark 1:11; Luke 3:22). From the Scriptures he grasps that his death and resurrection are the inevitable outcome of his mission (Matt 16:21; 20:18-19; Mark 8:31; 10:33-34; Luke 9:22; 18:31-33), and he explains his work in terms of the Scriptures and their fulfillment (Luke 24:27). Telford Work comments that "if Jesus' self-awareness was an effect of his anointed priesthood ... and not merely his status as incarnate Word, then it is also in large part a function of Jesus' relationship with Scripture."[50]

As B. B. Warfield observes, in the New Testament "a duplex life is attributed to him [Jesus] as his constant possession."[51] In the God-man we see humanity and divinity in unity. He has direct and immediate knowledge of God, and he receives the knowledge of God. Although these are distinct, they are not opposed. There is a wonderful and mysterious harmony. It is not that divine knowledge denies or replaces human knowledge, but rather that Spirit-given knowledge of God

---

Clark, 2009), 68.

49. John Owen, "Pneumatologia," in vol. 3 of *Collected Works* (Edinburgh: Banner of Truth, 1966), 159-88; Sinclair Ferguson, *The Holy Spirit* (Downers Grove, IL: InterVarsity, 1996), 35-56; Myk Habets, "Spirit Christology: Seeing in Stereo," *Journal of Pentecostal Studies* 11, no. 2 (2003): 199-234.

50. Telford Work, *Living and Active: Scripture in the Economy of Salvation* (Grand Rapids: Eerdmans, 2002), 171; and see N. T. Wright, *Jesus and the Victory of God* (London: SPCK, 1996), 536-37.

51. Benjamin B. Warfield, "The Human Development of Jesus," in *Selected Shorter Writings of Benjamin B. Warfield*, ed. J. E. Meeter (Nutley, NJ: Presbyterian and Reformed, 1970), 1:164, states that the question of Jesus' knowledge is "a topic very much under discussion nowadays." See also Thomas C. Oden, *The Word of Life*, vol. 2 of *Systematic Theology* (San Francisco: Harper, 1989), 204; Donald G. Bloesch, *Jesus Christ: Savior & Lord*, Christian Foundations (Downers Grove, IL: InterVarsity, 1997), 70-71.

conforming Jesus' human knowledge to the full knowledge of the Son without transforming the human into the divine. It is the same pattern as in the two wills of Christ, in which human obedience in the power of the Spirit conforms with the eternal will of God.

In all of this, Christ's knowledge is mediatorial; that is, he knows God so that we may know him. So he becomes head of a new humanity among whom God is known. Because Jesus Christ knows the Father by the Spirit, those who share in his Spirit also come to know God (1 Cor 2:9-16).[52]

The high point of John's presentation of this theme is Jesus' prayer in John 17. There Jesus states that he has revealed the Father to the disciples on the basis of what he has been given by the Father, and as the disciples receive it they recognize that he has come from the Father (John 17:6-8; see 17:25). This recognition of Jesus as from the Father has a double effect. On the one hand, it means that they acknowledge Jesus for who he is and believe in him; at the same time, it means that they come to know the Father in and through Jesus. This passage underscores what is correct in Bultmann's overstatement that Jesus reveals nothing but that he is the Revealer.[53] Knowing Jesus truly is knowing that we know God in him, and knowing God is knowing that we know him in Jesus, and all of this comes from the revelation of the Father to the Son.[54]

In terms of the theme of this paper, Christ's own knowledge is fully human and also fully divine. This most fully establishes the place of reason. The New Testament Christ is not an Apollinarian figure who has a divine mind alone, or even the neo-Apollinarian version whose human knowledge is a section of the divine mind or human consciousness with a divine subconscious. Christ's knowledge is fully human knowledge, in harmony with divine knowledge. As Christ knows God as a man, he knows according to reason, he knows as the human capacity of knowing

---

52. See Douglas F. Kelly, *Systematic Theology Grounded in Holy Scripture and Understood in the Light of the Church*, vol. 1, *The God Who Is: The Holy Trinity* (Fearn, Ross-shire, UK: Mentor, 2008), 28-32.

53. Rudolf Bultmann, *New Testament Theology*, trans. K. Grobel (New York: Scribner, 1955), 2:66.

54. See Marianne M. Thompson, *The God of the Gospel of John* (Grand Rapids: Eerdmans, 2001), 140-41.

and understanding is sanctified and put to its full and proper end. On that basis he enables us to know God.

CONCLUSION

I am glad that our topic has been framed as "revelation and reason." There are different pairings used for similar discussions: "faith and reason," "theology and reason," "theology and philosophy." Each is an important topic and deserves discussion. One of the burdens of my paper is that the "revelation and reason" question is the most basic. Christian faith should follow revelation as the proper human response to what God makes known about himself. God's self-revelation is the external cognitive foundation (*principium cognoscendi externum*) of theology. The work of the Spirit evokes in us faith in God as he has revealed himself, and so the illumination of the Holy Spirit is the internal principle (*principium cognoscendi interernum*) that brings knowledge of God to human consciousness.[55] Thus theology, the human account of knowledge of God, follows faith, and faith follows revelation. All of which is to say that to ask how revelation relates to reason will provide the right basis for then considering how reason relates to faith and how, then, reason and philosophy function in theology.

The traditional Reformed view is that reason is a good servant but a demonic master. This extended theological reflection underscores that conclusion. Reason must be chastened. We are quick to measure all things, and especially God, by our own understanding and comprehension. The gospel of Jesus Christ shows that our capacity is not only limited but that in sin humanity is committed to misunderstanding and opposing God's truth. That is the point of the theology of the cross; left to ourselves we will be theologians of glory.

The answer to the rebellion of reason is not the destruction of reason. For revelation establishes reason in two senses. First, it shows the validity of reason, even for the things of God. The presence of the Logos in the flesh means Christ has mediatorial knowledge. He reveals and is revelation because he has been given the gift of knowledge of God accommodated to human reception. Reason has its place.

---

55. Herman Bavinck, *Prolegomena*, vol. 1 of *Reformed Dogmatics*, ed. John Bolt, trans. John Vriend (Grand Rapids: Baker, 2003), 213; see 39.

Revelation establishes reason in another sense as well. It is because we are redeemed into communion with God and receive knowledge of him that we can think properly.

Revelation in Christ does not displace or subvert reason. It chastens it, but not to discard it. This is a case of grace perfecting nature, not destroying it. The path to perfection is through judgment and repentance. Reason must be sanctified, in the full Reformed sense of mortification and vivification. It must be stripped of pretensions and brought to heel before it can be raised to know God. So raised, in Christ and by the Spirit, human reason enters into its God-ordained vocation to know God and to view all things in their relation to him, for his glory and to guide the redeemed in living for God.

WORKS CITED

Allen, R. Michael. *The Christ's Faith: A Dogmatic Account*. London: T&T Clark, 2009.

Allison, C. FitzSimons. *The Cruelty of Heresy: An Affirmation of Christian Orthodoxy*. Harrisburg, PA: Morehouse, 1994.

Anderson, James. *Paradox in Christian Theology: An Analysis of Its Presence, Character, and Epistemic Status*. London: Paternoster, 2007.

Anselm. *Cur Deus Homo*. In *The Major Works: Anselm of Canterbury*. Edited by Brian Davies and Gillian R. Evans. Oxford: Oxford University Press, 1998.

Ayres, Lewis. "Shine, Jesus, Shine: On Locating Apollinarianism." *Studia Patristica* 40 (2006): 143–58.

Bauckham, Richard. "Jesus as the Revelation of God." In *Divine Revelation*, edited by Paul Avis, 174–200. London: Darton, Longman & Todd, 1997.

Bavinck, Herman. *Reformed Dogmatics*. Vol. 1, *Prolegomena*. Grand Rapids: Baker, 2003.

Beeley, Christopher A. "The Early Christological Controversy: Apollinarius, Diodore, and Gregory Nazianzen." *Vigiliae Christianae* 65, no. 4 (2011): 376–407.

Bloesch, Donald G. *Jesus Christ: Savior & Lord*. Downers Grove, IL: InterVarsity, 1997.

———. *A Theology of Word and Spirit: Authority and Method in Theology*. Downers Grove, IL: InterVarsity, 2005.

Brown, Harold I. "Rationality." In *The Oxford Companion to Philosophy*, 2nd ed., edited by Ted Honderich, 744–45. Oxford: Oxford University Press, 2005.

Bultmann, Rudolf. *New Testament Theology*. Translated by K. Grobel. New York: Scribner, 1955.

Calhoun, Robert L. *Scripture, Creed, Theology: Lectures on the History of Christian Doctrine in the First Centuries*. Eugene, OR: Cascade, 2011.

Coakley, Sarah. "What Chalcedon Solved and Didn't Solve." In *The Incarnation: An Interdisciplinary Symposium on the Incarnation of the Son of God*, edited by Stephen T. Davis, Daniel Kendall, and Gerald O'Collins, 143-63. Oxford: Oxford University Press, 2002.

Craig, William L. "The Coherence of the Incarnation." *Ankara Üniversitesi Ilahiyat Fakültesi Dergisi* 50, no. 2 (2009): 151-64.

Diamond, Cora. *The Realistic Spirit: Wittgenstein, Philosophy, and the Mind*. Cambridge, MA: MIT Press, 1995.

Evans, Craig A. *Word and Glory: On the Exegetical and Theological Background of John's Prologue*. Sheffield: JSOT Press, 1993.

Ferguson, Sinclair. *The Holy Spirit*. Downers Grove, IL: InterVarsity, 1996.

Ferrara, Dennis Michael. "Hypostatized in the Logos: Leontius of Byzantium, Leontius of Jerusalem and the Unfinished Business of the Council of Chalcedon." *Louvain Studies* 22, no. 4 (1997): 312-27.

Forde, Gerhard. *On Being a Theologian of the Cross: Reflections on Luther's Heidelberg Disputation, 1518*. Grand Rapids: Eerdmans, 1997.

Galvin, John P. "From the Humanity of Christ to the Jesus of History: A Paradigm Shift in Catholic Christology." *TS* 55 (1994): 252-73.

Geisler, Norman L., and W. D. Watkins. "The Incarnation and Logic: Their Compatibility Defended." *Trinity Journal* 6 (1985): 185-97.

Grabill, Stephen J. "Natural Law and the Noetic Effects of Sin: The Faculty of Reason in Francis Turretin's Theological Anthropology." *WTJ* 67, no. 2 (September 2005): 261-79.

Gregory of Nazianzus. "Epistle 51 of St Gregory the Theologian to Cledonius, against Apollinarius."www.monachos.net/content/patristics/texts/158-gregory-to-cledonius.

Habets, Myk. "Spirit Christology: Seeing in Stereo." *Journal of Pentecostal Studies* 11, no. 2 (2003): 199-234.

Hart, Trevor. "Revelation." In *The Cambridge Companion to Karl Barth*, edited by John B. Webster, 37-56. Cambridge: Cambridge University Press, 2000.

Hick, John. *The Myth of God Incarnate*. London: SCM, 1977.

————. *The Metaphor of God Incarnate: Christology in a Pluralistic Age*. 2nd ed. Louisville: Westminster John Knox, 2006.

Hoblík, Jiří. "The Holy Logos in the Writings of Philo of Alexandria." *Communio Viatorum* 56, no. 3 (2014): 248-66.

Kelly, Douglas F. *Systematic Theology Grounded in Holy Scripture and Understood in the Light of the Church*. Vol. 1, *The God Who Is: The Holy Trinity*. Fearn, Ross-shire, UK: Mentor, 2008.

Kolb, Robert. "Luther in an Age of Confessionalization." In *The Cambridge Companion to Martin Luther*, edited by Donald K. McKim, 209-26. Cambridge: Cambridge University Press, 2003.

————. "Luther on the theology of the cross." *Lutheran Quarterly* 16, no. 1 (2002): 443–66.

Leslie, Andrew. "The Reformation a Century Later: Did the Reformation Get Lost Two Generations Later?" In *Celebrating the Reformation, Its Legacy and Continuing Relevance*, edited by Mark D. Thompson, C. Bale, and Ed Loane, 281–308. London: Apollos, 2017.

McGrath, Alister E. *The Genesis of Doctrine: A Study in the Foundation of Doctrinal Criticism*. Grand Rapids: Eerdmans, 1997.

McIntyre, John. *The Shape of Christology: Studies in the Doctrine of the Person of Christ*. 2nd ed. Edinburgh: T&T Clark, 1998.

Moreland, J. P., and William L. Craig. *Philosophical Foundations for a Christian Worldview*. Downers Grove, IL: InterVarsity, 2003.

Muller, Richard A. *Post-Reformation Reformed Dogmatics: The Rise and Development of Reformed Orthodoxy, ca. 1520 to ca. 1725*. Vol. 3, *The Divine Essence and Attributes*. Grand Rapids: Baker, 2002.

Oden, Thomas C. *The Word of Life*. San Francisco: Harper, 1989.

Ostella, Richard A. "The Revived Apollinarianism of Moreland and Craig in *Philosophical Foundations for a Christian Worldview* (IVP, 2003)." Presented to Evangelical Theological Society Midwest, March 28, 2014. Available online at www.westminsterreformedchurch.org/True%20Humanity%20and%20Deity%20of%20Christ/ETS2014FinalDraft.Apollinarianism.pdf.

Owen, John. "Pneumatologia." Vol. 3 of *Collected Works*. Edinburgh: Banner of Truth, 1966.

————. *The Reason of Faith*. In *The Works of John Owen*, edited by William H. Goold. London: Johnstone & Hunter, 1850–1855.

Padgett, Alan G. "Faith Seeking Understanding: Collegiality and Difference in Theology and Philosophy." In *Faith and Reason: Three Views*, edited by S. Wilkens, 85–130. Downers Grove, IL: InterVarsity, 2014.

Pannenberg, Wolfhart. *Jesus—God and Man*. 2nd English ed. Translated by Lewis L. Wilkins and Duane A. Priebe. Philadelphia: Westminster, 1977.

Rahner, Karl. "Current Problems in Christology." In *Theological Investigations*, vol 1, 149–200. Baltimore: Helicon, 1965.

Rehnman, Sebastian. "Alleged Rationalism: Francis Turretin on Reason." *CTJ* 37, no. 2 (November 2002): 255–69.

————. "Graced Response: John Owen on Faith and Reason." *Neue Zeitschrift für systematische Theologie und Religionsphilosophie* 53, no. 4 (2011): 431–49.

Runia, David T. *Philo in Early Christian Literature: A Survey*. Minneapolis: Fortress, 1993.

Sanders, Fred. "Chalcedonian Categories of the Gospel Narrative." In *Jesus in Trinitarian Perspective*, edited by Fred Sanders and Klaus Issler, 1–41. Nashville: B&H, 2007.

Snodgrass, Klyne. "The Gospel in Romans: A Theology of Revelation." In *Gospel in Paul: Studies on Corinthians, Galatians and Romans for Richard N. Longenecker*, 288–314. Sheffield: Sheffield Academic, 1994.

Swinburne, Richard. "The Coherence of the Chalcedonian Definition of the Incarnation." In *The Metaphysics of the Incarnation*, edited by Anna Marmodoro and Jonathan Hill, 153–67. Oxford: Oxford University Press, 2011.

Thompson, Marianne M. *The God of the Gospel of John*. Grand Rapids: Eerdmans, 2001.

Turretin, Francis. *Institutes of Elenctic Theology*. 3 vols. Phillipsburg, NJ: P&R, 1992–1997.

Warfield, Benjamin B. "The Human Development of Jesus." In *Selected Shorter Writings of Benjamin B. Warfield*, edited by J. E. Meeter, 158–68. Nutley, NJ: Presbyterian and Reformed, 1970.

Witherington, Ben, III. *John's Wisdom: A Commentary on the Fourth Gospel*. Louisville: Westminster John Knox, 1995.

Work, Telford. *Living and Active: Scripture in the Economy of Salvation*. Grand Rapids: Eerdmans, 2002.

Wright, N. T. *Jesus and the Victory of God*. London: SPCK, 1996.

Young, Frances M., and Andrew Teal. *From Nicaea to Chalcedon: A Guide to the Literature and Its Background*. 2nd ed. London: SCM, 1983.

12

Free Speech

Scripture in the Context of Divine Simplicity and Divine Freedom

Steven J. Duby

At the end of the nineteenth century, Dutch Reformed theologian Herman Bavinck made the general statement that the early church tended wholly to equate divine revelation and Holy Scripture ("it seemed as if there was nothing behind Scripture"), while various modern theologians have tended to reduce Holy Scripture to a mere human record of revelation.[1] In his *Church Dogmatics* Karl Barth offers one way of navigating between these two tendencies by contending that, while the Bible does not have "the attribute of being the Word of God"—in Barth's view, the word of God may be termed "God himself in Holy Scripture"—the Bible nevertheless becomes the word of God whenever it effectively bears witness to Christ by the gracious work of the Holy Spirit. Behind Barth's decision not to identify the Bible as the word of God in a direct manner is not only a strong distinction between Christ as the Word of God and the Bible as the word of God but also a concern to uphold God's freedom and his lordship over the Bible: "God is not an attribute of something else, even if this something else is the Bible. God is subject, God is Lord. He is Lord even over the Bible and in the Bible."[2]

Barth's insistence on God's lordship over the Bible presents an important challenge for those who still wish to identify the Bible as

---

1. Herman Bavinck, *Prolegomena*, vol. 1 of *Reformed Dogmatics*, ed. John Bolt, trans. John Vriend (Grand Rapids: Baker, 2003), 381.
2. *CD* I/2, 457, 513–14.

revelation or as the word of God in a direct sense.[3] In particular, it underscores the need for an account of Scripture that is attentive to matters such as the nature of divine action and revelation and the relationship between God's transcendent freedom and God's accessibility in his self-disclosure. Among others, Kevin Vanhoozer, for example, has taken up this challenge and begun significant work at the intersection of the doctrine of Scripture and the doctrine of God. He argues that the words of Scripture "do not become but are the word of God."[4] At the same time, by grounding the doctrine of Scripture in God's triune communicative agency and making use of speech-act theory, Vanhoozer is able to bring together the propositional content and the personal action of God that are both integral to the concept of revelation.[5] The Bible is indeed the word of God inscripturated, though not as a text detached from God's activity but rather as a "field and form of divine communicative action."[6]

With the likes of Vanhoozer and others, I believe that Scripture should be identified as the constant word of God, or as a continual form and locus of divine revelation, and that this identification is best carried out at the nexus of bibliology and theology proper, where we can take into consideration the relationship between the words of the text and the revelatory action of God, and the relationship between God's sovereign freedom and his accessibility to us. In this essay I offer a contribution to the discussion of Scripture in relation to divine action by exploring some pertinent implications of the doctrine of divine simplicity. I do not intend to offer a defense of divine simplicity here, but it may be helpful to state briefly what it means. In short, it is the catholic teaching that God is not composed of parts but is instead really

---

3. It should of course be clear that this does not entail confusing the Bible and the person of Christ. Identifying the Bible as an ongoing form of revelation entails taking the category of revelation to be broader than just the person of Christ.

4. Kevin J. Vanhoozer, "Triune Discourse: Theological Reflections on the Claim That God Speaks (Part 2)," in *Trinitarian Theology for the Church: Scripture, Community, Worship*, ed. Daniel J. Treier and David Lauber (Downers Grove, IL: InterVarsity, 2009), 54.

5. Kevin J. Vanhoozer, *First Theology: God, Scripture and Hermeneutics* (Downers Grove, IL: InterVarsity, 2002), 127–58.

6. Kevin J. Vanhoozer, "Word of God," in *Dictionary for Theological Interpretation of the Bible*, ed. Kevin J. Vanhoozer (Grand Rapids: Baker, 2005), 854.

identical with his essence, existence, and attributes. This claim is rooted chiefly in God's aseity: since nothing stands above or behind the triune God to establish his being, God's essence, existence, and attributes all are just God himself considered under various aspects. The persons of the Trinity are not "parts" composing a greater divine whole but are rather three distinct personal modes of subsisting of the whole divine essence. Furthermore, God is not composed of potentiality and actuality; instead, his being is entirely actual or "pure act." [7] I will show that, assuming the legitimacy of the doctrine, divine simplicity helps to confirm that, while Scripture is indeed the word of God written, this coheres with the freedom of God in his revelation. In this connection I will argue that God's simplicity illumines that God or God's action, however low and however unremitting his revelatory condescension may be, never comes under the control of his creatures. As we will see, this is because simplicity reframes the nature of divine action and in so doing offers a fresh corroboration of the transcendence of God's communicative activity in Scripture. Furthermore, divine simplicity reframes also the nature of human knowledge of God, elucidating well both the incomprehensibility of God and the genuine knowability of God. Therefore, after examining how simplicity underscores the transcendence of the action of God's revelation in Scripture, we will also explore its implications for the transcendence of the *content* of God's revelation in Scripture.

DIVINE SIMPLICITY AND DIVINE ACTION

The bearing of the doctrine of divine simplicity, especially its claim that God is pure act, on the freedom and transcendence of God's speaking in Scripture can be seen when we consider biblical descriptions of God's plenitude and omnipotence. The Old and New Testaments emphasize that God is, as Barth would have it, "rich in himself."[8] This is implied where God is called the "living God" over against lifeless, impotent idols

---

7. For contemporary expositions and defenses of divine simplicity, see James E. Dolezal, *God without Parts: The Metaphysics of God's Absoluteness* (Eugene, OR: Wipf and Stock, 2011); Steven J. Duby, *Divine Simplicity: A Dogmatic Account*, T&T Clark Studies in Systematic Theology (London: Bloomsbury, 2016).

8. *CD* II/1, 334.

(2 Kgs 19:15-19; Jer 10:1-16; Acts 14:15; 1 Thess 1:9). The God of Israel lacks nothing and needs nothing from his creatures (Ps 50:7-15). Rather, he possesses all that is good in himself and generously shares that goodness with creatures (Ps 24:1; Acts 17:24-28; Rom 11:36; Phil 4:19). Significantly, the action of God whereby he accomplishes his works is not a matter of exertion. He calls creation into being by sheer command (Pss 33:6, 9; 148:5; Rom 4:17). Because he has life in himself, God the Son is capable of raising the dead by the power of his word (John 5:25-26). Likewise, he can overthrow the man of lawlessness by the mere "breath of his mouth" and the "appearance of his coming" (2 Thess 2:8).

Accordingly, God informs his people that nothing is difficult for him to accomplish. Sarah laughs at the thought of having a child in her old age, but God responds and asks, "Is anything too hard for the LORD?" (Gen 18:12-14 ESV). Jeremiah employs the same language to speak of God's ability to create the heavens and the earth, to deliver Israel out of Egypt with signs and wonders, to give Judah over to Babylon and to restore her to the land again: "Nothing is too hard for you" (32:17; see 32:27). Furthermore, the activity of God according to Scripture is eternal and constant. God did not start to exercise his intellect and will with the beginning of creation. Instead, he knew and loved and chose his people "before the foundation of the world" (Eph 1:4-5; 2 Tim 1:9). Indeed, in the triune life of God, the divine intellect and love are exercised even without any reference to creatures: the Father loved the Son "before the foundation of the world," and we are then brought into the fellowship of that prevenient love (John 17:20-24). In his relationship to the economy, God is ever "working," even through the Sabbath intervals that punctuate the lives of his creatures (John 5:17). He is constantly sustaining the world (Col 1:17; Heb 1:3), and, in the words of the psalmist, "he who keeps Israel will neither slumber nor sleep" (Ps 121:4). Juxtaposing the constant activity of God and the ease with which he acts, Augustine thus observes, "You, Lord, are always working and always at rest."[9]

Of course, there are texts in which God is said to sleep: "Rouse yourself! Why do you sleep, O Lord? Awake, do not cast us off forever" (Ps 44:23; cf. 12:5; 59:5; Isa 28:21; 33:10). Yet, as John Chrysostom observes,

---

9. Augustine, *Confessions*, trans. Henry Chadwick (Oxford: Oxford University Press, 1991), 13.52, p. 304.

where God is said to sleep, this does not indicate inactivity on God's part but rather patience and forbearance.[10] When God rouses himself to act, it is not a matter of exertion or an elevation of God's actuality and efficacy; rather, it is a matter of God's already complete, multifaceted actuality breaking forth at fresh points in time according to God's wise judgment and according to the needs of his creatures. Thus, Hilary of Poitiers writes that God accomplishes his works without the various motions that creatures require in order to perform their works. God is always active in his omnipotence, and "no labor is required where there is no weakness."[11]

The nonexertive character of divine action and the pure actuality of God gathered from Scripture and encapsulated in the doctrine of divine simplicity imply the conclusion of older theologians that divine action is nothing but God's essence operative under a certain relation to created objects and circumstances.[12] In other words, God acts by what he already is as God (that is, by his own essence). This is different from creaturely action, where the creature is moved from inactive potency to actuality and thereby increases in force and efficacy. This is why God is said not to undergo motion—not because he is immobile in the popular sense of the word but, instead, because he is active *a se* and eternally and thus does not pass from inertia to activity. Though the claim that God is pure act is sometimes taken to mean that God is impersonal or cannot engage in personal action, the notion that God is pure act in fact accentuates that God's personal action is so lively in his own being that it is not augmented but rather simply turned outward or applied by God to us for our good when God meets us in the economy.

---

10. John Chrysostom, *On the Incomprehensible Nature of God*, Fathers of the Church 72 (Washington, DC: Catholic University of America Press, 1984), 8, pp. 214-15.

11. Hilary of Poitiers, *The Trinity*, trans. Stephen McKenna, Fathers of the Church 25 (Washington, DC: Catholic University of America Press, 1954), 9.72, p. 394.

12. So Thomas Aquinas: God's action is *ejus essentia cum relatione ad creaturam* (*Summa Theologiae*, in vol. 4 of *Opera Omnia*, Leonine ed. [Rome: Ex Typographia Polyglotta, 1888], Ia 45.3, ad 1, 467). Compare Dutch orthodox theologian Peter van Mastricht: "nec operatio penes ipsum est, nisi essentia operans ... hic operatio divina duo concludat: essentiam Dei actuosam, et ejus relationem ad opus" (*Theoretico-Practica Theologia*, 2nd ed. [Utrecht: Water, Poolsum, Wagens, and Paddenburg, 1724], 3.1.4, p. 273).

This identity of God's action with his essence in the doctrine of divine simplicity entails that God's action cannot be circumscribed or taken over by creatures. For God's essence is infinite and exceeds every field of created reality (cf. 1 Kgs 8:27; Isa 40:12–26; Jer 23:24). The consequent immensity of God's action means that it cannot become encased or comprehended under any media or loci of divine revelation. This will of course have implications for the transcendence of God's communicative action in Scripture. Yet, en route to explaining this, it is worth noting that, since God's simplicity also reminds us that God's essence is indivisible, the identity of his action with his essence under a certain relation also has implications for the genuineness of his active presence in speaking in the Bible. Stephen Charnock points out that "whatsoever is compounded of parts may be divided into those parts, and resolved into those distinct parts which make up and constitute the nature."[13] God, however, has no such parts and is therefore wholly and immediately himself in his action. On the one hand, the infinity and indivisibility of the divine essence reinforce that God's action, which is God's essence working under a relation to creatures, will always transcend created media, for there is no "part" of God that can be separated from God's being and reduced to a feature of created reality. As Hilary comments, wherever God is, he is there in the simple wholeness of his indissoluble being.[14] On the other hand, this also highlights that God is fully himself in his revelatory action. With creatures, essence possesses various capacities for action, but those capacities may lie dormant for long periods of time, and, when creatures do actualize those capacities, there is always some difference between the underlying principle by which they act (essence) and the action itself. With God, however, the identity of God's action with God's essence under a certain relation implies that there is no ontological space between what God is in his essence and what God is in his action toward us.[15]

---

13. Stephen Charnock, *The Existence and Attributes of* God (Grand Rapids: Baker, 1996), 1:187.

14. Hilary, *The Trinity* 2.6, p. 40.

15. To be clear, this does not necessarily call into question all usefulness of the distinction between the "immanent Trinity" and the "economic Trinity." The triune God is not enclosed or exhaustively known by his economic action. At the

What, then, are the specific implications for God's speech in Scripture? We have noted that Barth thought God would surrender his freedom and lordship over the Bible if the Bible were continually the word of God, but divine simplicity reframes the nature of God's revelatory action and sheds light on the transcendence of that action. When we say that the Bible does not *become* the word of God but rather continually *is* the word of God, we are saying that God continually speaks the locutions written in the Bible. As God speaks those locutions, he is acting by his essence. In authoring Scripture with its human authors and committing himself to speaking continually in Scripture, God, or God's revelatory action, is therefore not domesticated by the text of Scripture. For God's infinite, indivisible essence simply cannot undergo such domestication. As infinite, the action and being of God exceed the field of the sacred text. As indivisible, they have no constituent, finite parts that might be disconnected from God's infinity and left behind, as it were, in the text, resulting in a diminishing of God's transcendence. Rather, the force with which God speaks in the Bible is that of his very essence, which resists any circumscription or reduction. Yet, precisely because of this, we can also trust that God is uninhibited in his speech in Scripture. He can and does continually address us in the Bible with no concern that he might somehow compromise himself in condescending verbally to reveal himself to us.

In sum, God's simplicity, particularly his pure actuality, impresses on us both the transcendence and sovereignty of his speech in Scripture and also the depth of his immanence in this speech. It may at first appear reverent to deny that God would so bind himself to communicating to us in a book that this book could be identified as the constant word of God. It can be argued, however, that it is in fact an underestimation of the greatness of God that would lead us to attempt to protect God's transcendent freedom by rejecting the notion of him continually addressing us in lowly, creaturely terms. If we think that the fullness and transcendence of God might be threatened by his condescension, we might feel the need to mitigate his condescension. By contrast, if we recognize that God's greatness is, in the infinite actuality

---

same time, there are not two instances of the Trinity; the "immanent Trinity" is the Trinity that accomplishes God's works *ad extra*.

and indivisibility of his being, entirely incapable of any attenuation whatsoever, then we are free to affirm God's ongoing speech in the humble language of the prophets and apostles. There is no concern that a traditional account of Scripture as the word of God will somehow weaken the majesty of God. Some have suspected that a classical doctrine of God, of the sort in which simplicity can be found, might have been designed to keep God from ever truly relating to his creation. But, properly understood, divine simplicity confirms that God's incorruptible plenitude and transcendence foster a rich understanding of his immanence: he is able to act continually in the field of the biblical text without ever worrying about losing himself in so doing. Such is, I submit, the significance of God's simplicity for his freedom and sovereignty in the *action* of his revelation in Scripture. Next we consider divine simplicity in connection with the *content* of his revelation in Scripture.

DIVINE SIMPLICITY AND THE CONTENT OF GOD'S REVELATION

Moving beyond the implications of divine simplicity for divine action, we now examine the manner in which God's simplicity bears on human knowledge of God and helps us to see that the continual accessibility of the content of God's revelation in Scripture does not render God an object that can be mastered by the human mind. God's works in the economy, including his speech in Scripture, truly make God known to us. Indeed, they make known not just God's relationship to creation but also God himself. This means that the (created) media of revelation do not exhaust the content of revelation. Yet, at this point, when we have identified the Bible as revelation and when we recognize that biblical revelation gives us knowledge of God himself, divine simplicity helps us still to honor the transcendence of the content of God's self-revelation in the Bible, or, put differently, the incomprehensibility of God.

God's incomprehensibility is set before us in various biblical passages. In Exodus 3, where the LORD gives his name (אֶהְיֶה אֲשֶׁר אֶהְיֶה) to Moses before he goes to lead the people of Israel, there is an interweaving of hiddenness and revelation. For this reason, the passage is a helpful vantage point from which to reflect on the transcendence of

God in the midst of his ongoing self-disclosure in Scripture. On the one hand, though God answers the anticipated question of the Israelites in Exodus 3—"What is his name?"—he still declines to give a full description of himself. He deploys a tautology, "I Am Who I Am," to give assurance that he is to be trusted and at the same time signal that he will not place himself under the jurisdiction of human beings.[16] Bruce Waltke comments that in this passage "the Eternal lowers himself into a bush amid the dirt and rocks" and promises Moses "I am who I am for you."[17] However, Waltke happily does not separate this humble covenant faithfulness from the implications of the name for God's own being: God is *a se*, all-sufficient, "pure being without dependence," "pure power without limitation," "pure love without self-regard."[18] That Waltke is right to discern implications for God's own transcendent being can be seen in the broader canonical development of the name "I Am." In Deuteronomy 32:39 God emphasizes "I am he" to make the point that he alone is God and is the omnipotent giver of life. In Isaiah "I am he" is used to express God's singularity and eternal life (41:4; 43:10, 13; 48:12).[19] Christ himself invokes this thread of biblical teaching to convey his eternal existence when some wonder how he can speak authoritatively about the patriarch Abraham (John 8:58).[20] Finally, in Revelation, the divine name is unfolded in various pericopes where God is "the one who is and who was (and who is coming)" (1:4, 8; 4:8; 11:17; 16:5).[21] The

---

16. Compare Brevard S. Childs, *The Book of Exodus: A Critical, Theological Commentary*, Old Testament Library (Philadelphia: Westminster, 1974), 6. Particularly helpful on the note of divine trustworthiness in the passage is Terence Fretheim, *Exodus*, Interpretation (Louisville: John Knox, 1991), 63.

17. Bruce K. Waltke, *Old Testament Theology: An Exegetical, Canonical, and Thematic Approach* (Grand Rapids: Zondervan, 2007), 363, 366.

18. Waltke, *Old Testament Theology*, 366–67, 505. This more holistic approach stands in contrast to, for example, Gerhard von Rad, *Old Testament Theology*, vol. 1, *The Theology of Israel's Historical Traditions* (New York: Harper & Row, 1962), 180; Christopher R. Seitz, *Figured Out: Typology and Providence in Christian Scripture* (Louisville: Westminster John Knox, 2001), 140.

19. Of course, this eternal, abundant life and power of God expressed in the "I am he" statements is applied to the circumstances of creation for the good of God's people (43:25; 46:4; 51:12).

20. On the "I am" sayings of John's Gospel, see Richard Bauckham, *The Testimony of the Beloved Disciple: Narrative, History, and Theology in the Gospel of John* (Grand Rapids: Baker, 2007), 246–47.

21. So Richard Bauckham, *The Theology of the Book of Revelation*, New Testament

point is that across the canon of Scripture the divine name "I Am" indicates not only God's covenant faithfulness but also God's eternal life and
incomprehensible plenitude. It is not a matter of idle speculation, then,
to say, with John of Damascus, that the God of Holy Scripture is not a
limited being but "like a sea of essence infinite and unseen" (πέλαγος
οὐσίας ἄπειρον καὶ ἀόριστον).[22]

On the other hand, while the name "I Am" points toward God's
fullness and incomprehensibility, the name is given to communicate
knowledge of God's fullness to us in the biblical text. In Exodus 3, the
God who is "I Am" is the Lord (יְהוָה, a form arguably related to אֶהְיֶה[23]),
the God of Abraham, Isaac, and Jacob. The one who is eternally is the
one revealed in the history of the patriarchs. The redemptive-historical
exposition of the name "I Am" continues in Exodus 33-34. When Moses
seeks confirmation that God will go with him in leading the people and
entreats God to reveal his glory, God replies that he will manifest his
goodness and proclaim his name, יְהוָה (33:12-19a), which is then glossed
by the statement "I will be gracious to whom I will be gracious, and I will
show mercy on whom I will show mercy" (33:19b). The proclamation of
the name is cast in terms of announcing God's free grace and mercy.[24]
If someone sees the face of the LORD, they will die, but when the LORD
proclaims his name, Moses may still see his "back" (33:20-23). The LORD
then passes before Moses, proclaiming his name, "יְהוָה, יְהוָה, a God mer-
ciful and gracious, slow to anger and abounding in steadfast love and

Theology (Cambridge: Cambridge University Press, 1993), 28-30.

22. John of Damascus, *Expositio Fidei*, in vol. 2 of *Die Schriften des Johannes von Damaskos*, ed. Bonifatius Kotter, Patristische Texte und Studien 12 (Berlin: de Gruyter, 1973), I.9, p. 31. This certainly does not represent a depersonalization of God on the part of John, for he is clear that the infinite God is the one who knows, loves, wills, and acts according to his wisdom in the economy of salvation. The modern tension between God as absolute and God as personal is not an issue in John's thought.

23. So, for example, R. W. L. Moberly, *The Old Testament of the Old Testament* (Minneapolis: Fortress, 1992), 21-22.

24. The flow of the text entails that "I will be gracious ..." is materially apposi-tional to the divine name. One could also argue that perhaps even the grammar of the text itself suggests this: the waw of וְחַנֹּתִי ("I will be gracious ...") might have an epexegetical function (on which see for example Bruce K. Waltke and M. O'Connor, *Introduction to Biblical Hebrew Syntax* [Winona Lake, IN: Eisenbrauns, 1990], 39.2.4, pp. 652-53).

faithfulness, keeping steadfast love for the thousandth generation, for-
giving iniquity and transgression and sin, but by no means clearing the
guilty, but visiting the iniquity of the parents upon the children and
the children's children, to the third and the fourth generation" (34:6-7).

Human persons cannot comprehend God (see Ps 145:3; 1 Tim 6:16),
and sinful human persons cannot see him face to face without perish-
ing (see Isa 6:5; Heb 12:14; 1 John 3:2), but, in the teaching of Exodus
33-34, they can indeed know him by his many attributes: goodness, grace,
mercy, patience, love, faithfulness, justice, and so on. God's proclamation
of his ineffable name by his attributes in Exodus 33-34 is echoed in John
1, where Jesus "tabernacles" among us as the LORD did in Moses' day
and displays God's glory in his grace and truth (1:14).[25] Though no one
has ever seen God, Jesus has made him known (1:18). Chrysostom comments on John 1:18 that no human being has "perfect comprehension of
God." Even among the prophets none "saw God's essence in its pure state"
or "in its exact nature."[26] That is why Chrysostom says elsewhere that,
when Paul speaks of the imperfection of our knowledge in 1 Corinthians
13:8-12, Paul "does not know what God is in his essence. He knows," for
example, "that he is wise but he does not know how great that wisdom
is." It is not that Paul knows one "part" of God's essence but not another;
rather, he simply does not know the immensity of God's simple essence
or the mysterious working of God's providence and so must know God
by attributes such as wisdom, greatness, and so on.[27] As John Dama-
scene explains, since God does not exist in a category of things, finite
creatures cannot demarcate God's nature. Instead, we content ourselves
with "affirmations" (ὅσα ... λέγομεν ἐπὶ θεοῦ καταφατικῶς) such as goodness,
justice, and wisdom "concerning God's nature" (περὶ τὴν φύσιν).[28]

---

25. For the reference back to Exod 34, see for example Craig A. Evans, *Word
and Glory: On the Exegetical and Theological Background of John's Prologue*, JSNTSup
89 (Sheffield: Sheffield Academic, 1993), 79-83.

26. Chrysostom, *Incomprehensible Nature of God* III, p. 122.

27. Chrysostom, *Incomprehensible Nature of God* I, p. 65.

28. John of Damascus, *Expositio Fidei* I.4, p. 13. Later John states that what we
affirm about God does not signify "what he is according to essence" but rather
clarifies "either what he is not or some relation toward something of contrasting
things or something of things following the nature, or an energy" (*Expositio Fidei*
I.9, p. 31). At the constructive level, I would prefer to say that the divine attributes
"describe" or "gloss" God's nature rather than "follow" God's nature.

What is the particular relevance of all this to divine simplicity in connection with the transcendence of the content of God's revelation in Scripture? The doctrine of divine simplicity illumines the biblical dynamic, carried forward by various church fathers, of affirming God's eternal, incomprehensible plenitude and then understanding that plenitude in a limited (but still true) fashion by the many attributes God gives to us in Scripture. God's rich, infinite essence cannot be known precisely or exhaustively by the human mind, but each of God's attributes is really identical—is the same "thing" (res)—with his essence. They are not qualities inhering in God but are glosses of the whole perfection that God is as God. To appropriate some scholastic language, the attributes or perfections of God by which God's triune essence is known are one with God's essence, not "formally," as though the formal notion or definition of each could capture the fullness of the essence, but rather "identically" as wisdom, justice, goodness, and so on just are the essence of God taken under some aspect.[29] As in Exodus, so according to a traditional account of God's simplicity the divine attributes are critical to our knowledge of God himself. Yet, while they are spoken *de essentia* ("about the essence") and even are *ipsa essentia* ("the essence itself"), they are, in the strict sense of the word, *inadequate* concepts of God's incomprehensible plenitude.[30]

All of this implies that when we read Scripture as divine revelation and the very word of God and see that it speaks of God himself, we can never master the content of the revelation in Scripture and thereby puncture God's transcendence. It is not simply that we *should not* do so; the doctrine of divine simplicity underscores that we truly *cannot* do so. We lack the epistemic capacity to conceive all the fullness that the triune God is; we apprehend him but can never comprehend him. This frees us to affirm that Scripture is continually God's self-revelation without worrying that we are subjecting God to our intellectual mastery. Though the content of his revelation in the Bible is continually accessible to us, his transcendence is not in danger on that account.[31]

29. Mastricht, *Theoretico-Practica Theologia* II.3.19, p. 82.
30. Mastricht, *Theoretico-Practica Theologia* II.5.4, p. 93.
31. Although she is not specifically discussing divine revelation in Scripture, Katherine Sonderegger captures well the overarching dynamic when she says God

Though it may initially seem to the contemporary reader to be a presumptuous speculation about God's being, divine simplicity in fact discourages speculation by reminding us of God's incomprehensibility and committing us to thinking about God by way of his biblical attributes. And, once again, we can note that it is not that God's transcendence must be upheld by us distancing God from Scripture. As we have seen, a biblically rooted account of divine simplicity confirms that the action of God's revelation in Scripture exceeds the field of the text even as he continually speaks in it. Similarly, divine simplicity confirms that the content of God's revelation in Scripture exceeds our finite noetic capacity even as biblical description of God's triune perfection is an ongoing form and locus of revelation. For, even in revealing himself, God makes clear that the fullness of his being is incomprehensible to creatures.

CONCLUSION

In this essay I have taken seriously Barth's concern to maintain God's freedom and sovereignty in his self-revelation. However, I have also examined some points of intersection between bibliology and theology proper to make the case that the Bible can be identified as the (ongoing) word of God without forgoing the transcendence of the action and content of God's revelation. In this connection, the doctrine of divine simplicity reframes the nature of God's action, including his speech in Scripture. For God's action is really identical with his essence, which entails that God's ongoing communicative action exceeds the field of the text, indicating that God or God's action is not somehow encased within or reduced to the text itself even as he constantly addresses us in it. Divine simplicity also drives home the transcendence of the content of God's speech in Scripture. For what is revealed of God himself pertains to or glosses God's rich essence but does not demarcate or comprehend it. In this way I hope I have exhibited the potential fruitfulness of divine simplicity for helping the church to continue its historic affirmation of

---

humbly presents himself as an "object" "open to our investigation and praise" while the divine objectivity still "closes the intellect up in wonder. The richness of this mystery is inexhaustible, and we study it only in prayer" (*Systematic Theology*, vol. 1, *The Doctrine of God* [Minneapolis: Fortress, 2015], xii–xiii).

Holy Scripture as the word of God. The importance of that affirmation is expressed well by Bavinck:

> Holy Scripture is not an arid story or ancient chronicle but the ever-living, eternally youthful Word, which God, now and always, issues to his people. It is the eternally ongoing speech of God to us. ... In it God daily comes to his people. In it he speaks, not from afar but from nearby. In it he reveals himself from day to day, to believers in the fullness of his truth and grace. ... Scripture is the ongoing rapport between heaven and earth, between Christ and his church, between God and his children. It does not just bind us to the past; it binds us to the living Lord in the heavens. It is the living voice of God, the letter of the omnipotent God to his creature. God once created the world by the word, and by that word he also upholds it (Heb 1:2–3); but he also re-creates it by the word and prepares it to be his dwelling.[32]

WORKS CITED

Aquinas, Thomas. *Summa Theologiae*. In vol. 4 of *Opera Omnia*. Leonine ed. Rome: Ex Typographia Polyglotta, 1888.

Augustine. *Confessions*. Translated by Henry Chadwick. Oxford: Oxford University Press, 1991.

Barth, Karl. *Church Dogmatics*. Edited by G. W. Bromiley and T. F. Torrance. Translated by G. W. Bromiley et al. London: T&T Clark, 2009.

Bauckham, Richard. *The Testimony of the Beloved Disciple: Narrative, History, and Theology in the Gospel of John*. Grand Rapids: Baker, 2007.

———. *The Theology of the Book of Revelation*. New Testament Theology. Cambridge: Cambridge University Press, 1993.

Bavinck, Herman. *Prolegomena*. Vol. 1 of *Reformed Dogmatics*. Edited by John Bolt. Translated by John Vriend. Grand Rapids: Baker, 2003.

Charnock, Stephen. *The Existence and Attributes of God*. 2 vols. Grand Rapids: Baker, 1996.

Childs, Brevard S. *The Book of Exodus: A Critical, Theological Commentary*. Old Testament Library. Philadelphia: Westminster, 1974.

Chrysostom, John. *On the Incomprehensible Nature of God*. Fathers of the Church 72. Washington, DC: Catholic University of America Press, 1984.

Dolezal, James E. *God without Parts: The Metaphysics of God's Absoluteness*. Eugene, OR: Wipf & Stock, 2011.

---

32. Bavinck, *Prolegomena*, 384–85.

Duby, Steven J. *Divine Simplicity: A Dogmatic Account*. T&T Clark Studies in Systematic Theology. London: Bloomsbury, 2016.

Evans, Craig A. *Word and Glory: On the Exegetical and Theological Background of John's Prologue*. JSNTSup 89. Sheffield: Sheffield Academic, 1993.

Fretheim, Terence. *Exodus*. Interpretation. Louisville: John Knox, 1991.

Hilary of Poitiers. *The Trinity*. Translated by Stephen McKenna. Fathers of the Church 25. Washington, DC: Catholic University of America Press, 1954.

John of Damascus. *Expositio Fidei*. In vol. 2 of *Die Schriften des Johannes von Damaskos*. Edited by Bonifatius Kotter. Patristische Texte und Studien 12. Berlin: de Gruyter, 1973.

Mastricht, Peter van. *Theoretico-Practica Theologia*. 2nd ed. Utretcht: Water, Poolsum, Wagens, and Paddenburg, 1724.

Moberly, R. W. L. *The Old Testament of the Old Testament*. Minneapolis: Fortress, 1992.

Rad, Gerhard von. *Old Testament Theology*. Vol. 1, *The Theology of Israel's Historical Traditions*. New York: Harper & Row, 1962.

Seitz, Christopher R. *Figured Out: Typology and Providence in Christian Scripture*. Louisville: Westminster John Knox, 2001.

Sonderegger, Katherine. *Systematic Theology*. Vol. 1, *The Doctrine of God*. Minneapolis: Fortress, 2015.

Vanhoozer, Kevin J. *First Theology: God, Scripture and Hermeneutics*. Downers Grove, IL: InterVarsity, 2002.

———. "Triune Discourse: Theological Reflections on the Claim That God Speaks (Part 2)." In *Trinitarian Theology for the Church: Scripture, Community, Worship*, edited by Daniel J. Treier and David Lauber, 50–78. Downers Grove, IL: InterVarsity, 2009.

———. "Word of God." In *Dictionary for Theological Interpretation of the Bible*, edited by Kevin J. Vanhoozer, 850–54. Grand Rapids: Baker, 2005.

Waltke, Bruce K. *Old Testament Theology: An Exegetical, Canonical, and Thematic Approach*. Grand Rapids: Zondervan, 2007.

Waltke, Bruce K., and M. O'Connor. *Introduction to Biblical Hebrew Syntax*. Winona Lake, IN: Eisenbrauns, 1990.

13

Christ in Creation

Shortcut to Liberalism
or a Neglected Truth?

Andrew Moody

What is the nature of the relationship between the Logos, the second person of the Trinity, and creation? The Bible makes it clear that he is both the instrumental cause and sustainer of the universe—all things were made through him; he sustains all things by his powerful word (Col 1:16; Heb 1:3). But is there any relationship between the *form* of creation and the eternal Son? Does creation bear the stamp of the Word who mediates the creating work of the Father?

The idea that creation exemplifies Christ is ancient and widespread in Christian tradition. It is also frequently associated with theology that sidelines the gospel and Scripture. Yet an examination of the case for and against reveals a complex verdict. There seems to be a warrant for some form of exemplarism—but only in the light of Christ crucified and risen. Following this, a tentative case is made that Christ is often experienced in creation when he is proclaimed as Savior.

Historically many theologians have considered that all of creation is and must be an expression of the Logos. If the eternal Word is God's perfect, natural, and necessary self-expression (Son, Radiance, Word, Image, Stamp, etc.) then every other contingent, imperfect, and finite expression of God's will (such is creation) must have something to do with him. To put it another way, if there is anything that God *chooses* to do (such as create the universe), then the qualities he wants to see in that project must derive from his own qualities—all of which are first exemplified perfectly in his eternal Word/Image.

THE WORD AS THE SOURCE OF CREATURES

Ephrem the Syrian (d. 373) writes: "In every place, if you look, his [Christ's] symbol is there, and wherever you read, you will find his types. For in him all creatures were created and he traced his symbols on his property. When he was creating the world, he looked to adorn it with icons of himself. The springs of his symbols were opened up to run down and pour forth his symbols into his members."[1] Maximus the Confessor (d. 662) similarly speaks of how creatures each have their own form or *logos*—and that these *logoi* have their home in the Logos himself: "The many logoi are the one Logos to whom all things are related and who exists in himself without confusion, the essential and individually distinctive God, the Logos of God the Father. He is the beginning and cause of all things in whom all things were created, in heaven and on earth, visible and invisible, whether thrones or dominions or principalities or authorities—all things were created from him and through him and for him (Col. 1:15-17, Rom. 11:36)."[2]

In the medieval West the same idea appears as "exemplarism"—the term I will use for it henceforth. Here the eternal Son is the original and perfect exemplar of God, and thus the source for everything else that comes from God. For Thomas Aquinas (1225-1274), the going forth of the Son and Spirit is the original cause of the procession of creatures.[3] His Franciscan contemporary, Bonaventure (1221-1274), develops the same theme: "For, as it has been said, the Father begot his own likeness, that is, the Word coeternal with himself, and expressed a similitude of

---

1. From *Hymn on Virginity*, in S. J. Beggiani, "The Typological Approach of Syriac Sacramental Theology," *TS* 64 (2003): 543-57, 544-45.

2. "[The believer] will also know that the many *logoi* are the one Logos to whom all things are related and who exists in himself without confusion, the essentially and individually distinctive God, the Logos of God the Father. He is the beginning and cause of all things in whom all things were created, in heaven and on earth, visible and invisible. ... Because he held together in himself the *logoi* before they came to be, by his gracious will he created all things visible and invisible out of non-being," *Ambiguum* 7, in P. M. Blowers and R. L. Wilken, *On the Cosmic Mystery of Jesus Christ: Selected Writings from St. Maximus the Confessor*, Popular Patristics Series (Crestwood, NY: St. Vladimir's Seminary Press, 2004), 54-55.

3. See G. Emery, "Essentialism or Personalism in the Treatise on God in Saint Thomas Aquinas," *Thomist* 64 (2000): 521-63, 527-28.

himself, and in so doing he expressed all that he could. Hence the Word expresses the Father and the things he made."[4]

THE PERSISTENCE OF EXEMPLARISM

Yet this ancient theory is still with us—especially in the traditional wings of the church. We can see it in the poetry of Gerard Manley Hopkins with his vision of Christ as the *Heraclitean* Logos, expressed in "ten thousand places ... lovely in eyes not his."[5] We find traces of it in the "Radical Orthodox" movement and more clearly in the aesthetic theology of Orthodox writer David Bentley Hart: "as God utters himself eternally in his Word ... creation belongs to God's utterance of himself (as a further articulation, at an analogical remove, of the abundant 'eloquence' of divine love)."[6]

Occasionally the same ideas crop up in Reformed theology. In his unpublished work on the Trinity, Jonathan Edwards describes the begetting of the Son as a reflexive act of self-knowing (God's perfect self image) that is then the source for creation: "When God considers of making any thing for himself he presents himself before himself and views himself as his end, and that viewing himself is the same as reflecting on himself or having an idea of himself."[7]

Herman Bavinck also embraces the exemplarist scheme: "The Father expresses all his thought and his entire being in the one personal Word, and the idea of the world consequently is contained in the Logos. Accordingly, the Logos can be called 'a certain kind of form, a form which is not itself formed but the form of all things that have been formed' [Augustine, Sermon 117]. ... In him the Father contemplates the idea of the world itself. ... He is the Logos by whom the Father creates all things."[8]

4. From "Collations on the Six Days," in Bonaventure, *The Works of Bonaventure: Cardinal, Seraphic Doctor, and Saint*, trans. J. de Vinck (Paterson: St. Anthony Guild Press, 1970), 5:9.

5. See his poem "That Nature Is a Heraclitean Fire and of the Comfort of the Resurrection" (1888) and "As Kingfishers Catch Fire" (1877).

6. D. B. Hart, *The Beauty of the Infinite: The Aesthetics of Christian Truth* (Grand Rapids: Eerdmans, 2003), 289.

7. J. Edwards, *An Unpublished Essay of Edwards on the Trinity: With Remarks on Edwards and His Theology*, ed. G. P. Fisher (New York: C. Scribner's Sons, 1903), 133.

8. H. Bavinck, *Reformed Dogmatics*, trans. J. Bolt, ed. J. Vriend (Grand Rapids:

PLATONIC CHATTERING?

Yet for the magisterial reformers, such modes of thought can seem inherently suspect: too speculative; too reminiscent of Plato or Pseudo-Dionysius. They seem to indicate an attempt to know Christ apart from the incarnation and Scripture. Luther speaks of Bonaventure chattering vain imaginings along with "the heathen" Plato.[9] For him Christ is to be found solely in the swaddling clothes of Scripture and on the cross.[10] Calvin meanwhile, chides even Augustine for similar speculations: "Augustine, who is excessively addicted to the philosophy of Plato, is carried along, according to custom, to the doctrine of ideas; that before God made the world, he had the form of the whole building conceived in his mind; and so the life of those things which did not yet exist was in Christ, because the creation of the world was appointed in him. But how widely different this is from the intention of the evangelist."[11] These criticisms have bite. Exemplarism often sounds more like rationalist speculation than biblical theology. And there is no doubt that its notions of the Christ of creation or cosmic Christ can provide a pretext for liberal theology: If Jesus can be found everywhere as Logos, then why insist on the particular and exclusive claims of the incarnate and crucified Christ?[12] Both Maximus and Bonaventure are regularly enlisted to support inclusivist and mystical theologies that celebrate creation and honor other faiths while muffling the themes of sin, judgment, and atonement.[13]

Baker Academic, 2003), 2:425.

9. M. Luther, *The Table Talk or Familiar Discourse of Martin Luther*, trans. W. Hazlitt, The European Library (London: David Bogue, 1848), 4; see 50. See *LW* 54:112, no 644.

10. Luther, *Table Talk*, 26, 50; *Heidelberg Disputation* (1518), theses 19–21 (*LW* 31:40).

11. J. Calvin, *Commentary on the Gospel according to John*, trans. J. Pringle, repr. ed. (Grand Rapids: Eerdmans, 1956), 1:31.

12. As Douglas Farrow observes, "Christ everywhere means Christ nowhere." D. Farrow, *Ascension and Ecclesia: On the Significance of the Doctrine of the Ascension for Ecclesiology and Christian Cosmology* (Grand Rapids: Eerdmans, 1999), 12.

13. See for example J. Hart, *Cosmic Commons: Spirit, Science, and Space* (Eugene, OR: Wipf & Stock, 2013), 395–96; I. Delio, *Christ in Evolution* (Maryknoll, NY: Orbis, 2008), 53–65; E. H. Cousins, "Bonaventure and the Coincidence of Opposites: A Response to Critics," *TS* 42 (1981): 277–90.

OTHER PROBLEMS WITH EXEMPLARISM

There are other problems too.

One is that the framework seems very vague. What difference does it make to say that creation partakes of the Logos rather than just reflects the glory of "God" in a Romans 1:20 kind of way? What difference does it make to our understanding of specific parts of creation such as electromagnetism, honey, or participles to assert that these participate in Christ the Creator?

A more serious problem is that it can move attention away from the person of the Son to his filiality/exemplarity itself—from *him* to *what he is*.[14] It raises the question: Is creation's goal to be for the Logos (filiocentrism) or simply to be *like* him (filiomorphism)? If it is *solely* the latter, Jesus Christ becomes the supreme manifestation (or, more vaguely, establisher) of a universal telos;[15] salvation is conflated with sanctification; and the eschaton is remodeled into a general woolly notion of participation (or *methexis*).[16] Against such we might invoke

---

14. George Hunsinger's reported question (at the 2006 AAR/SBL meeting), concerning David Bentley Hart's *Beauty of the Infinite*, seems telling: "Why does ... this book talk so much about the form of Christ and the pattern of Christ as opposed to Jesus Christ himself?" From D. W. Congdon, "Summary of AAR/SBL," *The Fire and the Rose* (blog), November 2006 (accessed February 2010; the quote has been removed by a later revision).

15. So, for example, in the work of Teilhard de Chardin, and especially in Lionel Spencer Thornton, for whom the chief significance of the Logos-incarnation connection is a transformation wrought in the imagination, reason and will "towards those otherworldly standards of value which were realized personally by our Lord in his Incarnate life on earth." L. S. Thornton, *Conduct and the Supernatural: Being the Norrisian Prize Essay for the Year 1913* (London: Longmans, Green, 1915), 182. See also J. Macquarrie, *Twentieth-Century Religious Thought: The Frontiers of Philosophy and Theology, 1900–1960* (New York: Harper & Row, 1963), 269–73.

16. That these temptations are real is readily demonstrated. For example, Kathryn Tanner's application of the principle demands a switch of focus from "Jesus's passive sufferings on the cross" to his assumption of "all aspects of human existence"; K. Tanner, *Jesus, Humanity and the Trinity: A Brief Systematic Theology* (Minneapolis: Fortress, 2001), 75. The issue here is not the desire to widen the focus but the loss of the cross as its center. John Milbank provides more egregious examples of philosophical exemplarism. Waving away the actual person of Christ, he writes: "All that survives that is particular in this assumption is the proper name 'Jesus.' It is certainly the case that by telling stories about a character on earth called 'Jesus,' and by putting words into his mouth, the gospels minimally indicate reference to a 'reality' that is independent of their narration. ... [But] the gospels can be read in another way, which gives to the empty name a logical foundation in

the words of English Puritan John Flavel (1627–1691): "Christ and his benefits go inseparably and undividedly together. … Many would willingly receive his privileges, who will not receive his person; but it cannot be; if we will have one, we must take the other too: Yea, we must accept his person first, and then his benefits: as it is in the marriage covenant, so it is here."[17]

A CASE FOR EXEMPLARISM

And yet, despite these shortcomings, there are reasons to give exemplarism more careful thought.

First, its basic logic seems sound. According to Scripture, both the Son and creation are from the Father and bear witness to him—albeit to infinitely different degrees! The Son is the "the reflection of God's glory and the exact imprint of God's very being," according to Hebrews 1. Creation is *filled* with God's glory (Isa 6:3). It is quite legitimate to enquire about the relationship between these two expressions of God.

Second, it fits with some of the original sources of Trinitarian theology. The theory that creation has a prior exemplar certainly accords with certain kinds of Greek philosophy—and there is no doubt that Greek thought influenced some early patristic Trinitarianism.[18] But the idea that this exemplar is *a personal principle* has just as much to do with Jewish wisdom traditions. The Nicene fathers were convinced that passages such as Proverbs 1–8 or Wisdom 7:24–26 were, as Lewis Ayres

their universal proclamation. Along this path, I make my 'proper start'"; J. Milbank, *The Word Made Strange: Theology, Language, Culture* (Oxford: Blackwell, 1997), 150.

17. *The Method of Grace: In The Holy Spirit's Applying to the Souls of Men the Eternal Redemption Contrived by the Father and Accomplished by the Son,* in J. Flavel, *The Whole Works of John Flavel: Late Minister of the Gospel at Dartmouth, Devon* (London: W. Baynes & Son, 1820), 2:17. Modern heir of Puritanism J. I. Packer puts the matter still more pithily: "All constructions in which loving communion with the Father and the Son by the Spirit and unending praise and gratitude for redemption are not central are mere pagan fantasies. So we label them secular and strike them out of our reckoning." "Universalism: Will Everyone Ultimately Be Saved?," in *Hell under Fire: Modern Scholarship Reinvents Eternal Punishment,* ed. C. W. Morgan and R. A. Peterson (Grand Rapids: Zondervan, 2004), 180.

18. I mean particularly the theology of the apologists and Tertullian, who adopt the Stoic framework of the internal and nonpersonal Logos (*logos endiathetos*) that comes forth for the purposes of creation (*logos prophorikos*). For discussion of Athanasius and Wisdom, see K. Anatolios, *Athanasius* (London: Routledge, 2004), 110–75.

puts it, "fundamental points of reference and departure for discussing the divine being."[19]

Were they wrong? We might dispute their exegesis and their interest in apocryphal sources, but we can't blame them for seeing Christ in the Wisdom who worked as a craftsman alongside God (Prov 8:30), or the Wisdom of Wisdom 7, who is described as μονογενής (7:22) and "pure emanation of the glory of the Almighty" (7:25).

This is because these ideas are already in the New Testament. Jesus is the one in whom "all the treasures of wisdom and knowledge" are hidden (Col 2:3). He is the one in whom all things subsist and cohere (Heb 1:3; Col 1:17). Jesus is the one in whom God's fullness dwells (Col 2:9), the one who gives fullness to his people (Col 2:10)—and finally to all creation. In medieval terminology Jesus is the *exitus* and *reditus*: the one through whom things go forth from God, and the one in whom they return to him in perfection.

FOCUSING ON HUMANITY

All this seems to fit with the exemplarist scheme, but it does not completely vindicate it. To speak of Christ as creator, sustainer, and reconciler is not quite the same as Christ the template or formal source.

We come closer in the specific case of humanity, however. From Irenaeus theologians have made much of the connection between Christ the eternal image and humans,[20] *made in God's image*. Only Christ, God's true image, the argument goes, could perfect those made after the image. Or, as Nicholas Cabasilas puts it: "It was not the old Adam who was the model for the new, but the new Adam for the old. For those who have known him first, the old Adam is the archetype because of our fallen nature. But for him who sees all things before they exist, the first Adam is the imitation of the second."[21] This too might be written off as a

19. Lewis Ayres, *Nicaea and Its Legacy: An Approach to Fourth-Century Trinitarian Theology* (Oxford: Oxford University Press, 2004), 4, 40–52.

20. Limiting examples to the first centuries: Irenaeus, *Against Heresies* 5.6.1, 5.36.3; Athanasius, *On the Incarnation* 13.7,9; Clement of Alexandria, *Exhortation to the Greeks* 10; Hilary of Poitiers, *On the Trinity* 5.9; Gregory of Nyssa, *On the Making of Man* 6.3.

21. Nicholas Cabasilas, *The Life in Christ*, trans. C. J. De Catanzaro (Crestwood, NY: St Vladimir's Seminary Press, 1974), 190–91.

Platonist gloss—and it is interesting to note that even Philo describes humans as made in the image of God's Word.[22] But in this case there seems to be good scriptural evidence for it.

As the writer of Hebrews interprets Psalm 8, Christ in his resurrected glory realizes the true glory of humanity: "At it is, we do not yet see everything in subjection to them," he writes in Hebrews 2:8–9, "But we do see Jesus, who for a little while was made lower than the angels, crowned with glory and honor because of the suffering of death, so that by the grace of God he might taste death for everyone."

What's striking here is that Hebrews shows us how God's plans for humanity and Christ converge with the saving mission of Christ. God's creation of humanity in his image, with dominion over the "fish of the sea ... the birds of the air ... the cattle and ... every creeping thing" (Gen 1:26), is part of his plan to make his Son the heir (Heb 1:2) and to recapitulate all things in Christ (Eph 1:10). Humanity is thus, just like the exemplarist scheme suggests, an effect of Christ's Sonship—an expression of the eternal Son, and an anticipation of who he will become.

But this kind of exemplarism is more than filiomorphic. It is not just about a pattern—Christ recapitulating the stages and aspects of humanity. It is filiocentric—intensely personal and intensely soteriological:

- It is Christ who makes "purification for sins" who sits down at the right hand of the Majesty and inherits the excellent name (Heb 1:3–4).
- It is Christ who proves his trust in the Father (2:13) through suffering who is made perfect (2:10).
- It is Jesus who tastes death for everyone who is crowned with honor and glory and brings many sons to glory (2:9–10).

SEEING THE TRUTH OF EXEMPLARISM

Is all this too narrow? Is our response to the ancient and glorious vision of Christ in creation simply to turn back to the cross and humanity of Jesus and ignore the rest?

No, that is not what I'm saying. I strongly suspect that the exemplarist cosmic vision is true and that we will spend the rest of eternity

---

22. Philo makes the argument that humans are fashioned after the archetypal Image in *The Special Laws* 3.83 and *On the Creation* 25.

discovering how kingfishers, kestrels, and summer breezes all speak of Christ.

But the point is that we cannot begin there. Exemplarism, like all general revelation, only begins to really come true when we discover it in the light of the dying Lord and risen Savior. Without him there is too much we aren't told; too much sin fogging our vision; too much unfinished or unrevealed. As C. S. Lewis (a sturdy exemplarist if ever there was one)[23] observes: "We must not try to find a direct path through [nature] and beyond it to an increasing knowledge of God. The path peters out almost at once. Terrors and mysteries, the whole depth of God's counsels and the whole tangle of the history of the universe, choke it. We can't get through; not that way. We must make a detour— leave the hills and woods and go back to our studies, to church, to our Bibles, to our knees."[24] Lewis is right. And when we meet Jesus on our knees, in the Bible we may well discover that exemplarism is right too. We have good reason to expect that what Calvin says about Scripture functioning as spectacles to clarify and "gather" other impressions will also be true of Christ and creation.[25]

We have already seen how that works with humanity.

1. Humanity comes from the eternal relationship between the Father and the Son.

2. It is a broken and incomplete sign until Christ comes to redeem and fulfill it.

---

23. Lewis's exemplarism can be seen in *The Lion, the Witch and the Wardrobe*, where the children hear the name Aslan for the first time and immediately think of other parts of creation: "Peter felt suddenly brave and adventurous. Susan felt as if some delicious smell or some delightful strain of music had just floated by her. And Lucy got the feeling you have when you wake up in the morning and realize that it is the beginning of the holidays or the beginning of summer." C. S. Lewis, *The Lion, the Witch and the Wardrobe: A Celebration of the First Edition* (Grand Rapids: Zondervan, 2009), 67. Less evocative though more ambitious traces can be seen in a voyage to Venus, where the angelic beings sing praise to the triune creator: "All things are by Him and for Him. He utters Himself also for His own delight and sees that He is good. He is His own begotten and what proceeds from Him is Himself. Blessed be He!" C. S. Lewis, *Perelandra* (New York: Simon and Schuster, 1996).

24. C. S. Lewis, *The Four Loves* (Boston: Mariner Books, 1971), 21.

25. Calvin, *Institutes* 1.6.1.

3. By becoming man, Christ exemplifies himself (and thus his Father) in a new way.

We should expect to find similar patterns in all the created realities of our lives that intersect with this great story—things such as love, words, honor, trust, marriage, fatherhood, and sonship.

SENSING THE TRUTH OF EXEMPLARISM

But these are, in a sense, close to home—aspects of the human story. Is there any way that knowing Christ as Lord and Savior can help us discover him in chemistry, art, or economics?

Not through intellectual reflection, I think. There is simply no way to know how birds, beetles, or bacteria are like Christ unless Scripture tells us about it.

And yet, it is striking that encounters with Jesus the Savior are often accompanied by new *experiences* of the created order.

A few years ago I met an academic mathematician who told me that he'd become a Christian because the Jesus he heard about in the gospel "sounded like" mathematics. Since then I've had my ear out for this kind of thing, and I've come across many examples of it. When people have a new encounter with Jesus as Savior, there is often (not always; I stress that this is an uncovenanted blessing) a corresponding alteration in their perception of the world.

Sometimes this is prevenient and negative. One student investigating Christianity spoke about atheism "sucking the color out of life." A. N. Wilson, prior to his return to faith, talked about how frustrating it was to "listen to the music of Bach and realize that his [Bach's] perception of life was deeper, wiser, more rounded than my own."[26]

Other experiences coincide with the moment of conversion. Scientist Francis Collins recalls the spectacle of a frozen waterfall in the Cascade Mountains as the moment in which "I felt my resistance leave me."[27] Philosopher and apologist William Lane Craig remembers how

---

26. Staff Blogger, "Returning to Religion—An interview with A. N. Wilson," *New Statesman*, April 2, 2009, www.newstatesman.com/religion/2009/04/returning-to-religion.

27. S. Paulson, "The Believer: Francis Collins, Head of the Human Genome Project, Discusses His Conversion to Evangelical Christianity, Why Scientists Do

he "rushed outdoors—it was a clear, mid-western, summer night, and you could see the Milky Way stretched from horizon to horizon. As I looked up at the stars, I thought, 'God! I've come to know God!'"[28]

Jonathan Edwards provides a particularly interesting testimony. He recalls how his own youthful encounter with Christ was accompanied by a fresh appreciation of creation: "About that time, I began to have a new kind of apprehensions and ideas of Christ, and the work of redemption, and the glorious way of salvation by him. ... The appearance of everything was altered: there seemed to be, as it were, a calm, sweet cast or appearance of divine glory in almost everything. God's excellency, his wisdom, his purity and love, seemed to appear in everything."[29] Edwards says that those touched by revival often felt the same way: "Many, while their minds have been filled with spiritual delights, have as it were forgot their food; their bodily appetite has failed, while their minds have been entertained with meat to eat that others knew not of. The light and comfort which some of them enjoy, give a new relish to their common blessings, and cause all things about them to appear as it were beautiful, sweet, and pleasant. All things abroad, the sun, moon, and stars, the clouds and sky, the heavens and earth, appear as it were with a divine glory and sweetness upon them."[30]

CONCLUSION

Such experiences as these are no reliable basis for a theology, of course. Emotions can be stirred for all kinds of reasons. Yet I mention them at the end because of the way they potentially illustrate the two big ideas in this paper: first, that creation is fundamentally about Christ, and second, that discovery of this fact must begin in the context of meeting Christ, the Lord of salvation.

Not Need to Be Atheists, and What C. S. Lewis Has to Do with It," *Salon*, August 7, 2006, www.salon.com/2006/08/07/collins_6/.

28. W. L. Craig, "Personal Testimony of Faith," *Reasonable Faith with William Lane Craig* (blog), October 13, 2008, www.reasonablefaith.org/writings/question-answer/personal-testimony-of-faith/.

29. J. Edwards, *The Works of President Edwards in Four Volumes: A Reprint of the Worcester Edition*, 9th ed. (New York: Leavitt & Allen, 1856), 1:16.

30. Edwards, *Works of President Edwards*, 3:255.

My final exhortation is not for us to go off searching for mystical or aesthetic transport. Nor is it to return some variety of patristic, medieval, or modern aesthetic exemplarism. But I do want to commend the value of exploring a gospel-centered worldview that brings every part of life into the light of the Image of God who became flesh, died, and rose again for sinners. There may be greater intellectual riches for us there and possibly greater emotional resources too. Our appreciation of the central events of history—I mean the life, death, and resurrection of Jesus—might be increased as we contemplate the wider world in light of them.

WORKS CITED

Anatolios, K. *Athanasius*. London: Routledge, 2004.

Ayres, Lewis. *Nicaea and Its Legacy: An Approach to Fourth-Century Trinitarian Theology*. Oxford: Oxford University Press, 2004.

Bavinck, Herman. *Reformed Dogmatics*. Edited by J. Vriend. Translated by J. Bolt. 4 vols. Grand Rapids: Baker, 2003.

Beggiani, S. J. "The Typological Approach of Syriac Sacramental Theology." *TS* 64 (2003): 543–57.

Blowers, P. M., and R. L. Wilken. *On the Cosmic Mystery of Jesus Christ: Selected Writings from St. Maximus the Confessor*. Popular Patristics Series. Crestwood, NY: St. Vladimir's Seminary Press, 2004.

Bonaventure. "Collations on the Six Days." In *The Works of Bonaventure: Cardinal, Seraphic Doctor, and Saint*. Translated by J. de Vinck. 5 vols. Paterson: St. Anthony Guild Press, 1970.

Cabasilas, Nicholas. *The Life in Christ*. Translated by C. J. De Catanzaro. Crestwood, NY: St Vladimir's Seminary Press, 1974.

Calvin, John. *Commentary on the Gospel according to John*. Translated by J. Pringle. 2 vols. Grand Rapids: Eerdmans, 1956.

Cousins, E. H. "Bonaventure and the Coincidence of Opposites: A Response to Critics." *TS* 42 (1981): 277–90.

Craig, W. L. "Personal Testimony of Faith." *Reasonable Faith with William Lane Craig* (blog). October 13, 2008. www.reasonablefaith.org/writings/question-answer/personal-testimony-of-faith/.

Delio, Ilia. *Christ in Evolution*. Maryknoll, NY: Orbis, 2008.

Edwards, Jonathan. *An Unpublished Essay of Edwards on the Trinity: With Remarks on Edwards and His Theology*. Edited by G. P. Fisher. New York: C. Scribner's Sons, 1903.

————. *The Works of President Edwards in Four Volumes: A Reprint of the Worcester Edition.* 4 vols. 9th ed. New York: Leavitt & Allen, 1856.

Emery, G. "Essentialism or Personalism in the Treatise on God in Saint Thomas Aquinas." *Thomist* 64 (2000): 521–63.

Farrow, Douglas. *Ascension and Ecclesia: On the Significance of the Doctrine of the Ascension for Ecclesiology and Christian Cosmology.* Grand Rapids: Eerdmans, 1999.

Flavel, John. *The Whole Works of John Flavel: Late Minister of the Gospel at Dartmouth, Devon.* 2 vols. London: W. Baynes & Son, 1820.

Hart, David Bentley. *The Beauty of the Infinite: The Aesthetics of Christian Truth.* Grand Rapids: Eerdmans, 2003.

Hart, John. *Cosmic Commons: Spirit, Science, and Space.* Eugene, OR: Wipf & Stock, 2013.

Hopkins, Gerard Manley. "That Nature Is a Heraclitean Fire and of the Comfort of the Resurrection" (1888) and "As Kingfishers Catch Fire" (1877). In *The Collected Works of Gerard Manley Hopkins.* Oxford: Oxford University Press, 2006.

Lewis, C. S. *The Four Loves.* Boston: Mariner Books, 1971.

————. *The Lion, the Witch and the Wardrobe: A Celebration of the First Edition.* Grand Rapids: Zondervan, 2009.

————. *Perelandra.* New York: Simon and Schuster, 1996.

Luther, Martin. *Heidelberg Disputation* (1518). *LW* 31:39–70.

————. *The Table Talk or Familiar Discourse of Martin Luther.* Translated by W. Hazlitt. London: David Bogue, 1848.

Macquarrie, John. *Twentieth-Century Religious Thought: The Frontiers of Philosophy and Theology, 1900–1960.* New York: Harper & Row, 1963.

Milbank, John. *The Word Made Strange: Theology, Language, Culture.* Oxford: Blackwell, 1997.

Packer, J. I. "Universalism: Will Everyone Ultimately be Saved?" In *Hell under Fire: Modern Scholarship Reinvents Eternal Punishment,* edited by C. W. Morgan and R. A. Peterson, 169–94. Grand Rapids: Zondervan, 2004.

Paulson, S. "The Believer: Francis Collins, Head of the Human Genome Project, Discusses His Conversion to Evangelical Christianity, Why Scientists Do Not Need to Be Atheists, and What C.S. Lewis Has to Do with It." *Salon.* August 7, 2006. www.salon.com/2006/08/07/collins_6/.

Staff Blogger. "Returning to Religion—An interview with A. N. Wilson." *New Statesman.* April 2, 2009. www.newstatesman.com/religion/2009/04/returning-to-religion.

Tanner, Kathryn. *Jesus, Humanity and the Trinity: A Brief Systematic Theology.* Minneapolis: Fortress, 2001.

Thornton, L. S. *Conduct and the Supernatural: Being the Norrisian Prize Essay for the Year 1913.* London: Longmans, Green, 1915.

14

Revelation, *Sola Scriptura*, and Regenerate Human Reason

Mark D. Thompson

Modern theology has need of a more consistently theological account of revelation, Scripture, and the use of regenerate human reason. That would seem, at first glance, an outlandish claim to make in the wake of Barth's monumental *Church Dogmatics*, which he begins with a searching treatment of revelation as the self-communication of the triune God: "The basic problem with which Scripture faces us in respect of revelation is that the revelation attested in it refuses to be understood as any sort of revelation alongside which there are or may be others. It insists absolutely on being understood in its uniqueness. But this means that it insists absolutely on being understood in terms of its object, God."[1] These words are found at the very beginning of Barth's second chapter in *Church Dogmatics* I/1. His entire theological project is predicated on a refusal to separate the revelation of God from God the Revealer, his act from his being. The triune God is both the subject and the content of revelation, and that simple truth demands that our *doctrine* of revelation be theological in the strictest sense.

Nevertheless, the claim with which I began is not easily dismissed. The year 1932, when *Church Dogmatics* I/1 was published, was a long time ago, and a great deal has been written on the subject of revelation

---

1. "Das grundlegende Problem, vor das uns die Schrift hinsichtlich der Offenbarung stellt, besteht aber darin: die in ihr bezeugte Offenbarung will nicht verstanden sein als irgendeine Offenbarung, neben der es noch andere gibt oder geben könnte. Sie will schlechterdings in ihrer Einzigartigkeit verstanden sein. Das heißt abert: sie will schlechterdings von ihrem Subjekt, von Gott her verstanden sein"; *KD* 1/1, 311 = *CD* 1/1, 295.

since. Much of the focus has been on the reception of revelation, or the conditions of possibility for our reception of revelation, and this lends itself to a very different construction of the doctrine.[2] The doctrine of revelation sometimes becomes a subset of a more general theological epistemology, inhabited also by reason and the *consensus fidelium*. An entirely unnecessary nervousness leads some to seek to justify an appeal to revelation in Christian doctrine and practice by an increasingly complex set of theological prolegomena. Relaxed, joyful confidence in God's capacity to communicate his presence and purpose effectively to creatures—though they be both finite and fallen—a confidence that characterized the Reformers Luther, Calvin, Zwingli, and Cranmer, as well as Barth and more latterly John Webster, seems in generally short supply in the theological academy even given the recent resurgence of "theological exegesis."

What follows is an attempt to sketch what a theological account of revelation might look like, at least what it must not leave out, together with a somewhat briefer treatment of the Reformation slogan *sola scriptura* and the nature, function, and purpose of human reason within the divine economy of creation and redemption. This is not something that can or should be attempted *solo* or *de novo*. Three contemporary theologians in the evangelical Reformed tradition, who each exhibit the relaxed, nondefensive, joyful confidence in God and his word I have just mentioned, Peter Jensen, John Webster, and Kevin Vanhoozer, have very important contributions to make to a contemporary restatement of these doctrines in a determinedly theological mode.[3]

---

2. Jean-Luc Marion's 2014 Gifford Lectures, published as *Givenness & Revelation*, trans. S. E. Lewis (Oxford: Oxford University Press, 2016), are a case in point, providing an intriguing and deeply phenomenological approach the subject.

3. Peter F. Jensen, *The Revelation of God* (Leicester, UK: Inter-Varsity, 2002); Jensen, "God and the Bible," in *The Enduring Authority of the Christian Scriptures*, ed. D. A. Carson (Grand Rapids: Eerdmans, 2016), 477–96; John Webster, "Hermeneutics in Modern Theology: Some Doctrinal Reflections," in *Word and Church: Essays in Church Dogmatics* (Edinburgh: T&T Clark, 2001), 47–86; Webster, *Holy Scripture: A Dogmatic Sketch* (Cambridge: Cambridge University Press, 2003); Webster, "Biblical Reasoning," in *The Domain of the Word: Scripture and Theological Reason* (London: Bloomsbury, 2012), 115–32; Webster, "The Domain of the Word," in *Domain of the Word*, 3–31; Webster, "On the Theology of the Intellectual Life," in *God without Measure: Working Papers in Christian Theology*, vol. 2, *Virtue and Intellect* (London:

The proper starting point for such an enterprise, as in all theology, is most obviously the being and activity of the triune God.

THE GOD WHO REVEALS

The triune God of the Christian confession is a speaking God. In stark contrast to the idols of the nations, which "are like scarecrows in a cucumber field, and they cannot speak" (Jer 10:5), the living God addresses his creation. His limitless perfection includes this capacity to engage creatures directly with words. This fits within the broader category of God's self-communication. Christian theology is unavoidably committed to what Kevin Vanhoozer calls a "communicative theism." Of course Vanhoozer's notion of God's "communication" rightly goes deeper than the spoken or written word, "stretching into eternity and the Father's begetting of the Son and the proceeding of the Spirit."[4] Extended into the economy of creation and redemption, we must speak of the incarnation of the Word and the giving of the Spirit as communicative acts as well. The divine missions reflect the divine processions, and both can be characterized as communication. This is hardly a theological novelty. Almost three hundred years ago Jonathan Edwards noted, "The great and universal end of God's creating the world was to communicate himself. God is a communicative being."[5] All that God does involves the communication of his being and nature, as well as his purpose. Yet in such communication God's speech has a special role. It disambiguates the events and phenomena we experience. It locates particular people, events, and phenomena in the broader scope of God's sovereign intention and so enables us to explain their meaning with confidence.[6] It generates, sustains, and directs fellowship in faith and

---

Bloomsbury, 2016), 141–56; Kevin J. Vanhoozer, *Remythologizing Theology: Divine Action, Passion, and Authorship* (Cambridge: Cambridge University Press, 2010).

4. Vanhoozer, *Remythologizing Theology*, 226.

5. Jonathan Edwards, "Miscellany 332" [1728], in *The Works of Jonathan Edwards* (New Haven, CT: Yale University Press, 1994), 13:410. See "Miscellany 107b" [1724], in *Works*, 13:277–78.

6. This is what lies behind the provocative statement of D. Broughton Knox that "propositional revelation is the only revelation." "What is it then that makes the tribal migrations of the Israelites pregnant with revelation throughout the Old and New Testaments, while those of their related tribe, the Syrians, reveal only the one fact of God's general providence to which Amos alludes? Similarly, why are

hope. We must return to why this is so. However, in the meantime, we may say that a primary mode of God's communication in the economy is speech, and, given the recipients and the agency involved, that speech may with only slight qualification be identified as human speech.[7] God uses words, our words, to address us.

A testimony to God's activity of revealing himself and his purposes in human speech is ubiquitous in Scripture. God addresses the man and woman in the garden, necessarily in language they could understand, as he blesses them and warns them about the consequences of disobedience (Gen 1–2). The subsequent narrative is driven forward at every point by words spoken by God and addressed to human creatures: the call of Abram and the programmatic promise made to him (Gen 12:1–3), the call of Moses from the bush that is alight but does not burn (Exod 3:4–6), the call of Samuel sleeping at Shiloh (1 Sam 3), the promise to David and his descendants (2 Sam 7), the call of later prophets (Isa 6:8–13), the voice from heaven at the baptism of Jesus and again at his transfiguration (Matt 3:16–17; 17:5), the words at the end, "I am the Alpha and the Omega, the beginning and the end" (Rev 21:6). At points this word is mediated by a human or angelic messenger—Moses, the prophets, the apostles, or the angel Gabriel. That mediation in its various forms does not, however, get in the way of the identification of their words with the word of God. That identification is most acute when the incarnate Son speaks the words given to him by his Father.

---

the invasions of neighboring countries by the Assyrians, and the fate that overtook the Assyrians, revelational of God's character, while the intertribal warfare of, say, the Maoris, is not? It is not as though God's sovereign control is exercised any more over the one or any less over the other of these different events, but simply that to one have been added interpretative propositions and statements, but not to the other. It is the proposition which is the revelation, giving meaning to the event, to our minds. The conclusion is that revelation is essentially propositional" ("Propositional Revelation, the Only Revelation," *RTR* 19, no. 1 [1960]: 5–6). Note that Knox had earlier clarified what he meant by "propositional": "The denial of 'propositional revelation' is the denial that God reveals Himself to men through the medium of words, that is to say, through meaningful statements and concepts expressed in words; for such is the only sense that can be given to the word 'propositional' in this phrase" (2).

7. James I. Packer writes, "The Bible conceives of revelation as primarily and fundamentally verbal communication" ("Revelation," in *New Bible Dictionary*, 2nd ed., ed. J. D. Douglas et al. [Leicester, UK: Inter-Varsity, 1982], 1027).

He speaks with a singular authority yet insists that his words have been given to him by the Father who sent him (John 12:49; 14:23), and he can appeal to the words recorded by Moses and the prophets as "the word of God" without qualification (Matt 15:6; John 10:35). It comes as no surprise, then, that the writer to the Hebrews can sum up God's dealings in the created order with precisely such a reference to God's activity of speaking: "God spoke in many and various ways by the prophets, but in these last days he has spoken to us by a Son" (Heb 1:1-2).

The critical point is that the living God speaks, and the words he speaks are addressed to his creatures and so have extraordinary significance. His word can be heard, inscribed, and even translated. Rebuke and judgment are delivered on the assumption that this word can be understood and has been repudiated. Intriguingly, God's words carry their authority across the divide of human languages: they are open to translation. Even within the New Testament itself there is evidence of translation without a necessary loss of nature, authority, and power. Human finitude and diversity are not insuperable barriers to hearing the words in which God makes known himself and what he intends for his creation. Words from God have the power to bring life, to still the storm, to raise the dead, and to provide a genuine basis for hope.

Why such an emphasis on words? Apart from contemporary apologetic concerns, where the essentially verbal character of revelation is defended against attempts to locate the revelatory center in history or existential awareness or an unfolding ecclesiastical consensus, it is this pervasive witness of Scripture that provides the first answer to this question. As Graham Cole puts it, "From Genesis to Revelation, Scripture exhibits a communicative God in communicative action. ... God is rendered in the canon as a speech agent who promises (Gen 12:1-3), permits (e.g., Gen 2:16), warns (Gen 2:17), informs (Exod 3:14), and questions (e.g., 1 Kgs 19:9)."[8] To this we could add invites (Matt 11:28), summons (Mark 1:15), and commands (Matt 28:20).

Yet the significance of words lies in their capacity to generate and sustain a relationship between a speaker and a hearer. Among all the

---

8. Graham A. Cole, "Why a Book? Why This Book? Why the Particular Order within This Book? Some Reflections on the Canon," in *Enduring Authority*, ed. D. A. Carson, 458, 459.

other things that words can do, they can express commitment and deliver promises. They bind together the one who makes the commitment and the one to whom the commitment is made, the one who promises and the one who receives the promise. Peter Jensen laid particular emphasis on the relational importance of words as he argued from the verbal character of the gospel to the indispensability of the inscripturated word.

> A gospel that, through faith, overcomes alienation and restores fellowship between God and humanity, requires God's speech in human language to accomplish divine self-disclosure and faith. That is the nature of persons. Even between humans, language is the supreme instrument of human relationship. It is not the only means. We overcome the physical distance between us in a number of ways: we see each other; we observe, touch, and smell each other. We use signs and symbols to communicate, often at a very profound level indeed. But, in the end, it is the language we share which is the indispensable and peerless vehicle of disclosure, of invitation, of relationship, of faith.[9]

This reality too is anchored in the life and being of the triune God. Though we know little about the process involved, there is evidently an exchange of words between the Father and the Son in eternity. In the high-priestly prayer of John 17, Jesus speaks not only of "the glory that I had in your presence before the world existed" (17:5, indicating that not all that is said here is limited to the economy or the experience of the *incarnate* Son) but also of "the words that you gave to me" (17:8). Earlier he insisted, "No one knows the Son except the Father, and no one knows the Father except the Son and anyone to whom the Son chooses to reveal him" (Matt 11:27). This mystery of intra-Trinitarian relations and communication has not been made known to us in any detail. What we are given to say is that the words taught to us by the Spirit are intrinsically connected to God's self-knowledge: "no one comprehends what is truly God's except the Spirit of God" (1 Cor 2:11–13). Biblical texts such as these have led John Frame to venture that "God's word, his

---

9. Jensen, "God and the Bible," 487.

speech, is an essential attribute, inseparable from God's being."[10] There is something entirely appropriate about the Son being identified as the Word who was in the beginning, was with God, and was God (John 1:1). Frame again: "There are no unexplored depths in God's nature. He does not surprise himself. He is word. His word exhaustively expresses his being to himself, among the persons of the Trinity."[11]

There remains, though, something uncomfortably earthy, physical, even anthropomorphic, about attributing speech and especially human words to God, let alone arguing that these lie close to if not at the very heart of God's revelatory activity. Of course this may be just an example of what Webster calls "our natural antipathy to revelation taking creaturely form."[12] Barth would argue, "Who are we to say that God cannot do this if in fact he has done it?" The incarnation itself might seem impossible in principle until one is faced with the fact that the Word has indeed become flesh and dwelt among us. But the objections come with a degree of sophistication that means they are not easily dismissed. Rowan Williams has long spoken about the fragility of human language and a proper place for silence when facing "a God who can never be captured in one set of words, a God who is transcendently holy in a way that exacts from human language the most scrupulous scepticism and the most painstaking elaboration possible."[13] Most recently, in his 2013 Gifford Lectures published as *The Edge of Words: God and the Habits of Language,* he opines:

> Ultimately, what the various languages of revelation propose or imply is that our most fully aware and deliberate and freely accepted silences, when the speaker's agenda is most manifestly suspended, are moments where truthfulness is most evident, where there is the most potent and appropriate act of "representation." And because

10. J. Frame, *The Doctrine of God* (Phillipsburg, NJ: P&R, 2002), 475.

11. Frame, *Doctrine of God,* 475. "It is theologically right to say that in a sense God is revelation. God is a being who in his very nature is communicative. He speaks not only to creatures, but within his Trinitarian existence, Father to Son, Son to Father, both to the Spirit, and the Spirit to both of them" (Frame, *The Doctrine of the Word of God* [Phillipsburg, NJ: P&R, 2010], 42).

12. Webster, *Domain of the Word,* 12.

13. Rowan Williams, "Service to Commemorate the 450th Anniversary of the Martyrdom of Thomas Cranmer."

this is a representation of what we cannot ever in principle control or contain, we can say also that this is where the sacred appears—in whatever paradoxical sense we give to the word "appears" here. For those who accept the Christian revelation, this paradox is articulated with special clarity in the focal image of the bearer of ultimate revelation silenced and immobilized: a place where there is a convergence of two journeys of dispossession, divine and human.[14]

Elsewhere I have dared to suggest that a number of missteps are taken by Williams, not least associated with a particular and contested construal of transcendence, a neglect of the biblical presentation of God as the primal speaker using human words, a reluctance to distinguish clearly between true knowledge and exhaustive knowledge (we can never *contain* God in words, though the truth about God can be genuinely conveyed by words), and an overattachment to mystic apophaticism.[15]

In the twentieth century Karl Barth took issue with Paul Tillich's suggestion that the idea of divine speech or the divine word should be understood symbolically.[16] In doing so he emphasized both the reality and the fragility of human language—from his point of view even a kind of unsuitability as a vehicle of divine revelation.

We have no reason not to take the concept of God's Word primarily in its literal sense. God's Word means that God speaks. Speaking is not a "symbol." ... It is not a designation or description which on the basis of his own assessment of its symbolic force man has chosen for something very different from and quite alien to this expression. For all its human inadequacy, for all the brokenness with which alone human statements can correspond to the nature of the Word of God, this statement does correspond to the possibility which God has chosen and actualised at all events in His Church. ...

14. Rowan Williams, *The Edge of Words: God and the Habits of Language* (London: Bloomsbury, 2014), 184.

15. Mark D. Thompson, *Too Big for Words? The Transcendence of God and Finite Human Speech* (London: Latimer Trust, 2006).

16. Paul Tillich writes, "The word, determined by the Spiritual Presence, does not try to grasp an ever escaping object but expresses a union between the inexhaustible subject and the inexhaustible object in a symbol which is by its very nature indefinite and definite at the same time" (*Systematic Theology* [repr., Welwyn: James Nisbet, 1968], 3:270; cf. 1:138).

Let us simply stick to the fact, and not try to think beyond it, that in this form in which the Church knows God's Word—the one and only form which necessarily, because imperiously, affects us—in this form God's Word means that "God speaks," and all else that is to be said about it must be regarded as exegesis and not as a restriction or negation of this statement.[17]

Strangely, as Nicholas Wolterstorff has pointed out, Barth does not in fact go on to say very much about divine speech *as speech*, and he draws back from any unequivocal identification of the Bible as the word of God.[18] Rather, his attention is on the event, the impact of the personal presence of God in Christ, who is in fact *revelation* in Barth's terms. His presence might—by God's sovereign choice—be mediated by human words in all their fragility, but cannot be identified with them, even when the Bible writers—and Jesus himself as he appears in the Gospels—present them as words proceeding from the mouth of God (1 Kgs 8:15; 2 Chr 35:22; 36:12; Matt 4:4). Barth's account of *Deus dixit* has received a great deal of attention over the years, largely as a result of continuing disagreement over his doctrine of Scripture. Yet it hasn't really advanced our understanding of the critical role of human words as a vehicle of divine revelation.

The hint has already been given, but real progress in this area of taking seriously the critical role of divine speech and hence the word of God in the economy of creation and redemption has come through

---

17. "Dann haben wir keinen Anlaß, den Begriff 'Wort Gottes' nicht vor allem wörtlich zu nehmen. 'Gottes Wort' heißt: Gott redet. 'Redet' ist nicht ein Symbol. ... Eine vom Menschen auf Grund seines eigenen Urteils über größere oder geringere Symbolkräftigkeit gewählte Bezeichnung und Beschreibeung eines an sich ganz anderen, dem Sinn dieses Satzes ganz femden Sachverhalts. Sondern dieser Satz entspricht, gewiß in menschlicher Inadäquatheit, in der Gebrochenheit, in der menschliche Sätze dem Wesen des Wortes Gottes allein entsprechen können— der Möglichkeit, die Gott jedenfalls in seiner Kirche gewählt und verwirklicht hat. ... Eann halten wir uns einfach daran und denken nicht darüber hinaus: in der Gestalt, in der die Kirche Gottes Wort kennt—der einen und einzigen, die uns notwendig, weil gebieterisch etwas angeht—in dieser Gestalt heißt 'Gottes Wort': 'Gott Redet' und alles, was weiter von ihm zu sagen ist, mußt als Exegese, nicht aber als Einschränkung oder Negation dieses Satzes zu verstehen sein" (*KD* 1/1 137 = *CD* I/1, 132–33).

18. Nicholas Wolterstorff, *Divine Discourse: Philosophical Reflections on the Claim That God Speaks* (Cambridge: Cambridge University Press, 1995), 72–74.

the theological appropriation of speech-act theory, associated with philosophers of language John Austin and John Searle.[19] Kevin Vanhoozer has been a leader in this area. In his *Remythologizing Theology*, he provides an account of "the communicative quality of God's perfect life": "God in himself (*in se; ad intra*) enjoys never-ending, fully realized interpersonal communication: communion. The blessed communion— the triune life of God—involves the 'making common' of light and life. This *communicare* is the love of God."[20] There is an other-centeredness, a giving and receiving, at the heart of God's eternal triune life that makes sense of the biblical axiom "God is love"—not just "God loves," wonderful enough though that is, but "God is love" (1 John 4:8, 16). It is this intra-Trinitarian communication that, as Michael Allen writes, "freely spills over into creative and covenantal speech."[21] The two are to be kept together, Vanhoozer says: "What God communicates to us in time corresponds to what he eternally and perfectly is in himself. ... The economic drama (God's blessing creatures) thus corresponds to the immanent drama (God's blessedness in himself)."[22] Once again, this is where the continuing importance of words comes in: the Lord "takes the communicative initiative to enter into covenantal relation with Israel, and ... this covenant-making involves both oral and written communicative acts on God's part."[23]

So a theological account of revelation, anchored in the person and purposes of the triune God, played out in the divinely instituted, sustained, and directed economy of creation and redemption, cannot or must not ignore the significance of God's speech, addressed to and shaped for reception by his human creatures. However, as it does so it will not bypass the person of Jesus Christ, the Word become flesh who dwelt among us. Nevertheless, it is not simply Christ's "very

---

19. John L. Austin, *How to Do Things with Words: The William James Lectures Delivered at Harvard University in 1955* (Oxford: Clarendon, 1962); John R. Searle, *Speech Acts: An Essay in the Philosophy of Language* (Cambridge: Cambridge University Press, 1969).

20. Vanhoozer, *Remythologizing*, 244–45.

21. R. Michael Allen, "Knowledge of God," in *Christian Dogmatics: Reformed Theology for the Church Catholic*, ed. R. Michael Allen and Scott R. Swain (Grand Rapids: Baker, 2016), 11.

22. Vanhoozer, *Remythologizing*, 259–60.

23. Vanhoozer, *Remythologizing*, 263.

creatureliness [that] constitutes the act of revelation," as T. F. Torrance suggests.[24] Jesus appears among us in the context of a history of promises stretching back to the garden of Eden. He is not a mute presence among us. He situates himself and all he does in the context of the history of those promises, stretching out from Israel to the nations. As we have already noted, he speaks new words, words given to him by his Father. Preeminently he speaks of the gospel, both an announcement of the promised kingdom and a summons to repentance and faith as it draws near (Mark 1:15). Certainly it is in Christ himself (his person, words, and work) that all the promises of God find their "yes" (2 Cor 1:20). Yet the oft-repeated words of John Calvin bear repeating again: "This, then, is the true knowledge of Christ, if we receive him as he is offered by the Father: namely, clothed with his gospel."[25] As Barth himself recognized, "The personal character of God's Word is not ... to be played off against its verbal or spiritual character. ... The personalising of the concept of the Word of God, which we cannot avoid when we remember that Jesus Christ is the Word of God, does not mean its deverbalising."[26]

Against this backdrop the unique authority accorded to Scripture is given new depth. It is not arbitrary, nor is it shallowly grounded in a handful of prooftexts.

THE UNIQUE AUTHORITY OF SCRIPTURE

Scripture, like revelation itself, needs to be located in the divine economy of creation and redemption. The goal of the divine missions (*opera ad extra*), the free overflow of the other-centered divine processions (*relationes ad intra*), is that creatures might know, love, and delight in

---

24. T. F. Torrance, *Incarnation: The Person and Life of Christ* (Milton Keynes, UK: Paternoster, 2008), 186.

25. "Haec igitur vera est Christi cognition, si eum quails offertur a Patre suscipimus, nempe Evangelio suo vestitum" (Calvin, *Institutes* III.ii.6). Also, "we enjoy Christ only as we embrace Christ clad in his own promises" (*Nec vero aliter Christo fruimur, nisi quatenus eum amplectimur promissionibus suis vestitum*), *Institutes* II.ix.3.

26. "Die Persönlichkeit des Wortes Gottes ist also nicht etwa gegen seine Wörtlichkeit und Geistigkeit auszuspielen. ... Die Verpersönlichung des Begriffs des Wortes Gottes, der wir in Erinnerung daran, daß Jesus Christus das Wort Gottes ist, nicht ausweichen können, bedeutet nicht seine Entwörtlichung" (*KD* I/1, 142, 143 = *CD* I/1, 138).

their Creator. This fellowship, though, is cognitive as well as personal, affective, and spiritual, and it is generated and sustained by the word, which God introduces into the world. God speaks his word both as an act of revelation but also as a gift of providence. Indeed, in an important sense, revelation is a singular act of divine providence. Light and life are bound together. God in Christ "sustains all things by his powerful word" (Heb 1:3). The entire created order is sustained and led forward to its goal by the word of God.

Locating Scripture within the divine economy and expounding its nature and purpose in resolute connection to the divine missions keeps the Christian doctrine of Scripture from being isolated or abstracted from the person and work of Christ. It is surely an indication that something has gone awry if our doctrine of Scripture is constructed without reference to the One who is the Word incarnate, or with him at its periphery. The Law, the Prophets, and the Psalms bear witness *to him* (Luke 24:27, 44; John 5:39). The apostles are commissioned to be *his* witnesses (Acts 1:8; Matt 28:18–20). He stands at the very heart of the biblical message, Old and New Testament, and in Paul's words, speaking in the first instance of the Old Testament, these sacred writings "are able to instruct you for salvation *through faith in Christ Jesus*" (2 Tim 3:15).

Once again it is important to emphasize that the sending of the Son into the world occurs within a context of prior words, the promises of the Old Testament, and not *ex nihilo*. These words, given for the instruction and comfort of God's covenant people, cast their vision forward to the day when God will act in a decisive way, through the one he has chosen, to fulfill his promises and bring the whole of creation to its goal. Against that matrix of redemptive history and categories of thought (covenant, redemption, sacrifice, substitution, forgiveness, etc.), the ministry of the incarnate Son is rendered intelligible. Similarly, the words of the New Testament, arising out of the apostolic mission commissioned by the risen Christ, recalling, under the impress of the Spirit's ministry, "all that I have said to you," as Jesus put it (Matt 28:18–20; John 14:26; Col 1:28; 2:6–7), proclaiming him, encouraging and directing present and future disciples to live consistently in the light of who he is and all that he has accomplished—these words serve the saving purpose of Christ. All things, including the texts given at the hands of the prophets and apostles, are created through him and for him (Col 1:16). Whatever else these texts might do, their critical role is to testify to Christ and to play a part in the movement toward that day when every knee will bow before him and when, all things having been put in subjection to him, he delivers the kingdom to God the Father so that God may be all in all (Phil 2:9–10; 1 Cor 15:24–28). They bring the light, and engender that faith and hope, that enables creatures to arrive at their end: knowing and loving and delighting in their Creator. As John Webster puts it, "To accomplish his communicative mission, the exalted Son takes into his service a textual tradition, a set of human writings, so ordering their course that by him they are made into living creaturely instruments of his address to living creatures."[27] One might want to add, "not just any textual tradition, not just any set of human writings, but very specifically these written words, freely authored by those he called and commissioned to speak." These men "moved by the Holy Spirit spoke from God" (2 Pet 1:21). And it is their combined literary deposit (πᾶσα γραφὴ) that is θεόπνευστος (2 Tim 3:16).

Once again, Vanhoozer's communicative theism proves useful in maintaining the link between God and Scripture.

> I submit that the best way to view God and Scripture together is to acknowledge God as a communicative agent and Scripture as his communicative action. The virtue of this construal ... lies in its implicit thesis that one can neither discuss God apart from Scripture nor do justice to Scripture in abstraction from its relation to God. For if the Bible is a species of divine communicative action, it follows that in using Scripture we are not dealing merely with information about God; we are rather engaging with God himself—with God in communicative action. The notion of divine communicative action forms an indissoluble bond between God and Scripture.[28]

---

27. Webster, *Domain of the Word*, 8. See too Vanhoozer: "The crucial point is that Scripture is holy (set apart) and authoritative because it is ingredient in the economy of communication, that is, in the way in which the triune God ministers the Word of God in the power of the Spirit" (Vanhoozer, *Remythologizing*, 264).

28. K. J. Vanhoozer, *First Theology: God, Scripture and Hermeneutics* (Downers Grove, IL: InterVarsity, 2002), 35.

If this is right, though, it becomes even more important that we take very seriously the creaturely nature of the biblical texts. The human authors were consciously and creatively involved in the production of these texts. θεόπνευστος has never implied mechanical dictation, except in mischievous caricature. The biblical texts remain open to historical and literary analysis and investigation because they are genuinely human writings. Yet Webster is surely right to remind us that Scripture's "human characteristics, though real, are instrumental, ordered towards the divine act of speech, and to be understood in that connection."[29] Which is, of course, why these texts are distinct from all other written words. This is why the authority with which these words come to us stands over all other authorities. The authority of Scripture, which arises from its nature and origin in the communicative purposes of the living God, is none other than the authority of God.[30]

The reformation slogan *sola scriptura*, used, but sparingly, by Martin Luther, was not an absolute repudiation of all other authority. He for one was willing to read and weigh the writings of the fathers and the medieval theologians, the decrees of the popes and the decisions of church councils. He did this throughout his ministry at Wittenberg. But as he said to Cardinal Cajetan in Augsburg in October 1518: "The truth of Scripture comes first. After that is accepted one may determine whether the words of men can be accepted as true."[31] Luther could cite and make use of the writings of men, but by October 1518 he no longer considered them decisive. Two years later, in the wake of the papal threat of excommunication, he wrote, "I do not want to throw out all those more learned [than I], but *Scripture alone* to reign, and not to interpret it by my own spirit or the spirit of any man, but I want to

---

29. Webster, *Domain of the Word*, 28.

30. N. T. Wright, *Scripture and the Authority of God* (London: SPCK, 2005), 17.

31. *Prior est veritas scripturae, et post hoc, si hominis verba vera esse possunt, videndum*; M. Luther, *Acta Augustana* (1518), WA 2:21.5–6; *LW* 31:282. More than 150 years later François Turretin cited Basil the Great to the same end: "Let the divinely inspired Scriptures then judge for us and let the vote of truth be given to those among whom doctrines are found harmonizing with the Scriptures" (F. Turretin, *Institutes of Elenctic Theology* [1679–1685], ed. J. T. Dennison, trans. G. M. Giger [Phillipsburg, NJ: P&R, 1992], 1:162). The citation is from Basil's Letter 189, "To Eustathius the Physician."

understand it by itself and its spirit."[32] John Calvin understood, perhaps more than Luther, how difficult the task was that Luther had set for himself, but he was sure "it is better to limp along this path than to dash with all speed outside it."[33]

Scripture stands alone at the point of the final judgment on theological matters, matters of faith and life, because of its unique position in the economy of creation and redemption, its unique relation to the triune God whose authority is always absolute. Later theology distinguished between Scripture, the norm that norms all other norms (*norma normans*), and the other authorities to which one might appeal in these matters, the norms that are themselves normed (*norma normata*).

REASON REDEEMED YET AWAITING PERFECTION

What then about human reason? The basic line of approach has already been given. If a theological account of reason and its use is to be advanced, due attention needs to be paid to its existence within the divine economy. God's purpose in creation is fellowship with creatures, a fellowship that is, not entirely but certainly not least, a cognitive fellowship. God creates the capacity not only to hear but to understand the words he has spoken and to consider their consequences. As a created faculty, human reason is necessarily finite and contingent. Yet finitude and contingency are not necessarily negative things. These are part of the creaturely orientation to the word that God speaks. The man and the woman in the garden were to observe and make sense of their world, but in the context of fellowship with God. What the tree in the middle of the garden offered was the illusion of knowledge gained without reference to God, the exercise of an undisciplined and unaccountable reason. Yet, as Webster points out, human intellect, while created coordinate with God's intellect, is also incommensurate with it.[34] So what the primal pair grasped for at that critical moment was something that

---

32. "Nolo omnium doctor iactari, sed solam scripturam regnare, nec eam meo spiritu aut ullorum hominum interpretari, sed per seipsam et suo spiritu intelligi volo" (M. Luther, "Assertio omnium articulorum M. Lutheri per bullam Leonis X" [1520], WA 7:98.40–99.2 [emphasis added]).

33. "Satius sit in hac via claudicare quam extra eam celerrime currere" (Calvin, *Institutes* I.vi.3).

34. Webster, "On the Theology of the Intellectual Life," 144.

would unravel not only their fellowship with the Creator but also their own creaturely life. They flee from finitude only to fall, as Michael Allen puts it.[35] They could not "become like God," as the serpent promised, but entered the downward spiral into futility, senselessness, and perversity that the apostle Paul talks about in Romans 1. Their minds were darkened. Reason was distorted.

Yet again, Webster provides us with an insightful picture of the devastation consequent upon the fall.

> Sin is betrayal of our created nature and refusal to live out the vocation which that nature entails. Life in, with and under the creator involves three elements: glad consent to the nature and powers which in his love the creator has bestowed on us; the employment of our given powers in ways which move us to our creaturely fulfilment; fellowship with the creator. ... The children of Adam do not do these things. ... The freedom to consent becomes the freedom to dissent, to act against the purpose of the creator. We give ourselves permission to use our powers to fill out our nature in ways which the creator has not left open to us. ... We edge ourselves away from life in obedience to the creator's purpose.[36]

As he fills out that picture, Webster presents an intriguing conjunction of futility and curiosity—a craving for novelty, indiscriminate intellectual greed, a capitulation to pride and self-satisfaction.

Nevertheless, the economy of creation is at one and the same time the economy of redemption, and neither the tempter nor his handiwork has the final say. Through the redeeming missions of the Son and the Spirit, reason is recovered, rehabilitated, regenerated, and redeemed. Reason too encounters grace. The regeneration of reason is not an achievement but a gift, born of the Creator's own commitment to see through his original intention, to order the creation under the Lordship of the Son—"all things were created through him and *for him*" (Col 1:16). So regenerate human reason is disciplined by the gospel of grace and oriented toward the word that God has spoken. It is characterized by humility, a determination to operate within the limits God

---

35. Allen, "Knowledge of God," 14.
36. Webster, "On the Theology of the Intellectual Life," 147–48.

has set for it, in ministerial rather than magisterial mode, chastened and yet energized by the wholly undeserved mercy of God. Christian discipleship includes a determined discipleship of the mind—following and learning without an attempt to take the posture of a master. Michael Allen and Scott Swain put it well: "Grace does not undercut or circumvent intellectual reflection. Rather, grace comes as this promise: 'Think over what I say, for the Lord will give you understanding in everything' (2 Tim 2:7). The nature of God's gift is illumining. It does not augment our intellectual activity; it provides the context, conditions, and character for its proper functioning. ... Behold, the Lord makes all things new, including our sinful reason and our darkened suppression of the knowledge of the one true God."[37] There is still more to come. Our reason, though regenerate, awaits the consummation, like all else redeemed by Christ. It is not yet perfected. "Now I know only in part; then I will know fully, even as I have been fully known" (1 Cor 13:12).

CONCLUSION

This has just been a taster, really, of what an explicitly theological account of revelation, Scripture, and human reason might look like. It starts and ends with God, for after all theology is the knowledge of God and of all things in relation to God. The living God speaks. He is invested in communicative action. There are no insuperable obstacles to the realization of his communicative purpose. The prophets and apostles serve that purpose. So too does Scripture, which likewise operates within the economy of creation and redemption. Human reason, redeemed through the ministry of the Word and the Spirit, flourishes when shaped and disciplined by Scripture as the written word of God. For, to tweak a famous quote from Barth almost exactly a hundred years ago: what matters most is not what we say about God but what God says about God and about us and about our world—his world.

---

37. Michael Allen and Scott R. Swain, "Introduction," in *Christian Dogmatics*, 3.

WORKS CITED

Allen, R. Michael. "Knowledge of God." In *Christian Dogmatics: Reformed Theology for the Church Catholic*, edited by R. Michael Allen and Scott R. Swain, 7–29. Grand Rapids: Baker, 2016.

Allen, R. Michael, and Scott R. Swain, eds. *Christian Dogmatics: Reformed Theology for the Church Catholic*. Grand Rapids: Baker, 2016.

Austin, John L. *How to Do Things with Words: The William James Lectures Delivered at Harvard University in 1955*. Oxford: Clarendon, 1962.

Barth, Karl. *Die Kirchliche Dogmatik*. 14 vols. Zürich: Zolliken, 1932.

Calvin, John. *Institutes of the Christian Religion*. Edited by John T. McNeill. Translated by Ford Lewis Battles. 1536 ed. Philadelphia: Westminster, 1970.

Cole, Graham A. "Why a Book? Why This Book? Why the Particular Order within This Book? Some Reflections on the Canon." In *The Enduring Authority of the Christian Scriptures*, edited by D. A. Carson, 456–76. Grand Rapids: Eerdmans, 2016.

Edwards, Jonathan. "Miscellany 107b" [1724]. In *The Works of Jonathan Edwards*, 13:277–78. New Haven, CT: Yale University Press, 199.

———. "Miscellany 332" [1728]. In *The Works of Jonathan Edwards*, 13:410. New Haven, CT: Yale University Press, 1994.

Frame, John. *The Doctrine of God*. Phillipsburg, NJ: P&R, 2002.

———. *The Doctrine of the Word of God*. Phillipsburg, NJ: P&R, 2010.

Jensen, Peter F. "God and the Bible." In *The Enduring Authority of the Christian Scriptures*, edited by D. A. Carson, 477–96. Grand Rapids: Eerdmans, 2016.

———. *The Revelation of God*. Leicester, UK: Inter-Varsity, 2002.

Knox, D. Broughton. "Propositional Revelation, the Only Revelation." *RTR* 19, no. 1 (1960): 1–9.

Luther, Martin. *Acta Augustana* (1518). WA 2:6–26. For English translation, see *Proceedings at Augsburg 1518*, LW 31:259–89.

———. *Assertio omnium articulorum M. Lutheri per bullam Leonis X* (1520). WA 7:94–151.

Marion, Jean-Luc. *Givenness and Revelation*. Translated by S. E. Lewis. Oxford: Oxford University Press, 2016.

Packer, James I. "Revelation." In *New Bible Dictionary*. 2nd ed. Edited by J. D. Douglas et al. Leicester, UK: Inter-Varsity, 1982.

Searle, John R. *Speech Acts: An Essay in the Philosophy of Language*. Cambridge: Cambridge University Press, 1969.

Thompson, Mark D. *Too Big for Words? The Transcendence of God and Finite Human Speech*. London: Latimer Trust, 2006.

Tillich, Paul. *Systematic Theology* [1951–1963]. Repr. ed. Welwyn: James Nisbet, 1968.

Torrance, T. F. *Incarnation: The Person and Life of Christ*. Milton Keynes, UK: Paternoster, 2008.

Turretin, Francis. *Institutes of Elenctic Theology* [1679–1685]. Edited by J. T. Dennison. Translated by G. M. Giger. Phillipsburg, NJ: P&R, 1992.

Vanhoozer, Kevin J. *First Theology: God, Scripture & Hermeneutics.* Downers Grove, IL: InterVarsity, 2002.

———. *Remythologizing Theology: Divine Action, Passion, and Authorship.* Cambridge: Cambridge University Press, 2010.

Webster, John. "Biblical Reasoning." In *The Domain of the Word: Scripture and Theological Reason,* 115–32. London: Bloomsbury, 2012.

———. "The Domain of the Word." In *The Domain of the Word: Scripture and Theological Reason,* 3–31. London: Bloomsbury, 2012.

———. "Hermeneutics in Modern Theology: Some Doctrinal Reflections." In *Word and Church: Essays in Church Dogmatics,* 47–86. Edinburgh: T&T Clark, 2001.

———. *Holy Scripture: A Dogmatic Sketch.* Cambridge: Cambridge University Press, 2003.

———. "On the Theology of the Intellectual Life." In *God without Measure: Working Papers in Christian Theology,* vol. 2, *Virtue and Intellect,* 141–56. London: Bloomsbury, 2016.

Williams, Rowan. *The Edge of Words: God and the Habits of Language.* London: Bloomsbury, 2014.

———. "Service to Commemorate the 450th Anniversary of the Martyrdom of Thomas Cranmer." October 15, 2014.

Wolterstorff, Nicholas. *Divine Discourse: Philosophical Reflections on the Claim That God Speaks.* Cambridge: Cambridge University Press, 1995.

Wright, N. T. *Scripture and the Authority of God.* London: SPCK, 2005.

Contributors

WILLIAM J. ABRAHAM (DPhil, Oxford) is Outler Professor of Wesley Studies and Distinguished University Teaching Professor at Perkins School of Theology, Southern Methodist University. He is author of *Canon and Criterion in Christian Theology* and coeditor with Frederick D. Aquino of *The Oxford Handbook of the Epistemology of Theology*.

CAROLINE BATCHELDER (ThD, Australian College of Theology) teaches Old Testament and is the BTh Program Director at Alphacrucis College in Parramatta.

STEVEN J. DUBY (PhD, University of St Andrews) is assistant professor of theology at Grand Canyon University. He is author of *Divine Simplicity: A Dogmatic Account*.

CHRISTOPHER C. GREEN (PhD, University of Aberdeen) is director of Theology Connect, senior adjunct in theology at Azusa Pacific University, and director of Christian foundations at Plenty Valley Christian College (Australia). He is author of *Doxological Theology: Karl Barth on Divine Providence, Evil and the Angels*.

CHRISTOPHER R. J. HOLMES (ThD, Wycliffe College and the University of Toronto) is associate professor (systematic theology) in the Department of Theology and Religion at the University of Otago, Dunedin, New Zealand. His latest book is *The Lord Is Good: Seeking the God of the Psalter*.

CHASE R. KUHN (PhD, University of Western Sydney) is lecturer in Christian thought and ministry at Moore Theological College, Sydney. He is author of *The Ecclesiology of Donald Robinson and D. Broughton Knox: Exposition, Analysis, and Theological Evaluation*.

JOHN McCLEAN (PhD, University of Divinity) is vice principal and lecturer in systematic theology at Christ College, the Presbyterian theological college in Sydney. He is author of *From the Future: Getting to Grips with Pannenberg's Thought* and *The Real God for the Real World*, an introduction to Christian doctrine.

ANDREW MOODY (ThD, Ridley College, Melbourne) is an adjunct lecturer in systematic theology at several colleges around Australia and is also editorial director of The Gospel Coalition Australia website. He is author of *In Light of the Son* and *The Will of Him Who Sent Me*, and contributing author to *On Rowan Williams: Critical Essays*.

BRUCE PASS (BDiv, Moore College) is a doctoral candidate at the University of Edinburgh, researching the place and purpose of Christology in the theological method of Herman Bavinck.

DAVID I. STARLING (PhD, University of Sydney) is the head of the Bible and Theology Department at Morling College. He is author of *Hermeneutics as Apprenticeship*, *UnCorinthian Leadership*, and *Not My People: Gentiles as Exiles in Pauline Hermeneutics*.

CHRIS SWANN (BDiv, Moore College) is a doctoral candidate at St Mark's National Theological Centre and Charles Sturt University, researching the significance of discipleship in Karl Barth's theology of sanctification. He is also the director of training with City to City Australia, teaching practical theology for urban church planters and ministry leaders.

MARK D. THOMPSON (DPhil, University of Oxford) is the principal of Moore Theological College, Sydney, and the head of its Theology, Philosophy and Ethics Department. He is author of *A Sure Ground on Which to Stand: The Relation of Authority and Interpretive Method in Luther's Approach to Scripture*, *A Clear and Present Word: The Clarity of Scripture*, and numerous articles and book chapters.

DANIEL J. TREIER (PhD, Trinity Evangelical Divinity School) is Knoedler Professor of Theology at Wheaton College Graduate School. He is author of four books and coeditor of several others, including most recently a third edition of the *Evangelical Dictionary of Theology*. With Kevin Vanhoozer, he has written *Theology and the Mirror of Scripture*.

Scripture Index

Subject Index

eternal 28, 212, 213
human 95
political 47
religious 127
tree of 30, 98–99

light 16, 186, 229, 243, 244; see also
    Jesus Christ, as light
    and darkness 7, 7n20, 9–10, 10n31,
        11, 14n46, 25, 100, 187
    children of 15; see also God,
        children of
    creation of, see creation, of light
    heavenly 187
    physical 68
    spiritual 68

literacy, biblical 33

literature:
    apocalyptic 114, 114n4
    early Jewish 114

logic 39, 127, 189
    deductive 83
    inductive 83

logos 220, 220n2

Logos, the 9, 14, 14n46, 21, 22, 24, 49,
        158, 159, 191, 192, 193, 199, 219, 220,
        220n2, 221, 222, 223n15, 224n18;
        see also Jesus Christ
    agency of 192
    as God's communication 24
    as God's rationality 192
    as sustainer of universe 219
    divinity of 14
    relationship with creation 219, 222,
        223
    theology of 25

love 118, 124, 141
    Christian 142
    divine, see God, love of
    gift of 124
    human 55, 228
    object-oriented 45, 53, 54, 57
    of neighbor 57, 121
    of others 131, 138, 177
    reign of 131
    tradition of 54

Luther, Martin 156, 157, 164, 172,
        187–88, 222, 233, 245–46
    justification by faith 188; see
        also justification; faith,
        justification by; works,
        justification by
    theology of the cross 188, 188n18;
        see also theology, of the cross

MacIntyre, Alasdair 43
man, first 6, 7, 12, 13, 14, 235, 246–47;
    see also Adam; couple, first
Mangina, Joseph 167–68
manifestation, divine 63, 79
Martyn, J. Louis 115–16
mathematics 95, 228
matter (material) 6, 160
Mavrodes, George 64
Maximus the Confessor 220, 22
McGrath, Alister 156n6, 166
McMaken, W. Travis 176
meaning 50, 130
    of Scripture 41, 74, 131, 133, 134, 138,
        138n48, 142
    layers of 132
    multiple 131, 132, 133, 139
    philosophical challenges of 130
    questions of 40
meditation 146, 150; see also reason,
        relationship to meditation
    as apprehension 149
    as way to understanding 151, 152
    on divine truth 147
    on God's works 147
mercy 46, 47
metaphysics 22, 82, 176
methodism 84–85
Middle Ages 22
mind 68, 150
    divine, see God, mind of
    human 164, 182, 192, 193, 194, 211,
        215, 229
    new 118; see also Jesus Christ, mind
        of
    transformed 117

as divinely inspired 71-72, 73
as normative 64
as record of revelation 204; *see also*
    revelation, in Scripture
as truth 140
as witness to Christ 204, 243
as word of God 71, 206, 209, 211,
    217; *see also* God, word of
attacks on 183
authority of 140, 143, 242, 245, 246
canonization of 64, 71; *see also*
    canon; text, canonical
collection of 71
content of 75, 206, 211, 215, 216
doctrine of 71, 205, 240, 243
engagement with 139
figural reading of 128-29, 131, 132,
    133-35, 136, 137, 138, 139, 140, 141,
    142
hermeneutics of, *see* hermeneutics
historical study of 71, 74, 75
identity of 73-74
in politics 74
inerrancy of 72-73
infallibility of 72
interpretation of, *see* interpretation
literal sense of 131, 131n22, 132,
    133-34, 139
meaning of, *see* meaning, of
    Scripture
meditation on 197
origins of 74, 75
primacy of 184
reading of 128, 129, 132, 139
relevance of 139
text of, *see* text
theological account of 248
theological interpretation of (=
    TIS) 40, 128-29, 132, 134, 138,
    140, 142; *see also* exegesis,
    theological
transmission of 71
truth of 27, 245
unity of 174
use of 142-43
witness of 4, 139, 179, 236
writing of 71
Searle, John 241

secularity 54
seeing 152, 153
self:
    new 172, 179
    old 172, 178
senses:
    human 78, 151, 152, 157, 237
    spiritual 78
seraphim 100, 101, 107, 108, 109
sermon 40-41
Sermon on the Mount 173, 174
Servant Songs (in Isaiah) 101-107,
    101n65, 101n66
    first 101-103
    fourth 104-107, 108
servant, in Isaiah 91, 101
Seth (biblical character) 13
shalom 16, 26, 91
silence 238-39
sin 9, 11, 12, 66, 68, 80, 95, 105, 122, 137,
    163, 164, 175, 177, 179, 184, 193, 194,
    199, 214, 222, 226, 227, 247, 248
sinners 171
skepticism 40, 41, 52, 78, 84, 238
social media 54
society 6, 32, 43, 44, 50, 51, 52, 53, 54,
    57
    expectations of 27
    modern liberal 46
    of God 50
    postpolitical 57
    redemption of 46
    secular 54
    transformation of 46
    western 38
sociology 32
sola scriptura 233, 245, 246
Solomon (biblical character) 98n50,
    104
Son, the 14, 16, 50, 145, 146, 150, 168,
    171, 173, 195, 196, 219, 220, 224, 226,
    227, 235, 236, 243; *see also* Jesus
    Christ
    as the Word 22, 238; *see also* God,
    Word of